THE Alliance

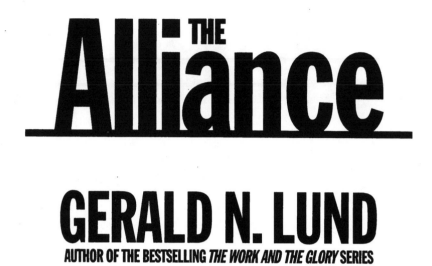

THE Alliance

GERALD N. LUND

AUTHOR OF THE BESTSELLING *THE WORK AND THE GLORY* SERIES

BOOKCRAFT

SALT LAKE CITY, UTAH

Bookcraft is a registered trademark of Deseret Book Company.

First printing redesigned paperbound edition, January 2000

Library of Congress Cataloging-in-Publication Data

Lund, Gerald N.
    The alliance.
    1. Title.
PS3562.U485A79 1983   813'.54   83-14359
ISBN 0-87747-982-8

Printed in the United States of America   72082-6507
34th Printing

THE Alliance

CHAPTER

1

Before the world ended, the place was known as Star Valley, Wyoming. For the past eighteen years they had called it simply "the valley." Eric Lloyd removed his broad-brimmed, crudely woven straw hat and wiped at his brow with his sleeve. The cornfield he was irrigating skirted the edge of the foothills and was slightly higher than the rest of the valley. From that vantage point he could see the whole sweep of it before him—the mountain ranges that hemmed it in on both sides, shoving some peaks up over ten thousand feet, still laced with winter snows; the neat patchwork of wheat, barley, corn, and alfalfa fields; the deeper green, more erratic lines of cottonwoods and willows along the creeks rushing down from the mountains to the Salt River; the meadowland dotted with dairy and beef cattle. From almost any spot in it, the valley presented a dazzling array of color and beauty, and Eric never tired of looking at it.

"Ricky! Ricky!"

Eric straightened and looked around, his gray eyes squinting in the early afternoon sunshine. For a moment the only sound was the soft gurgle of water as it slipped out of the irrigation ditch and into the furrows. Then the call came floating across the fields again. He replaced his hat and squinted into the sun, still unable to pinpoint the source of his sisters' voices. Then he saw the tops of two heads—one dark brown, one a golden blonde—bouncing up and down above the level of the chest-high field of corn.

With a smile, he took two quick swipes with the shovel, slicing through the thick grass and soft dirt of the ditch bank to open up another furrow, then stuck the shovel in the opposite bank with one quick thrust. His boots made a pleasant sucking sound as he uprooted his feet from the soft mud and moved to dry ground.

"Lori! Becky! I'm over here."

Two figures rounded the edge of the cornfield, then exploded into a spontaneous and uneven race toward him. Long-legged Lori, nine years old and three inches taller than her sister, easily outdistanced Becky. Her blonde hair streamed out in back of her as her face contorted with the efforts of victory. Becky, six and destined to be small all her life, tried valiantly to keep up, her ponytail bouncing as her feet pounded up little puffs of dust in the narrow path. They were both clothed in plain homespun woolen dresses with white pinafores. Deerskin moccasins covered their feet, standard wear for most of the children in the village during the summertime. Shoes laboriously cut and stitched from hand-cured and tanned cow hides were too expensive for anything but wintertime or Sunday wear.

"Ricky! Ricky!" Lori shouted as she slid to a stop, almost catapulting into the ditch. "School's out!"

"I get to tell! I get to tell!" Becky cried as she collided with Eric's legs.

"No more school," Lori gasped between heaving breaths, determined to win the verbal race as well.

"Lori!" Becky wailed, swinging at her sister with a fistful of crumpled papers.

"Whoa!" Eric commanded, sweeping them both into his encircling arms and pulling them down next to him in the grass. "First, both of you get your breath. Then we'll take turns."

They both nodded, grateful for the reprieve.

After a few moments, Eric released them. "Okay, now. Who wants to start?"

2

Becky, still fresh from the regimen of school, shot up her hand. But Lori, ever the practical one, said, "I get to tell him about the party. Then you can tell him about your report card first." She shot Becky one of her I-dare-you-to-disagree looks.

"Okay."

"Oh, Ricky, it was so neat." Her blue eyes danced with excitement. "Mr. Wilson checked in all our books and equipment, then we sang songs, had refreshments, played games, and—"

"Yeah," Becky broke in, her eyes wide. "We didn't do *any* work. Not any, *all* day." Her nose, liberally sprinkled with a light dusting of freckles, wrinkled with the wonder of it.

"Becky," Lori complained, "it's not your turn."

"Right," Eric said sternly, giving her a quick wink. "Let Lori tell me."

"We played Red Rover, and Run Sheep Run, and Kick the Can. I broke through the arms of Kenny Miller and Peter Carlson in Red Rover." She beamed with a broad, thoroughly uninhibited smile. "Mrs. Crookston said that I proved girls were as strong as boys."

Eric nodded soberly. "I have heard that's true." Then he shushed her gently, as she prepared to plunge in again. "Okay, it's Becky's turn now."

Becky's head ducked momentarily as she pawed quickly through her papers. When she looked up, she was radiant with excitement. "Look, Eric," she said, thrusting her report card at him, "I got all ones except in writing and spelling, and those are two pluses."

"And I only got two twos, too," Lori blurted, holding her own card out for inspection.

Eric took the cards, smoothed them out on his legs, and leaned over to study them.

"My," he said finally, "you both did really well. Mom and Dad will be proud of you."

The girls beamed happily.

Eric peered more closely, comparing the two papers, then looked at Lori. "I thought you and Becky walked to school together."

"We do."

"Then how come you have six tardies and Becky has none?" The six for Lori was not a great surprise to Eric. Her immense curiosity about the world caused her to stop and inspect every new flower, chase any errant toad, or sometimes just brought her to a stop in the middle of the road to daydream for a moment or two. But the discrepancy puzzled him, for Becky was always a willing partner in such delays.

Becky cocked her head to one side, her brown eyes earnest. "Oh," she said helpfully, "Mrs. Crookston is real nice. She doesn't even mark us down when we are retarded."

Eric nearly choked, then whooped with laughter.

"Not *retarded*," Lori said in disgust. "*Tardy.*"

Becky blushed and lowered her eyes, her thick lashes lying softly on her cheeks. "Oh, yeah," she said, that irrepressible grin breaking through her embarrassment. "That's what I meant." Then she giggled, causing Eric to laugh out loud again.

He leaned over and hugged her. "That's my Becky."

Lori suddenly jumped up. "Look!" she cried. "Here comes Stephanie."

Eric stood up as their older sister, astride her sorrel mare, came at a hard lope from the direction of the village.

"Eric!" she cried, pulling the horse up to a sliding halt and leaping off to face them. "Dad is back. He wants you in the village right now. All the men are meeting at the church."

"Dad?" Eric echoed in surprise. "He and Cliff aren't supposed to be back for two more days."

"I know, but last night they saw lights."

"What kind of lights?"

She shook her head. "They were a long way away. But Dad said that they looked like the headlights of automobiles! Coming down old U.S. Highway 89 from the north."

"Car lights? How can that be? How could there be automobiles?"

"What's an automobile?" Becky asked, looking up at her brother and sister.

Stephanie ignored the question and thrust the reins into Eric's

4

hand. "I don't know how it can be, but Dad is worried. So go! The meeting has already started."

Eric swung up, kicked the mare in the flanks, and leaned over her neck as she leaped forward into a pounding run.

Eric's eyes snapped open, and it took him a moment to realize he had dozed off again. He shifted his weight, trying to find a more comfortable position against the rough bark of the tree, then glanced up at the sun through the boughs of the pine trees. It was now just past its zenith and starting its downward slide toward the west. He had ridden all night, finally joining up with Cliff shortly after dawn. But Cliff had not given him any time to rest. They had immediately headed north again, not stopping until a little before noon. His eyelids felt as heavy as the anvil irons in Ralph Maddox's blacksmith shop.

Eric turned his head slightly and studied the lean whip of a man, now in his seventy-first year, who sat a few feet away. His bony frame was cushioned in a small mound of pine needles, and his elbows rested on his knees, holding the binoculars to his eyes with steadiness. The afternoon breeze moaned in the pine branches above them, then softly ruffled Cliff's short-cropped hair, once saddle-brown but now mostly gray. Except for that slight motion, he could have passed as part of the forest, a gnarled old stump clad in brown deerskin. Somewhere behind them a red squirrel scolded harshly, breaking the gentle quiet of the forest.

Eric shook his head. It must have been that kind of single-minded concentration that had made Dr. Clifford Cameron one of the foremost neurosurgeons on the West Coast—and the most consistently successful hunter in the village.

The Appaloosa mare and the black gelding tethered a few feet behind them stopped their stamping and turned toward the canyon below them, their ears cocked forward. "Cliff," Eric said softly, "the horses hear something."

There was no response for almost a full minute; then a deep grunt and a low whistle from Cliff brought Eric's head up sharply. He peered down into the canyon below them, where the steep, thickly forested mountainside formed a V and allowed the Salt River to disappear from sight. Even to the naked eye it was evident that the bright orange object emerging from the gorge about half a mile from where they sat was not natural to the forest.

"It is!" Cliff exclaimed, his voice tinged with awe. "It's an automobile!" He lowered the glasses, stared at Eric for a moment without seeing him, then swung back to peer through the binoculars once more. "And there's another one! Can you believe it? After eighteen years—cars!" Cliff was rarely awed by anything, and Eric felt a tiny shiver, half fear, half excitement, run down his spine.

"Look!" Cliff commanded, tossing the glasses to Eric.

It took Eric a moment to find the vehicles, but then he too stared. Through the binoculars, he could see both vehicles clearly. They were not unlike the automobiles he had seen many times in books and in old videotapes, and yet they were different. Clear, bubble-shaped covers sat atop squat, nearly square bodies. Oversized tires held them well above the weed-strewn highway, giving them an awkward, overbalanced look. Though the hot afternoon sunshine glinted off the bubble, Eric could make out several figures inside each car. They were coming slowly, almost cautiously, moving not much faster than a man could walk.

He handed the glasses back to Cliff, his expression puzzled.

"Listen!" Cliff commanded, peering through the glasses again. "No motor sounds. Nothing! We would've heard a regular car's engine at least a mile away in these mountains. That means—" He leaned forward intently. "Look! Here comes another—no, it's not a car, it's a truck."

The third bright orange vehicle moved out of the canyon, but without the glasses, all Eric could tell for sure was that it was much larger than the lead vehicles.

"It's an open truck filled with men." Once again Cliff lowered the glasses to stare at Eric. "In uniform. Blue and orange, like the cars." He turned back, and Eric watched his lips moving as he counted silently. "There are close to thirty of them."

Cliff didn't speak again, and Eric stared at the scene below as one orange truck after another emerged from the trees. Finally

Cliff stood up. He shoved the field glasses back into the battered case and shook his head. "Two cars and ten trucks, one of which is carrying a bulldozer. I count about a hundred men in the first three trucks—the others seem to be empty. I can't see any weapons, but the men are all in uniform." He picked up his rifle and stared down at the long column moving toward them. "A veritable army."

"They can't be just another group of Marauders." It was not a question. The occasional bands of men roaming the countryside raping and pillaging the pockets of survivors were like packs of wolves—vicious, savage creatures of the wild scavenging from the weak, then, likely as not, turning on one another. Their only weapons were clubs, axes, any other crude tools they could steal or make. Trucks, bulldozers, uniforms? No, they weren't just another band of Marauders.

Cliff shook his head and scratched at the thick, grizzled stubble that lined his cheeks. Eric watched him closely, amazed how little weariness showed through the deep creases that lined his face. He, like Eric, must have been up most of the night, but it showed hardly at all. He seemed like a weatherbeaten piece of granite, impervious to all external forces.

"But trucks! Cars!" Eric exclaimed. "That implies civilization, industry, technology."

"High technology," Cliff agreed, his eyes troubled. "No engine noise means either they're electric—which seems unlikely for any long distances—or they're nuclear powered."

"Nuclear? Is that possible?"

The doctor shrugged. "Who knows? There certainly weren't nuclear-powered automobiles before." His face reflected a curious mixture of hope and longing and worry.

Eric had seen that same look on the faces of those in the village who were old enough to remember before. He had also sensed it in his father, though he usually refused to talk about the times before life in the valley. Dipping into the pitcher of the past, his father often said, can only sour the cup of the present.

"What do you suppose they want?" he asked, staring down at the passing procession, now less than five hundred yards below the ridge where they sat.

That seemed to pull Cliff out of his thoughts. He turned and walked swiftly to where the horses were tethered. "That is what we're supposed to find out. It will take them about twenty minutes or so to loop around the road and reach the spot where we dropped that tree across the highway. We can be there in half that. Let's get into position."

They cut directly down the back side of the ridge, the way they had come up earlier. In ten minutes they reached a place where they had a clear view of the road and the clearing where they had dropped a big pine across it and blocked it off.

Cliff pulled up and pointed with his rifle toward a thick clump of undergrowth. "You stay up here. That'll give you a clear line of fire to the road where they'll have to stop." His face softened slightly. "But don't, for heaven's sake, get jumpy until I've had a chance to see if they're friendly. Okay? You'll be close enough you should be able to hear what we say clearly."

"Yes, but—"

"Once I'm sure it's safe, I'll wave you down."

"Cliff," Eric protested, "I want to come down with you. If something goes wrong, I can't be much help from up here."

Cliff let his voice ease into what Eric's father called his corn-pone drawl. "Ricky, my boy, if somethin' goes wrong, Ol' Doc can handle hisself. You git yo'self off to where yo' daddy is settin' up at the river crossin'. You hear me, boy?"

"But Cliff!"

"Eric!" The sharpness in Cliff's voice sliced off further protest. "That's an order. We've had people come to our little valley before—some friendly, some with murder in their hearts—but we've never had a group this large or this well equipped. It's my fervent hope that they come in peace." His eyes darkened momentarily. "Surely after what the world has seen—surely they come in peace."

As quickly as it had come, the dark mood had gone, and his mouth set into a firm line. "But if not, your job is to slow up this column and then get to your dad as soon as possible. Tell him what's happening. Understood?"

Eric took a deep breath. "Yes, sir."

Cliff's hands, surprisingly gentle for their bigness, came up and rested briefly on Eric's shoulders. "I'll be fine. In fact, I have to admit, I'm actually tingling with excitement. Imagine—people! Civilization! You've no idea what that could mean." Then he was gone, moving through the trees like the patterns of shadow and sunlight in the forest.

Eric watched him go, keenly aware that of all men, only his father engendered a fiercer sense of attachment and loyalty than did this man. His drawling reference to Eric as Ricky, and himself as Doc, brought old memories flooding back. Everyone in the village except his father and mother called Clifford Cameron "Doc." And for as long as he could remember, Doc had always called him Ricky. That had changed six years ago, shortly after Eric's eighteenth birthday. It had been late fall, and he had accompanied Doc and his father on a week-long hunting trip to supplement their winter meat stocks. Just after sundown of the third day, they had found a huge bull moose grazing in a marshy area of the forest. Eric could still vividly remember the huge rack of antlers, silhouetted against the sky.

Eric's father had taken the shot, but to their surprise the moose gave a wild bellow, then crashed away into the brush. Positive it had been hit, the three had cautiously started out after it, his father taking the point, Eric and Doc about twenty yards back and thirty yards apart. The light was rapidly fading, but large splashes of blood were easily discernible in the wet grass. His father had just entered a thick stand of pines when the underbrush off to the right of Doc exploded. Out hurtled a black mass of fury, weighing over eighteen hundred pounds and standing seven feet high at the shoulders. With a startled cry, Doc spun around—too fast. His feet shot sideways in the mud, and he went down.

To this day, Eric still maintained he had reacted in blind panic, but he dropped to one knee and snapped off a quick shot over the prone figure. It was as though he had used a scythe on the moose's front legs. Nearly a ton of raging flesh slammed into the mud and slid to a shuddering halt less than ten feet from Doc's scrambling figure. The bullet had caught the bull just below his left eye and shattered in his brain.

Both of the older men expressed their breathless thanks, but it was later that night, as the long strips of moose meat were being cured in a heavy smoke, that Eric had started to say something to Cliff, calling him Doc. He had raised his hand, interrupting him. "Why don't you call me Cliff?" Even now, the memory sent a thrill of warmth shooting through Eric. And that was the last time—until just a few minutes ago—that Cliff had called him Ricky.

Eric shook his head impatiently at the sudden surge of emotions, laid the rifle butt against his cheek, and sighted in on the fallen pine tree.

CHAPTER

2

The first man to the tree was tall and angular. As he took off his orange helmet, Eric could see that his thinning hair was plastered to his head with sweat. Unfortunately, he had stopped sooner than Eric expected, leaving only the lead vehicle in sight and the rest of the column hidden in the trees.

As two other men moved up to join him, the leader's voice carried clearly up to where Eric lay concealed. "Look at this. This tree didn't just fall across the road. It's been cut, and in the last day or two."

So at least they are Americans. Eric could detect no trace of accent, and that relieved him somewhat. Each man was clad in orange and blue and had what appeared to be a weapon strapped to his hip. And yet from this distance it was difficult to tell exactly what kind of weapon. It looked too long for a pistol, and yet too short for a rifle.

"It looks like it was done deliberately to block the highway."

"Well, if it was, they chose their spot well." The leader gestured to one of the men. "Bring up one of the trucks. We can use a winch to move it. It's not worth getting the tractor off."

"I wouldn't do that, not just yet."

11

It was comical in a way. Had the fallen tree instantly righted itself, it could not have created a more stunned reaction. All three men visibly jumped at the sound of Cliff's voice and whirled to stare at the figure that had appeared from nowhere.

The leader was the first to recover. "Hello," he called nervously, starting toward Cliff.

The muzzle of Cliff's Winchester 30.06 raised slightly. "Just stand easy," he drawled, "until we get a little better acquainted. Who are you, and where do you come from?"

The tall man stopped, but if he was deterred by Cliff's coolness, Eric couldn't detect it in his voice. "My name is Bruce Byers. I am the commander of the First Corps of Guardians." He waved toward the unseen column. "We're from the city of Shalev."

"Never heard of it," Cliff said.

"That's not too surprising. It's up north, where Kalispell, Montana, used to be. The name comes from the Hebrew word meaning peaceful."

"You're a long ways from home."

"Yes, about five hundred miles."

"What brings you this far south?"

"We heard there were people living in a valley south of here."

The surprise in Cliff's voice made Eric smile. "Oh, really? Whereabouts?"

The leader shook his head. "We're not exactly sure. That's assuming there is a village." It was evident he was fishing.

Cliff rejected the bait. "And if you find them?"

"We're hoping they might be pleased to hear others have survived, that there are cities and civilization. We'd like them to join us, help us rebuild America."

"Cities?"

"Yes. Shalev has nearly seventy thousand people—it's the largest. There are four main cities in the Alliance, and numerous smaller towns and villages."

"Seventy thousand?"

"Right. Close to a quarter million of us, altogether."

"That's incredible! We had no idea any groups that large had survived. Especially anywhere close to us."

12

"Yes, and while we don't have everything like it was before Termination, we have a very comfortable life. Electricity, schools, automobiles. We even have a university and a symphony orchestra."

"Termination," Cliff mused softly, making Eric strain to hear his words. "An appropriate title. We simply refer to it as before or after." He lowered his rifle and stepped forward, extending his hand. "I'm Dr. Clifford Cameron, from the village you're looking for."

"Wonderful! Dr. Cameron, we're delighted to find you." The man gave a small laugh. "Or rather to have you find us."

"Yes. I apologize for the initial wariness, but—"

"I understand," the other said quickly. "We have to watch some of those wandering around the country too. Well, if you'd care to join us, we'll get this tree out of the way and push on to your village." He looked up at the late afternoon sky. "If we hurry, we can be there before nightfall."

Eric could hear the edge in Cliff's voice as he stepped back suddenly. "By nightfall?"

"Yes. Not that we can't travel after dark, but . . ."

"I thought you didn't know where the village was," Cliff said slowly.

"Oh," the other man said, his voice tinged with nervousness. "We don't. I was just assuming it must be fairly close. I mean— well, you're here, and I just thought . . ." His voice trailed off, and it was obvious even he knew how flimsy his words sounded.

Eric was suddenly wary. The man was lying, and poorly at that, though he wasn't exactly sure why. He jerked the rifle up again and notched back the safety. Cliff laughed softly. "Oh, I see. Well, you're right. It isn't really that far from here. In fact, I have my horse up in the trees. Why don't I just cut over the mountain and tell the village the good news. Just follow this old highway. We'll meet you where the highway crosses the river about five miles further on. It's the first bridge. You can't miss it. Then we can show you the way into the valley."

"But, Dr. Cameron, it would be so much better if you'd help us find the way."

Cliff shook his head, then raised his hand in farewell and started moving away. "Really, you'll be fine. Just stay on this highway. I'll be there before you. I'm much too excited to wait. The people will be so surprised."

"Dr. Cameron," the leader said sharply. All three men in the bright orange suits pulled their weapons up. "I'm afraid I really must insist."

Eric squeezed the trigger, and his first shot caught the tall leader high in the shoulder, jerking him around violently. One of the other men evidently fired, though later Eric realized there had been no sound of a shot. Cliff's low grunt was audible even at this distance as he spun around with a jerk, then jackknifed forward into the grass.

Eric snapped off another shot, but the two men dove for cover, and he saw a puff of dust as the bullet tore into dry ground. As excited shouts for help filled the air, Eric grabbed the binoculars and focused them quickly on Cliff's still figure. For a long moment, Eric stared at the motionless figure, the shock hammering at his reason. Savagely he jammed the glasses back into their case and snatched up the rifle again. He squeezed off a shot at a quick flash of orange below him and grunted in satisfaction at the sharp cry of pain and the crash of a heavy body in the brush.

"He's up on the ridge!"

"Stay down! Stay down!"

"Circle around him."

"Stay low!"

Eric was aware of the voices below, but with cool precision, he brought the rifle stock firmly against his cheek and began methodically emptying the magazine at the biggest target in the clearing. His first shot ricocheted with an angry whine off the orange vehicle's bubble, so he lowered the sights a fraction of an inch. First one tire exploded, then another. The remaining four shots stitched a neat pattern in the orange and blue hood.

With one last anguished glance at Cliff's inert form, he slithered backwards over the crest of the hill, then leaped to his feet and burst into a hard run toward the horses.

14

Eric tethered the horses in a thick clump of cottonwoods near the river, took the rifle out of its scabbard, and shouldered the saddle bags, which he had stuffed with hand-wrapped sticks of dynamite yesterday afternoon. Numbing shock hardened into a tight fist in his stomach whenever he thought of Cliff. He turned and trotted swiftly through the trees, pushing away a hunger for revenge so strong it was almost like acid on his tongue. His only task now was to stop that column long enough to give the village time to prepare their defenses.

The mountain air was still, filled with the heavy aroma of pine, and the heat of the afternoon was now at its fullest. As he came out of the trees and onto the old highway, a blue jay burst out at him, furious that he had startled it without warning. But if Eric heard it, he gave no sign, for he had a fury of his own driving him.

He jogged about two hundred yards up the road, then stopped to survey the scene. Sometime in the two decades since the Wyoming Highway Department had ceased to exist, the flood-waters of the Salt River had risen high enough to chew away at the base of what had once been U.S. Highway 89. Most of the outside lane had collapsed into the hungry waters. Given enough time, Eric could have planted his explosives in such a way as to drop the rest of the pavement into the river and block any hope of passage. But he didn't have that time. Even allowing for the fact that the intruders had to move the tree before they could continue, he couldn't have gained much time on them.

It could have been better, but the river's work would suffice for his purposes. The vehicles could still squeeze through, but they would have to slow down to a crawl. Eric strode over to a heavy clump of brush clinging to the steep hillside at the edge of where the gaping slash in the pavement began. The crunch of tires and treads suddenly amplified, and he dove behind the bush, pushing into the heavy tangle of branches. Peering out, he saw the first vehicle round the bend and come into sight. The last rays of the sun caught the bright orange metal and turned it into flaming gold. He huddled deeper into the protecting foliage, grateful that his dark brown shirt and pants blended into the deep shadows of the oak brush.

As he stared at the approaching line of vehicles, Eric felt grimly satisfied. There was only one car now instead of two.

Not unexpectedly, the lead vehicle stopped at the edge of the pavement that had been ripped away by the flood waters. Eric heard the door open, then the crunch of footsteps coming toward him. He tensed, raising the muzzle of his rifle slightly.

"What do you think?"

"I don't know." The steps moved closer. "It looks solid enough." Again Eric felt a brief flash of satisfaction. Neither voice belonged to the tall, hollow-cheeked man who had shaken hands with Cliff. Cliff was dead, but he hadn't gone totally unavenged.

"The bank isn't undercut at all. I think we'll be okay. Just tell the others to stay as far to the right as they can."

"Right." The footsteps moved back quickly. The low hum of the motor increased in intensity, and even before the doors were shut, the car began to creep forward.

Eric opened the flap of the saddle bag and quickly pulled the friction fuse out. It was simple enough—two patches of sulphur, like match heads, in which the fuse had been imbedded. He pushed the leaves of his hiding place aside gently and watched as the car passed slowly across the narrow strip of pavement; then he turned back to gauge the speed of the first truck. With a quick slap he grated the two sulphur heads together, and as they flared into life, catching the fuse, he started to count.

One. Two. Three. He grasped the root of the oak brush firmly and swung out.

Four. Five. The clump of brush kept him hidden from the driver of his target, but as he started the arching, upward swing of the saddle bags, the sudden movement caught the attention of the driver in the second truck. Eric knew that once the charge blew, he was going to have to get out and get out fast.

Six. Seven. Eric heaved the twenty pounds of explosives up over the edge of the pavement and under the truck, then frantically dove back under the bush and dug his face into the graveled hillside, throwing his free arm over his head.

The blast was deafening. Though the major part of the con-
cussion was deflected off the pavement and went over Eric's head,
he felt as if he were lying prone on the back of a bucking horse. He
bounced once, half turning as he tried to hold on, but his fingers
tore free, and he slid two or three feet down the steep embank-
ment. As he dug in his fingers to halt his plunge, he instinctively
looked up.

The explosion had caught the truck almost exactly under the
midsection and bounced it around a quarter turn to the right,
leaving the left back wheels hanging precariously over the edge of
the pavement. Even as his brain registered the wild scene—
tumbling orange bodies, the screams of men, the sharp pain in his
ears, the raw agony of clawing into gravel—it also registered his
danger. In just a few seconds an angry swarm of blue and orange
hornets would be zooming in on him.

He grabbed his rifle and leaped out, plunging down the slope,
his boots leaving deep gouges in the soft gravel and dirt.

"There he goes!" he heard someone shout. "Get him!"

But Eric was already into the trees and running hard for the
horses.

C H A P T E R

3

As Eric came around the bend and the weed-strewn highway straightened out again, he pulled up on the reins, bringing the horses to a sliding halt. About fifty yards ahead of him, directly in front of the concrete bridge that spanned the turbulent river below, a huge barricade of trees and logs and earth had been erected. It completely blocked the highway, cutting all access to the bridge.

Before he had gone ten feet more, he heard a cry off to his right. Suddenly men sprung up everywhere, swarming out at him from behind the barricade, out from the trees, and up from the steep riverbank.

"It's Ricky," someone shouted. When he saw the tall figure of his father among those at the barricade, he kicked the horses into a trot.

"Ken," Eric said, as he swung down and thrust the reins at the nearest man, "can you cool these horses down and then water them? I've pushed them pretty hard." Without waiting for a reply, he turned to face his father.

"Where's Cliff?"

Eric looked down and his shoulders sagged. "He's dead."

Karl Lloyd flinched, as though slapped across the face.

"They shot him down without warning."

His father's face, normally a deep tan, turned the color of wet clay, and his lips tightened into a tight line. "Marauders?"

"No. You and Cliff were right about the lights. There are cars and trucks. It's a regular army. Over a hundred men." That brought renewed exclamations from the villagers. Eric went on quickly. "Cliff went down to talk to them. At first they seemed friendly. They know about the village and are looking for us. Cliff got suspicious and tried to disengage, and they opened fire."

"We heard shooting and an explosion," one of the men said.

Eric shook his head, still dazed by the searing reality of seeing Cliff go down. "Their weapons don't make a sound. It was really strange. I was up on the ridge and opened fire, but it—" His voice caught in his throat, and he went on angrily. "Cliff made me stay out of sight. There was no way I could get to him. I—it all happened so fast."

Karl Lloyd laid his hand on his son's shoulder. "Where are they now? How far behind you?"

"I dynamited one of their trucks three or four miles back and blocked the road. But it won't take them long to clear that up. At most they're probably an hour behind me. Maybe less."

His father swung around to face the men. "All right, we'd better get ready. We know now that they don't come in peace." He took one of the men next to him by the elbow. "Fred, get Eric a fresh mount, and—"

Eric jerked up. "What?"

"I want you to go back to the village, start the—"

"No, Dad! We've got to stop them here. You need me here!"

Karl shook his head, his eyes resolute. "We'll try to stop them here, but if we can't, they'll roll right on into the valley. I want you and Travis to take the rest of the dynamite, mine every bridge, every culvert along the road to the village. Anything that will delay them."

"Travis is at the village," Eric pleaded. "Send someone to tell him what's happening. I want to be here when they come."

"Travis doesn't know how to work with dynamite. Besides, he's only been with us a month. He's a good man, but not proven.

19

Not in this kind of a conflict. I will feel much better with you there."

"The village needs you, Ricky." That came from a man near the back.

"He's right, Eric," Karl said soberly. "We need you here, but the village needs you more. If you see them enter the valley, let Travis light the charges. You get the people up Dead Rock Canyon and into the high country."

Eric suddenly surrendered, remembering his useless protest with Cliff, feeling the same sick feeling he had felt then.

Fred Carlyle trotted up, a large dun quarter horse in tow. "Your rifle is in the scabbard, Ricky," he said, handing him the reins.

Eric looked quickly around the circle of tight-lipped, grim-faced men. The only sound was the soft rushing of the river off to their left. These were the men with whom he had grown up, played, hunted, worked, worshipped. The sick feeling became a heavy dread pressing down on him. Finally his gaze met his father's.

"We'll have a few surprises for them here," his father said quietly. "Maybe we can turn them back, but we can't take that chance. Take care of your mother and sisters."

Eric nodded numbly, then swung up into the saddle.

"The Lord be with you." It was Karl Lloyd's standard farewell when anyone left the village for any length of time, but now it pierced Eric like the thrust of a knife.

He took a deep breath. "And with you," he answered softly. Then with a savage jab of his heels, he sent the dun exploding into a hard lope around the barricade and across the bridge toward the valley road.

Travis Oakes had evidently been watching down the valley, for he came trotting down the main street, rifle in hand, and met Eric just beyond the first houses of the village. "Eric," he called, "what are you doing here? Where are the others?"

"At the river bridge," Eric answered as he pulled up the horse and swung down. He gave the lathered animal a quick slap on the

20

rump, as he pulled the rifle out of the scabbard and turned to face Travis. "Come on, we've got big trouble." He started up the street, leaving Travis staring at him.

Travis broke into three quick steps to join Eric. He was an inch or two shorter than Eric's six-foot height and of a stockier build, with a dark handsomeness and a quick smile that had sent every unmarried female over twelve years of age into flights of hopeful, tittering anticipation. But he had quickly proven to be a valuable addition to the village and had been accepted as one of them. As he caught up and matched strides with Eric, he asked, "What is it? What's wrong?"

"Cliff and Dad were right. They were automobile lights. A whole column of men and vehicles is moving toward us. They killed Cliff."

Travis stopped abruptly, stunned. "What?"

"Yes." Eric went striding on, once again making Travis hasten to catch up with him. "It's a whole army of men." Eric looked around, suddenly noticing the lack of activity in the village. "Where is everybody?"

Travis was startled momentarily by the question. "Uh— they're in the schoolhouse. We were—uh—they're having a meeting, trying to keep the kids occupied."

"Good," Eric said, oblivious to the sudden change in Travis. "That will save time getting everybody together. We may have to evacuate the village." He pulled up short, causing Travis to bump against his arm. "Listen!" he commanded, raising his hand.

They both cocked their heads as the faint echo of rifle fire rolled up the valley toward them.

"It's started!" Eric said, grabbing Travis by the elbow. "They've reached the bridge already. We've got to hurry."

"What is going on?" Travis demanded. "There shouldn't be shooting. What if they come in peace?"

"Cliff's dead!" Eric snapped angrily. "They don't come in peace." He dragged Travis into motion, talking quickly, outlining what had to be done, then answering Travis's rapid-fire questions about the events of the past few hours.

As they rounded the corner and started up the street that ended at the white frame schoolhouse, Travis was shaking his head. "It's all wrong," he muttered. "Those stupid, blundering idiots!"

Eric spun around angrily. "You think it's stupid to protect ourselves?"

That pulled Travis out of his thoughts, and he shook his head. "I don't mean the villagers. I mean those idiot fools in the blue and orange uniforms."

"Oh." Eric took two more steps, then stopped short again, staring at Travis. "How did you know they were wearing blue and orange uniforms?"

Travis looked past Eric, then jerked his thumb behind him. "Did they look like that?" he asked softly.

Eric turned in time to see two men step out from behind a nearby building. They were clad in bright orange and blue one-piece uniforms and orange helmets. Each pointed a stubby, long-barreled pistol directly at Eric. Instinctively, Eric started to whirl, bringing up his rifle, but Travis was quicker; he snatched the rifle out of Eric's grasp, jumping back from him.

Three more men in similar dress came running out from behind the schoolhouse as Eric stared, dumbfounded.

"All right," Travis barked. "Get him inside with the others. Something has gone wrong. We've got to get down to the river bridge and stop a massacre."

"You're one of *them!*" Eric cried hoarsely, the understanding hitting him like a runaway hay wagon.

Travis smiled sadly. "How do you think they knew where the village was?"

Eric had risen to the balls of his feet, his fingers extended like the talons of a hawk. With a cry of rage, he launched himself at Travis, but as swift as he was, the nearest man was quicker. The barrel of the weapon swung a fraction of an inch. There was no sound, but Eric was caught in midair, as though hit by an invisible sweeping steel boom that instantly stopped his forward flight and hurled him backward. He bounced once hard against a hitching post, then slumped forward, face down in the street.

CHAPTER

4

Considering how important it was to the total function of Central Control, and indeed to the total function of Shalev and the entire Alliance of Four Cities, the Monitoring Room was really quite unremarkable. About thirty feet long and twenty feet wide, it was painted in pale blue and orange, as was much of the rest of Central Control. As one entered from the main hallway, the wall to the right was bare except for a door marked "Authorized Personnel Only." Behind that door stood a dozen large CPUs—the central processing units for the entire computer system, the heart of Shalev and the Alliance of Four Cities.

But it was the wall to the left that made the Monitoring Room what it was. Along the entire length of the wall was a built-in cabinet system containing four computer consoles with keyboards. These monitoring consoles were overshadowed by the two large tracking screens filling the whole wall above them. If the CPUs held the heart of the system, these screens were the eyes. On them, the computers could pinpoint any one of the seventy thousand citizens of Shalev in a few seconds, a flashing light showing the person's location on a grid map of the city.

Travis Oakes stopped outside the door to the Monitoring

Room and rechecked his orange and blue dress uniform, tugging the jacket downward. Four weeks of farm work had tightened his waist muscles, he noted, not without some satisfaction. His fingers briefly straightened the Guardian emblem on his lapel; then, satisfied, he took a deep breath, opened the door, and slipped inside.

After the simple rooms and furnishings of the village, the gleaming glass and steel computer consoles and digital readout panels of the Monitoring Room stood in sharp contrast. He stopped and looked around, letting the room's familiarity soak back into him.

His eyes fell on the figure bent over one of the consoles, and he felt a sudden quickening of his pulse. Nicole Lambert had not yet noticed him, so absorbed was she in studying the screen in front of her. He stepped back, content for a moment to study her in profile. The one-piece jumpsuit of the Guardians couldn't fully hide the graceful cut of her figure. Had Travis been the sculptor, he might have changed her facial features slightly, lowered the cheekbones a touch, perhaps placed her large, green eyes a fraction of an inch closer together. Her mouth, which curved softly under an exquisite nose, he would have left exactly as it was now. It pulled the rest together perfectly, making her altogether more than satisfactory.

She leaned forward slightly and frowned. Her brows pulled together, giving her a girlish look, as though she were scolding an errant pet. Then she flashed a look of triumph and began typing rapidly on the keyboard. When she finished, she tossed her head in satisfaction, and her soft brown hair bounced back into place, settling gently on her shoulders.

Travis could name half a dozen women who might surpass Nicole in outward beauty, but not one who combined outward loveliness with the inner vibrancy, the spirited intelligence that this woman radiated. Every conversation proved to be a refreshing challenge. It was this vitality that most intrigued him, perhaps because it was so rare in the women of Shalev.

Travis frowned. Research and Development had been promising the Major a solution to that problem for years, but as yet the promises were unfulfilled, and a wooden sameness permeated all too many of the women he had been interested in. He shook his head, suddenly aware how glad he was to be home. Then he stepped forward. "Nicole," he said softly.

Her head turned, then her eyes widened. "Travis!" In an instant she was on her feet and into his arms.

He spun her around once, a little surprised by the warmth of her welcome. As he sat her down, she pulled back, blushing deeply, obviously a little surprised. "I—we didn't expect you until tonight. Communications said you radioed in last night from Serenity."

"I did, but a few of the men took a vote—" he grinned and squeezed her hand—"with a little encouragement from me, and decided to drive all night. The rest of the men are bringing in the villagers and should be here by tonight. Except for one, and we brought him with us. But anyway, we're back."

Her eyes dropped slightly, the thick tangle of lashes turning them a beguiling turquoise. "I'm glad."

"Does that mean I was missed?"

She looked up and smiled, almost shyly. "You know you were."

Travis's brown eyes teased her as he held up her left hand. "I see my warning worked."

"What warning?"

"I told the men who stayed behind that if I came home and found a ring on your finger, they would get permanent duty on the Outer Perimeter."

She laughed lightly and pulled a face at him. "So that's why no one would eat lunch with me."

"You'd better believe it. But to make up for it, how about dinner tonight?"

"Oh, I'd love to, but seriously, aren't you exhausted?" She studied his face, deeply tanned since she had last seen him, and saw the weariness in his eyes. Suddenly she realized how much she had missed him, and she was tempted to throw her arms around him again. But she merely reached down and took his hand. "It must have been terrible."

Travis took a deep breath, then let it out slowly. "It wasn't very pretty."

"What happened?"

"I have to give a full report right now to the Major. He'll meet us in Detention, in the observation room. He'd like you there."

Nicole's head jerked up. "Me?"

He nodded, then pointed to her console. "File off what you're doing and let's go."

"Why does he want me there?"

"They're going to start implanting the people we brought back, and—"

"I don't want to be there, Travis," she said, stepping back. "I always hate that. You know that."

"Hey, listen! Let me finish. The Major doesn't want you to be there for the implantations, but he has three or four men he wants to bring into the Guardians. One especially—the one we brought back with us—is going to be a real challenge. His father was killed trying to stop us."

"How awful! But if he's that much of a problem, why use him?"

"Because if we can bring him over, he would be perfect as a commander of the Perimeter Forces. He's as much at home in the forest as in the village. He's resourceful, innovative, and adaptable—a natural leader. Within one week after my arrival in the village, I knew he was the one the Major has been looking for." He touched her arm. "The Major wants you in on the turn-around from the very beginning. So turn off your machine and let's go."

Nicole's face softened. "Okay. I didn't mean to stand here questioning you." She stepped to the bank of instruments, punched a couple of keys on the keyboard, then shut the machine off. "Okay," she said, turning back to face him.

On an impulse, he stepped forward, took her in his arms, and kissed her. For an instant, her body stiffened in surprise, but then she responded in a soft, warm acceptance of his embrace. When he pulled back, her eyes were wide, searching his. "Mr. Oakes," she said softly, "is that what you learned from the girls in that village?"

"I missed you, Nicole. More than I expected."

She cocked her head to one side. "I think you very neatly sidestepped my question, but I find your answer quite acceptable. Now, do we walk down to Detention like this, or do we act more like the two proper, senior members of the staff we're supposed to be?"

Travis smiled, stepped back, and bowed. "After you, Miss Lambert."

The Major had not yet arrived, and as Nicole and Travis entered the small, narrow observation room, Nicole moved to the window and studied the figure lying on the cot in the cell with his face toward her. He didn't have Travis's rugged handsomeness, but his features were pleasant, with a square chin and strong mouth. His hair was rough cut and dark brown, but lightened by hours in the sun. The sun had also left his face and neck a deep tan. His hands were farmer's hands and his clothes plainly homemade. "Is that the one?"

Travis stepped up next to her. "Yes. Eric Lloyd."

"He's young."

"Twenty-four. Same as you."

"But I expected an older man. Is he married?"

"Hey!" Travis growled. "What kind of question is that? I know he's good looking, but—"

She dug her elbow into his side. "Come on. You said his father was killed. Does he have any other family? That could make a difference in how quickly he responds."

"His mother is here. He has a sister who's twenty-one and two younger sisters, one nine and the other six. They're all fine."

"Will they be implanted?"

"Of course."

Nicole frowned, thinking of the six-year-old. "Families of the Guardians are exempt from implantation. Why won't that be true for his?"

Travis shrugged. "That's up to the Major, but his policy in cases like this is to go with a Stage Two for now, pull them back to

Stage One when the candidate begins to prove himself, then remove them completely once we are sure he is completely turned. That way he'll have some leverage."

He was watching her closely for her reaction, but Nicole continued to stare through the one-way glass. "Has he been sedated the whole time?"

"Yes. We used the stun gun on him and then put him under sedation before he came fully out of it. But we gave him the last injection late last night, so it should be wearing off any time now."

"So he'll have no idea where he is?"

"None. And he doesn't know about his father either. That happened after he was captured."

She shook her head. "Then he is going to have a lot of reason for hating us. That is going to make it very difficult. I—"

At that moment the door pushed open, and the Major strode in. "Travis!" He quickly crossed the room and gripped the younger man's hand. "Welcome back."

"Thank you, sir. It's good to be back."

"Hello, Nicole. How are you?"

"Fine, sir, thank you."

He stepped to the window and peered through. "This is our boy?"

"Yes," Travis nodded, "that's him. Eric Lloyd."

"Good. Let's go into the conference room and sit down." He took Nicole's elbow. "Did Travis tell you I'd like you to monitor this one, Nicole?"

"Yes."

"Good. Come in with us. I want you to hear Travis's report." He guided her out of the room and down the hall to a conference room. He helped her with her chair, motioned Travis toward another, and sat down himself, crossing his legs carefully so as to keep straight the knife-sharp creases in his navy blue, pin-striped business suit. Nicole smiled inwardly. He was, as usual, absolutely immaculate. Not a strand of his short, gray hair was out of place, and his shoes gleamed like polished obsidian. Though in his early fifties, he was as tall and trim as a sixteen-year-old. His pleasant face appeared more solemn because of a perfectly groomed mustache and horn-rimmed glasses that made his pale blue eyes seem larger than they were. He looked more like a banker or an accountant than the most important and powerful man in the Alliance of Four Cities.

"What went wrong?" In his usual blunt way, the Major dismissed further formalities. "How come thirteen Guardians are dead?"

Travis took a deep breath. "Well, let me start at the beginning. As I indicated in my reports, I had no trouble being accepted in the village. After I was let off by the men, I spent three days circling around to come in from the south. I had food enough for only one day, so by the time I stumbled into the valley, I looked pretty authentic."

"They had no idea where you were from?"

"No. I told them I had been with a small group of families living in northern Utah who had been caught by a group of roaming bandits—the villagers called them the Marauders. I said I was the only survivor."

"Good, good."

"I hid the radio transmitter away from the village." Travis smiled. "It wasn't always easy to slip away. That's why I missed a couple of reports."

"I understand."

"Anyway, the village accepted me very quickly. In fact," he added modestly, "normally, Eric would have been left in charge of the village defenses. His father is the accepted leader for the village, but surprisingly, Eric is viewed as the second in command." He paused. "Well, actually, that isn't really too surprising once you come to know Eric. He is very much like his father—bright, resourceful, courageous, and personable. I told Nicole that he's a natural leader, and the villagers see that too."

He took a breath. "But anyway, Eric's father wanted Eric to join Doc Cameron, so he took the men down to the river and left me in charge of the village defenses. That, of course, made the capture of the village much easier."

The Major nodded, obviously pleased. "For you to gain their confidence to that degree in less than a month's time, that is remarkable." He leaned back, putting his hands together to form a steeple. "So what went wrong? We've never had this much trouble taking a group before."

"Two things. First, Captain Byers was delayed by a flash flood. He lost almost half a day and decided to travel at night to get back on schedule."

"No!" the Major said angrily. "I warned them not to do that."

"I know, but he figured he was still nearly thirty miles from the village, and it would be all right. But unfortunately, Eric's father and Dr. Cameron were out hunting. They camped on a high ridge, and—" He shrugged.

"Cameron is the brain surgeon?"

"Yes. Eric's father hightailed it back to the village to warn us and sent Eric with some dynamite to join—"

"They had explosives?" Nicole broke in.

"Yes, Eric's dad was a chemist and an explosives expert. They make their own. They also have reloading equipment and make their own gunpowder as well." He turned back to the Major. "Anyway, we would still have been all right. Lights meant civilization. The village was wary but very excited, eager to see who we were."

"It was Cameron who made the first contact?"

"Yes. Eric was hidden in the trees, covering him with a rifle. At first Captain Byers made out as if they were looking for some unknown village. Then he inadvertently let it slip that he knew how far away it was. Doc was instantly suspicious and started to back off. Bruce panicked and tried to stop him. That's when Eric opened fire, and Bruce was hit."

"How is Captain Byers?" the Major asked.

"Still in a lot of pain. We took him straight to surgery this morning. The surgeon thinks he may never fully recover the use of his right arm."

"It's not that I have no sympathy," the Major said curtly, "but he's reaping the results of his own shortsighted stupidity. Well, either way, he is now relieved of his command."

Nicole looked up quickly. The Major's impatience with shoddy performance was legendary, but Bruce Byers was one of the original Guardians and second in command to the Major.

"Go on," the Major commanded, prodding Travis out of his own evident shock at Byers's dismissal.

"Well, that essentially set the course of events. Eric slipped away and ambushed the convoy a few minutes later with a satchel of dynamite. We lost three men there, with nine others seriously injured, and, of course, one of the trucks. Eric then joined the others at the bridge and told them what was happening. That ended all hopes of a peaceful meeting. They were waiting in ambush for the column, and we lost six more in the first volley. Lieutenant Carter, who had taken over from Byers, returned fire, and the battle was on. We lost four more men in the next two hours, with several others wounded. We also lost another truck when they blew the bridge out from under it."

The Major slammed his fist against the table. "Thirteen dead, nearly two dozen wounded. And all because of sloppy execution of orders. This is intolerable!"

"How many villagers were killed?" Nicole broke in, watching the weariness etch deeper in Travis's face.

"Six. Some of the best men in the village."

"But how?" Nicole asked. "Strict orders were issued to put the weapons on stun capacity only."

"Both Byers and Carter swear they never rescinded that order. But evidently, some of the men took it upon themselves to open up to full power." Travis's eyes were dark. "And who can blame them when they were under fire like that? Remember, they lost six, but we lost thirteen!"

"And for nothing!" the Major snapped. "That's the tragedy."

Travis took a deep breath and then looked up. "As you know, I was in radio contact with the group the chopper let off about twenty miles south of the valley. That was two days before Byers was spotted, and I had led them into position in the foothills overlooking the village. Once the others left, we took the village easily. That was when Eric returned and told me what was happening at the river. I took immediate action, but it was too late to do much except end it quickly."

"You did well, Travis," the Major said, leaning forward in his chair. "I should have had you take over the column from the first. Byers is obviously getting too old for a field command." He shrugged off the thought, his irritation slowly fading. "So tell me about the village," he added gently, sensing Travis's discouragement. "They seem to have been quite well off compared to others we've found."

"Yes. Eric's father, Karl Lloyd, was in the Army, in the—"

"Colonel Karl Lloyd?"

"Yes, sir, did you know him?"

"Knew *of* him. He had a brilliant reputation among all the services. Perhaps the best chemist we had. And he was killed?"

"Yes, sir."

"Ah," the Major sighed. "That is a tragedy."

"He was a fine man, sir. Anyway, he had concluded that the nations had lost their senses. He resigned his commission and gathered a small group of others around him. They started preparing for what was coming. They purchased a large ranch in the upper part of what was then Star Valley, Wyoming. They took classes in wilderness survival, collected books on basic skills, even began looking for equipment that did not depend on petroleum, and so on. Unfortunately, it hit sooner than they expected."

"Sooner than any of us expected," the Major added sadly. "But then who could have predicted the total insanity we saw?"

"Well, he called it pretty close, except for the timing. He predicted that once it began, everyone would unleash everything they had in the ensuing chaos. He also guessed correctly that nuclear strikes would not be the only danger, that chemical and biological warheads would be as common as nuclear ones. And so he chose his spot well. Star Valley had no industrial or military sites close by. It was relatively isolated, hidden between two substantial mountain ranges, and the prevailing air currents would carry much of the fallout away from them. Even then the group roughed it out through the winter in the mountains. Lloyd's wife died of pneumonia, and they lost several others. I guess it was pretty bad. Eric was six at the time. When spring finally came, they decided the valley was finally safe, so they moved down."

"Then the valley didn't escape being hit?" Nicole broke in.

"Yes and no. There were no direct strikes, but some biological agents and radioactive fallout drifted in from the west. Not a great amount, but sufficient to decimate the valley's population. When the Lloyd group finally moved in, they picked up about thirty or forty survivors who were still there."

"And so they set up their own community?" the Major asked.

"Yes. The men Karl Lloyd had persuaded to join him were all top-notch in every way. Dr. Cameron was a leading neurosurgeon. Monroe Wilson was an electrical engineer. Ralph Maddox owned a major machine and tool business, and so on. But it was more than the skills. Lloyd wouldn't take anyone who wasn't outstanding in his personal character as well. Most were deeply religious and active in church. They had to be strong family men, men of integrity—the best kinds of people. Karl Lloyd often said, as he told me about their survival, that if God hadn't taken a direct hand in their lives, they would never have made it. That commitment to God influenced the whole village. Every Sunday, all work stopped. Everyone went to church, then spent the rest of the day with their families."

Nicole studied Travis's face, touched by the obvious feelings he felt for the people he had helped to capture. "You said Eric has two younger sisters?" she asked.

"Yes, half-sisters actually. Karl Lloyd married one of the women from the valley after several years. She had lost all of her family in the sickness. She's a very fine woman too."

"And technologically?"

"Oh, they built a small generating plant on the river to provide their basic electrical needs. Once the surrounding areas were decontaminated, they made scavenging trips to nearby towns and villages, such as Idaho Falls and Logan. They brought back commodities that they could not manufacture themselves—light bulbs, medical supplies, tools, and equipment. They also gleaned the best books from several libraries to help in the education of their children. They even raided a video shop. For years they had a video tape recorder, with about two dozen movies on tape, but gradually it wore out and the tapes gave out. They still talk about the old movies."

33

"So other than a minimal level of technology," the Major said, "they were essentially a nineteenth-century farming community."

"That's right. All in all, they lived very well off the land, both through farming and hunting."

The Major stood up. "Great!" he said enthusiastically. "Some excellent farmers are exactly what we need. And won't it be a thrill for them to have tractors and electric pumps for irrigation!"

"You do plan to send most of them to Serenity, don't you?" Travis asked.

"All of them. I had originally planned to use three or four men from the village, but I've changed my mind," he said. "We need the men too badly for farming. If we hadn't lost those six—"

"We also lost thirteen Guardians," Travis reminded him.

"Yes, I know. But we have the other villages we are working on right now. If all goes well, we'll obtain sufficient replacements for the Guardians from them. Right now we desperately need help in getting Serenity fully operational, or we're going to lose the wheat harvest. So all of the villagers will be implanted. Except for the Lloyd boy, of course. He's exactly what we have been looking for." He turned to Nicole and smiled. "Are you ready for a real challenge?"

"Yes, sir, I think so."

"Good. Travis won't be much good to us on this one." He turned to him. "The boy will blame you for his father. You know him best, but you'll have to work from the background."

"Yes," Travis agreed. "I still feel terrible about that."

"I know. But you aren't to blame. You did a great job for us." He clapped Travis on the shoulders. "I want you to take a couple of days off before you take over your new command."

Travis's head jerked up. "Command, sir?"

The Major waved his hand impatiently, but there was a twinkle in his eyes. "Yes, of course. Byers's command. Who did you think I would give it to?"

Before Travis could respond, he turned to Nicole. "I want you to work on Lloyd directly with me. He's too important to me to botch up. We'll begin Friday."

CHAPTER

5

With a groan, Eric pulled himself up into a sitting position and grabbed his head to keep it from rolling onto the floor. Then he stared at the blue expanse of sky in front of him. Why was a white washbowl hanging in midair? And a mirror? Somewhere in the dim recesses of his mind, he recognized the bloodshot eyes and stubble-strewn face staring back at him. But why a mirror in the middle of the sky?

With a sigh he decided it was a problem of infinite complexity and limited interest. He collapsed back onto the bed, noting with fuzzy satisfaction that the sink and mirror rolled out of sight. Now he saw only the sun. He blinked. It was a tiny sun, shaped like a light bulb. The thought wrenched his eyes into focus, and he jerked to a sitting position again. It *was* a light bulb, protruding from a ceiling of the same sky-blue color as the walls.

He shook his head to clear the fog smothering his mind and began to reexamine his surroundings, this time more slowly. A small bar on the side of the washbowl held a set of dark blue towels. Above the basin on a small wooden shelf sat a shaving mug, a hairbrush, a safety razor, a bar of hand soap, a toothbrush.

He looked down, his mind clearing slowly. He was sitting on a cot built into the wall. A navy blue blanket was tucked neatly under the mattress, and near the top was a gleaming white pillow, slightly rumpled. A simple wooden stool sat near the head of the bed. To his right, a bright blue metal door stood slightly ajar. He leaned over to see through it and noted a small room with a shower stall and toilet. Just beyond the door, a rod below a shelf held several hangers with clothing that looked vaguely familiar to him. Suddenly he realized they were his own clothes. He glanced down and saw that he was still clad in his dark brown shirt and trousers. Somehow that comforted him, yet it puzzled him too.

Shutting his eyes, Eric massaged his temples gently with his fingertips. Then he stood up and moved over to the mirror to stare at himself, noting the gauntness of his face and his bloodshot eyes. He ran his hand quickly through his hair, then scratched at the heavy black stubble on his jaw. He needed a shave badly. His mother would light in on him like a coyote on a wounded rabbit if she saw— Finally the circuits in his brain connected. The village! His family! Cliff! It all came back with stunning clarity—the ambush at the river, Travis Oakes smiling sadly at him just before the hammer blow to the chest took him out. So where in the world . . . ?

He moved instantly toward the far corner of the room. There was a door, but with no knob or latch of any kind. He ran his fingers along the thin crack, but the door was too finely fit. Not even a sheet of paper would slip through.

He sat back down on the cot. Now he understood the thick mud in his head. Somehow he had been drugged and taken away—but where? Obviously far from the village. And what about his family? Were they here too?

Suddenly Eric looked down and stared at his left wrist. Bound snugly around his wrist was a watch with a gold band. His father, Cliff, and a few others in the village had once worn digital watches, though the batteries had given out years before. This watch was slightly larger and thicker than theirs had been, but it was unmistakably a watch. As Eric held it up for a closer look, the numerals 9:18 were sharp and distinct. In the upper corner was a tiny "A.M." He studied it closely. Two small buttons protruded on the right side. Curious, he pushed the upper one. To his surprise, the numerals disappeared, and bright yellow letters began flowing slowly across the face. TODAY IS TUESDAY, JUNE 5. THE TEMPERATURE IN SHALEV IS 76°, RELATIVE HUMIDITY IS 63%, WINDS ARE OUT OF THE SOUTHWEST AT 4 MPH, BAROMETRIC PRESSURE IS 29.02 AND STEADY. The letters ceased flowing for a moment, then TODAY IS TUESDAY, JUNE 5. THE TEMPERATURE . . .

Eric released the upper button and pushed the lower. Once again a message moved slowly across the tiny screen. IMPROVEMENTS TO LAKESHORE PARK ARE SCHEDULED TO BE COMPLETED EARLY NEXT WEEK. FURTHER ANNOUNCEMENTS ABOUT THE RIBBON-CUTTING CEREMONIES WILL BE FORTHCOMING. . . . TRAGEDY STRIKES—CARL QUILTON, OF NORTH HEIGHTS, WAS SERIOUSLY MAULED BY A GRIZZLY BEAR WHILE BACKPACKING IN GLACIER PARK. HIS WIFE AND TWO SONS DROVE THE ANIMAL OFF WITH THEIR SCREAMS. QUILTON IS LISTED IN CRITICAL CONDITION AT SHALEV GENERAL HOSPITAL. PARK RANGERS WARNED CAMPERS AND . . .

Shalev. Eric shook his head. He had heard that name before. Then he remembered. The man who had killed Cliff said they had come from Shalev. Half-baffled, half-fascinated, Eric turned his arm, looking for some kind of clasp, but there was nothing. The watchband was uniformly the same all the way around. He put all four fingers of his right hand under the watch's face and pulled strongly. A sharp, intermittent buzzing caused him to jump. WARNING! WARNING! WARNING! flashed on and off the face. Then the letters flowed again, only this time they were not yellow, but blood red. THE WRIST COMPUTER CANNOT BE REMOVED. UNDUE PRESSURE ON THE BAND HAS TRIGGERED THIS ALARM. PLEASE RELEASE PRESSURE IMMEDIATELY TO AVOID AUTOMATIC PUNISHMENT MODE. The letters winked off, then almost instantly began again. WARNING! WARNING! WARNING! . . .

Suddenly, as he stared at the flashing thing on his wrist, Eric felt the frustration inside him boil over, and the sharp buzz only infuriated him further. With a yank that dug the band into his flesh, he put his fingers under the band and tried to tear it off his wrist. A sharp gasp exploded from his lips as his left arm suddenly went rigid with pain. His muscles knotted into iron-hard balls of agony, and his arm jerked violently. With a cry of pain he grabbed at his arm. Instantly the agony stopped, and his arm dropped limply into his lap.

Stunned, Eric stared at the innocent-looking little box on his wrist, his chest rising and falling rapidly. THE PUNISHMENT MODE IN YOUR WRIST COMPUTER WAS TRIGGERED BY UN-WARRANTED PRESSURE ON THE BAND. TO AVOID FURTHER ELECTRICAL SHOCK, DO NOT PULL THE BAND. The bright red letters repeated the message, then blinked off, and Eric was left staring at the numerals, 9:20, and a tiny "A.M." in the upper corner.

Madeline Lloyd let out her breath slowly. Judy, their bus driver and guide, a young woman majoring in child development at the University of Shalev, was right. The city *was* beautiful. No, Madeline amended. It was stunning. Images she had long ago decided would never be seen again in her lifetime were assaulting her senses on every side.

A farm woman all her life, she was still a little dazed by it all. The three-day journey in the trucks had been exhausting, but after they had finally arrived, they were fed a delicious meal, taken to modern quarters, and allowed to shower and then sleep in comfortable beds. As they had on the trip here, the orange-uniformed men continued to closely guard all males fifteen and over and keep them separated from the women and the children, but they promised that the separation would be maintained only one more day, and then the people would be reunited.

At least some will be reunited. Madeline bit her lip and forced her mind away from Karl and the wrenching pain in her heart.

After breakfast, the women and children had been loaded onto buses to begin a tour of the city. At first it had seemed absurdly out of character. On the surface everything was so normal, and yet they were prisoners, ripped from their homes through treachery and death and carted off like so many cattle.

"This is one of our newest sections of the city," Judy was saying, cutting into Madeline's thoughts. "The city council has taken the city, section by section, and replaced all the homes that were here before Termination. It has been an expensive and lengthy project, but now the homes are modern, energy efficient, and attractive places for our people to live. Not only are the houses all heated by electricity, but the cars are electric and virtually all industry is powered by electricity.

"With only about two hundred thousand people in the Alliance of Four Cities—we call it the AFC—we obviously do not have everything as it was before." She looked up into the rearview mirror and smiled. "My father still talks about coffee and cigarettes, but my mother says it was the best thing that ever happened to him. Other products found in warm climates, such as citrus fruit, bananas, pineapple, and several spices, we just do without. I would like to taste them some day. Rumor has it that an expedition may be sent south to see if any of those plants have survived and could be cultivated in greenhouses up here, but so far nothing has come of that.

"Metal products, especially aluminum and steel, are turned out in small quantities but are very limited and quite expensive. However, production is slowly expanding. We've reopened the copper mines around what used to be Butte, Montana, and have a large refinery near there."

Curious in spite of herself, Madeline called to the cheerful young guide, "You say the cars are electric. Does that mean you don't have petroleum?"

"No. We do have one fairly good-sized oil field in production east of here, near Browning. And there are several smaller areas. But most of that goes for the chemical and plastics industries. Our engineers have developed a heavy-duty, rechargeable battery, so virtually all vehicles in the AFC are electric."

As the bus stopped at a traffic signal, Judy half turned in her seat and smiled back at her passengers. "The older people—those who lived before Termination—still complain a lot about what we don't have, but as one writer put it, we have ice cream, television, and nylon stockings. What more could a person want?"

The bus turned a corner and entered a beautiful parkway with a center island of grass and flowers so brilliant that they dazzled the eye. About a block ahead of them, Madeline could see a quadrant lined on three sides with large, modern buildings of brick and glass.

"We are now entering Alliance Square," Judy said proudly.

Stephanie leaned forward in her seat. "Oh, Mother, look at the buildings."

"What you see before you is the heart not only of our city, but of the entire Alliance." The bus pulled into a turnaround so the passengers had a clear view. "Alliance Square houses offices for all three levels of government. Those along the north side are the AFC buildings, or the equivalent of the federal level. The square building with the round dome houses the Senate and the judicial offices. The brown brick mansion is where the president, Peter Dobson, lives. As before, all our officials are elected by the people."

She turned and pointed. "Along the south side here are the Shalev city offices and the Flathead District Council chambers."

Becky suddenly jumped up and pressed her nose to the window. "Oh, Lori! Look! Look at the water." She turned to her mother, her brown eyes wide with wonder.

Madeline Lloyd smiled as Judy explained, "That's the Shalev Fountain. Shalev is a Hebrew word that means peace. As you can see from the sign, the building directly behind the fountain is the Museum of Remembrance. It's a very special place for us all. It contains a collection of things from the world before Termination—things to help us realize what we are 'missing,' such as war, terrorists, crime, poverty, drugs, alcoholism. The museum houses weapons, relics, and documents from those horrible times so that we can teach our children how blessed we are in the AFC." Again she turned around and smiled at the group. "You see, in Shalev and the Alliance, all of those things have been totally eliminated."

40

Madeline looked up quickly. Totally eliminated? How could that be? She leaned forward, noting the amazement on the faces of the others as well.

Judy continued her explanation. "The museum was built to help us better appreciate what we no longer have—or better, what we really do have here. In it is a room for each of the wars America fought. There is a Civil War room, World War One and Two rooms, a room for Korea, one for Viet Nam, and, of course, one for the War of Termination. And we—"

"Eliminated?" Madeline asked. "How is it possible that *all* such things have been eliminated?"

Judy stiffened slightly, and for the first time her pride seemed to falter. "That is too complicated for me to explain to you here." She took a quick breath. "That is another reason for your orientation session this afternoon. They will explain all of that to you."

As she turned the wheel and started the bus again, Stephanie pointed to a long, brick building that occupied the entire west side of the quadrant. "Did she say what that building was?" Though nearly three stories high at the front, it butted up against a low pine-covered ridge. Only a front entrance interrupted the entire expanse of brick. It had the appearance of a brooding fortress with no eyes and one gaping mouth.

"No, ask her."

"Judy?"

The bus stopped, and their guide turned around. "Yes?"

"What is that building?"

Again, for a fraction of a second, Madeline saw the guide's smile falter, then snap back into place. "That is where you are going to have lunch in about ten minutes."

"What is it?"

"That is Central Control, headquarters for the Guardians."

"The who?"

"The Guardians." She started the bus, lurching it forward. "Now around the next corner we have the University of Shalev. It is—"

"Judy," Madeline said clearly, "are the Guardians the men in the orange and blue uniforms?"

41

She paused. "Yes."

A sudden chill swept the bus like a blast in a winter storm, and sensing it, Judy fell silent.

Madeline brooded for several moments, lost in the bitterness of memory. Suddenly she noticed four boys waiting at the intersection for the bus to pass, staring up at her and smiling. Then she realized they weren't smiling at her, but at Stephanie. She turned around in time to see Stephanie smile shyly back at them, which brought a quick wave from the nearest boy.

Once again Madeline felt a wrenching leap in her heart. Stephanie was strikingly beautiful, having inherited her father's dark hair and her real mother's finely cut features and slimness of body. And yet in the village there were only three eligible young men.

Maybe Shalev would change all that. The hope swelled inside her, and she would have given it full sway if it weren't for an ominous sense of foreboding that gnawed at her. *War eliminated? No more crimes? Then why are six bodies buried under the pines down near the river? And why are we in Shalev, imprisoned like sheep in a pen?*

"Oh, Mother, " Stephanie cried, "look at their clothes!"

They were passing a group of girls, apparently just leaving school. The women on the bus stared at the soft fabrics, the vibrant colors, the stylish cut, the variety of skirts, blouses, dresses, and pants. And nylons! Madeline almost cried aloud. After eighteen years of homespun and buckskin, hand-knit stockings and woolen sweaters, here were nylons and high heels, sandals, tennis shoes, purses that were more than thick leather pouches, necklaces, earrings, lipstick. How long it had been! How long had she forced her mind to forget there had once been such things? She turned away quickly and blinked back tears when she saw Stephanie's fingers touching her own rough, homespun blouse.

The waitress was about the same age as their driver, with a short haircut and smiling brown eyes. She came up to Becky and placed a large, round tray of food on the table. "Hi. My name is Molly."

"Hi," Becky responded shyly.

"What's your name?"

"Becky Lloyd."

"How do you do, Becky. Is this your sister?"

"I'm Lori," Lori responded, beaming.

The waitress stuck out her hand. "Hi, I'm Molly. You like hamburgers?"

Both girls nodded quickly.

"Have you ever had an ice cream soda?"

Stephanie laughed. "Even I haven't had one of those since I was tiny."

"Would you like one too?" Molly asked. "I didn't think about that."

"Yes, I would," Stephanie replied, a bit embarrassed, but eager nevertheless.

Molly lifted two frosty glasses off the tray and set them in front of Lori and Becky. "Now normally you would have to wait to have your sodas until after you've eaten your dinner. But since you've never had one, maybe we could let you snitch just one taste. Is that okay, Mother?"

Madeline smiled and nodded.

"Be careful," Molly said, sticking a straw in each glass. "It'll tickle your nose."

"What's that, Mama?" Lori asked, pointing.

"That's a straw, honey," Madeline answered, suddenly realizing how many things had been lost to her children.

"Remember when Eric showed you how to blow bubbles with a reed?" Stephanie said. "It's just like that, only you have to suck on it."

Becky took a quick sip, her cheeks sucking inward. As the carbonated liquid hit her mouth, she grimaced and gave a quick shudder. "Ummmmm," she said, "that's good."

Molly laughed with delight at the contradiction between Becky's words and expression.

"Oh, Mama," Lori cried, "that is good."

"Well," Molly said, "I'm a success. How does a breaded veal cutlet sound to you, Mrs. Lloyd, and . . . "

43

"Stephanie."

"Stephanie. Does that sound okay?"

"Delicious."

They were nearly through eating when suddenly Stephanie grabbed Madeline's arm. "Look, Mother, it's Travis."

A sudden hush fell over the dining room as every eye turned to the figure in orange and blue and followed it as it moved to the platform at the front of the room. The Lloyds were sitting near the rear of the dining hall, but even from that distance it was obvious that Travis Oakes was very nervous. He shuffled, then reshuffled some notes in his hand, then looked up, cleared his throat, and plunged in.

"I have conducted many of these orientation sessions," he began quietly, "but never has one been more difficult for me personally. I know that if it weren't for us, some of you would not be sitting here today without fathers, without husbands, without brothers. Nothing I can say will lessen the tragedy of that. But I want you to know that extremely unfortunate circumstances brought about that situation, not deliberate intent. I want you to know that every widow will be cared for, every fatherless child watched over. Shalev cannot bring those six men back to you, but we can try to lessen the impact of the tragedy on your personal lives."

As he continued, sober, earnest, and pleading for their understanding, Madeline watched him closely, then dropped her glance and continued eating her lunch. She had once hoped this man might be her son-in-law, that he might show some interest in Stephanie. Now all she could think about was Travis's betrayal.

"—and while it will be difficult for you to understand at this point," Travis was saying, "very shortly you will see that your coming to Shalev and the Alliance of Four Cities will be the turning point of your lives. Our purpose this afternoon is to orient you to our little pocket of surviving civilization, to show you what we have achieved.

"In a way, your children have grown up in the village with neither the advantages nor the disadvantages of so-called civilization. They have had virtually no experience with television, movies, transportation, modern conveniences, and so on. But on the other hand, neither have they had much experience with crime, violence, pollution, discrimination, greed, war, and similar 'benefits.' Their opportunities for education and culture have likewise been extremely limited.

"I could go on and on, but suffice it to say that in the Alliance we are prepared to offer you all of the advantages of civilization, and none of the disadvantages. When I say none, I mean that literally. You will find no crime here. None! I know that seems incredible, but we are not talking about *low* crime, we are talking about *no* crime! You can walk the streets of Shalev any time of the day or night and never fear a mugging, an assault, or a rape. None of those things exist here. None! There are no robberies, no burglaries, no shoplifting, no vandalism. In fact, it's difficult to find locks in Shalev, except for simple ones that maintain privacy or protect small children from getting into danger."

Becky slurped the last of her soda through the straw, yawned, then leaned against her mother's arm. Madeline gave her a quick squeeze. Thoroughly bored now also, Lori pushed her plate away and laid her head on her arms. Stifling a yawn herself, Madeline turned back to Travis. Scheduling a heavy lecture after a meal was not the wisest course of action, she decided.

"Because I have come to know you, to respect you, I am thrilled to tell you that in the Alliance of Four Cities, there is no poverty, no unemployment, no drugs, no street gangs, no alcohol, no slums, no bars, no pollution. We have free elections, free enterprise, freedom to grow and be what we want to be. We have art, music, education, trade, business, science, and industry."

He smiled for the first time. "Sounds like a dream, doesn't it?"

"Speaking of dreams," Stephanie said out of the corner of her mouth, as she slumped lower in her chair, "I wish he'd hurry up and finish and let us go take a nap."

"Shhhh!" Madeline said, fighting the heaviness in her own eyes.

"Well," Stephanie grumbled, "how long is he going to drone on?"

Five minutes later, Madeline was beginning to ask herself the same question. Travis had turned off all the lights to show slides of the Alliance and Shalev. That was all it had taken. Stephanie had now joined Lori with her head on her arms, and Becky had wiggled sideways in her chair until her head was in her mother's lap. Her breathing was deep and regular.

Madeline looked around. Perhaps Travis was excited about what he was saying, but he was obviously the only one. Over two-thirds of the heads were down and several others were tipped way back, mouths open, dead to the world. The soft sound of snoring was evident whenever Travis paused in his narrative. Even as Madeline watched, Rose Browning, who was sitting at the table in front of them, surrendered, and her head dropped forward with a snap.

Somewhere in the back of Madeline's head, an alarm clanged dully. Something was not quite right, and she tried feebly to sort it out in her head. Some drowsiness after lunch in a dark and stuffy room was normal, but it was barely one in the afternoon. Something was wrong! Then she decided that whatever it was, it wasn't that important after all, as her own chin dipped lower and lower until it rested on her chest. Travis droned on, lulling her over the edge into a blissful, inviting cloud of sleep.

CHAPTER

6

Madeline turned her eyes slowly, letting things come into focus. A wall panel with oxygen spouts, a call button, light switches, bars on the side of the bed all seemed so natural and yet so strange.

Suddenly a figure in white loomed over her and spoke. "Mrs. Lloyd? Hello, how are you feeling?"

"What?"

"How are you feeling now?"

With a conscious effort, Madeline considered the question and finally nodded. She felt a dull ache at the base of her skull, but other than that, nothing seemed wrong. "Okay," she mumbled.

"Good. I'll be back in a moment. Dr. Abernathy wanted to know as soon as you came out of the sedation so he can start prepping your child."

Madeline tried to stop the disappearing figure, but her body moved in slow motion, and the nurse was gone. She lay there for several minutes, gradually becoming more aware of herself and her surroundings. But greater awareness brought only greater confusion. She remembered now the conquest of the village, the trip to Shalev, and the tour of the city, but why was she in a hospital?

She pushed up onto one elbow, found the call button, and pressed it, coming fully alert now.

Quick footsteps clicked out in the hall, and the door pushed open. Madeline wasn't sure if it was the same nurse or not, but the smile was warm and gracious. "Oh good," the nurse said before she could speak, "you are coming out of it now. I'm Mrs. Carter."

"Hello." Madeline pushed up further, and the nurse hurried to her side and fluffed the pillow up behind her. "Uh—where am I? Why am I in a hospital?"

"Dr. Gould is waiting to explain all that to you. As soon as you feel up to it, I'll take you down to the surgery wing. The drug should be pretty well gone in another minute or two."

"The other nurse—or was it you?—said something about my children."

Again she gave Madeline a warm smile. "No, that was Miss Rasmussen. She went to tell Dr. Abernathy that they can start prepping your child."

"Prepping?"

"Yes, preparing for the operation. Dr. Gould wants—"

Madeline sat bolt upright, "Operation? What operation? What has happened?"

The nurse patted her arm. "There's nothing to worry about. Dr. Gould will explain that too." She retrieved a long robe from the closet, stepped outside for a moment, and returned pushing a wheelchair. "If you're ready, we can go."

Deeply alarmed, Madeline swung her legs out of the covers and over the side. "I don't need a wheelchair," she said, but as she stood up her legs nearly buckled, and Mrs. Carter grabbed her quickly.

"Come on," she soothed, "that sedation can fool you. This is what I'm here for." She helped Madeline with the robe, then sat her down in the chair and bent over to lift her feet onto the foot rests. Madeline stared ahead, barely aware of the nurse. *Child? Which child? Operating for what?* She felt as though she'd been dropped into an unfamiliar world, and no one was going to help her identify where she was.

As they moved briskly down the corridor, Madeline's eyes

were wide. It was a modern hospital in every sense of the word, with the same smell of antiseptic and soap and sickness as every other hospital she had ever been in. Nurses, orderlies, and patients moved here and there, and the intercom chimed and called for this doctor or that doctor. As they approached the elevators, a Pink Lady smiled at them. Madeline felt as if she had somehow been thrust back twenty years in time.

While they were waiting, Madeline suddenly pointed to her left wrist. "What's this?"

"That's your wrist computer," Mrs. Carter said, anticipating the next question. "Everyone in Shalev has one." She held up her own arm, and the Pink Lady did the same.

"Wrist computer?"

"Yes, it's like a watch, but more. Much more."

"But why—"

"Mrs. Lloyd," the nurse interjected, "I know this is all a little overwhelming to you, but if you'll just be patient for a few more minutes, Dr. Gould will explain it all to you. Just be patient."

Dr. Gould, a short, balding man, was dressed in green operating robes and hat, with a surgical mask hanging around his neck along with a stethoscope. He smiled at Madeline as Mrs. Carter wheeled her up, but the smile was brief and only touched the surface of his face.

"How do you do, Mrs. Lloyd. I'm Dr. Gould." He nodded to Mrs. Carter. "Thank you, nurse."

Mrs. Carter smiled at Madeline quickly and disappeared back around the corner.

Before the doctor could speak, Madeline's anxiety took control. "What's going on?" she demanded. "Why am I here?"

"Mrs. Lloyd, our time is relatively short at the moment, so I'll get right to the point. A full explanation will be given to you later. But briefly, as an incoming citizen of Shalev, you've undergone what we call implantation."

"Implantation?"

"Yes. A tiny piece of electronic equipment has been implanted at the base of your skull. Please," he said, catching her hand as it jerked upward, "be careful of the dressing."

Gingerly she raised her arm and touched the bandage at the hairline of her neck, staring at him as she explored it. "But why?"

"That will be explained later, as I said. It's standard procedure for all citizens. Your children are also undergoing this operation."

"What?" She started up out of the chair, but he pushed her back down firmly.

"It's a minor operation. I assure you they're all right. In fact, your two oldest daughters are already awake and doing fine."

"My two oldest—" She stumbled to a halt, her eyes focusing on the surgical mask that hung at his throat. A sense of horror more numbing than the sedation was crushing down on her, and she felt a sudden clamminess down her spine. "Who gave you permission to operate on my children?"

He sighed, like a teacher wearying of a particularly slow pupil. "Mrs. Lloyd, this will all make perfect sense later. But it's not a question of permission. It's a government requirement."

"A government requirement?"

"Mrs. Lloyd, I know this is all a bit of a shock, but we don't have time to go through all that now. We have a problem with your youngest daughter."

"Becky?" she cried. "What's wrong?"

"No, no," he said hastily. "It's nothing serious. We just, well, we have a problem. She threw up her lunch—" He managed a brief smile, meant to show his fatherly concern, but which filled Madeline with revulsion. "Too much hamburger and ice cream soda, I guess. Anyway, she came out of the sedation too early."

"Sedation?" Madeline shook her head, her mind reeling.

"Yes, you were all given a sedative with your lunch today. You've been asleep for about four hours. We find it's much easier on both you and us."

It came back to her then, the growing weariness during Travis's lecture, the dull sense of alarm as she slipped into unconsciousness. The sickness and the revulsion and the horror were turning now, swiftly changing to a burning rage. "It?" she nearly shouted. "What do you mean it? It makes what easier?"

A searing pain wrenched her stomach, causing her to gasp sharply. She tried to ignore it as the rage against this awful man engulfed her. "What are you saying?" she cried, leaping up to confront him. "Who are you? What right do you have—?" But a scream of agony cut her off, doubling her over.

Dr. Gould watched, his eyes expressionless as she finally straightened, biting back the pain, her face white. "Mrs. Lloyd," he said, shaking his head sadly, "anger will only hurt *you*. It will not help your daughter. Do you want to help your daughter or not?"

Madeline was dazed and shaken, not sure what was happening. The pain. His hammering words. But his final question registered, and she heard herself answering, "Yes, I do. Where is she?"

"Normally we use only a local anesthetic when we do implantations, but the patient must hold absolutely still. That's why we sedated all of you. But Becky's sedation has worn off, and the anesthesiologist would rather not put her under a general anesthesia when she has been throwing up. That presents a problem, for she must be perfectly motionless while we do the implantation, and Becky has been hysterical for the last hour and a half. She's terribly frightened and wants her mother."

"Oh, Becky," Madeline whispered, still unable to shake off the horrifying dreamlike quality of what was happening.

"Unfortunately, you'd already been sent to surgery, so we've had to wait for you to recover. Now, time is critical. The next busload of people have to be implanted before their sedation wears off." He looked at his hands, then finally raised his head. "Mrs. Lloyd, I don't like to put it this way, but I must. We have no option. Your daughter must have this operation now. If you can calm her down, we can do it with a local anesthetic. If not, we'll have to put her under. She'll probably be fine, but there's a greater risk that way. Do you understand that?

She leaped up, knocking away his hand as he tried to stop her. "I only understand—" She gasped as someone took a red hot iron and rammed it up from her stomach into her chest. She grabbed for the wheelchair. "I won't let you touch my daughter!" she shouted. Then her body jerked violently, and she started to topple over, the wheelchair tipping beneath her weight.

51

Dr. Gould grabbed her, pulling her back upright. For a moment she thought she was going to faint, and she didn't resist as he pushed her firmly back down into the wheelchair.

"Mrs. Lloyd," he said, leaning over and peering into her face, "you must control your anger. It's your implantation that's causing the pain you're experiencing now."

She shook her head, drawing deep, hungry breaths of air. "No. It's my stomach."

"Just trust me. I'll explain it all to you later. But you must not get angry, or the pain will return. Do you understand that much?"

She didn't, but she slowly nodded.

"Good. Now I'll say it again. You can either help us with your daughter or you can refuse. Either way we will proceed. Will you help us, or do we do it without you?"

She nodded, not daring to think, not daring to feel, lest she call back the searing pain. Tears welled up, and her lower lip trembled. "Yes, I'll help you. Where is she?"

As they wheeled the hospital bed down the long hallway toward her, Madeline saw the tiny figure hunched up in a pitiful little ball, exhausted sobs racking the body. She felt a sharp pain in her heart far more intense than the blows that had hammered at her stomach. She swept Becky up into her arms, clinging to the trembling little body as desperately as Becky clung to her. For five minutes they sat in the hallway until finally the sobs subsided, the heart stopped its furious pounding, and Becky pulled away and looked around. Though her eyes were still swollen and her cheeks a blotchy red, her normal adventuresome spirit was returning, and when Mrs. Carter brought green gowns for both Becky and her mother and they went into surgery, she was bouncing with the newness of it all.

"Okay, young lady," Mrs. Carter said, patting the operating table. "Let's trade beds."

"That's a bed?" Becky cried, wrinkling her nose.

"Yup. A pretty funny one, isn't it?"

"What's that?" Becky was pointing to a circular device made

of stainless steel and lined on the inside with thick foam rubber. It was attached to the head of the bed.

"That, kiddo, is where your head goes. How's that for silly?"

"My head?"

"Yes, ma'am. Lie on your tummy, and rest your chin right here. Your mommy will come and sit in the chair here where you can see her."

The nurse helped Becky rest her head in the cup, then began to adjust the stainless steel clamps. "I'll just tighten this until it's nice and comfy, and that way your head will be real still while the doctors fix you up. Okay?"

"Yes. This really is silly."

Becky giggled happily, a sound that tore through Madeline like a serrated blade of steel. A scream started somewhere in the back of her throat, swelling up inside her until she had to clench her teeth to stop it from bursting out. Then just as suddenly, the silent scream was snuffed out by rolling waves of pain smashing at her body. Her knees buckled, and she sat down quickly, averting her face, glad that the surgical mask hid all but her eyes.

The nurse watched her sadly for a moment, then picked up a hypodermic needle from the tray and showed it to Becky, whose eyes suddenly grew wide with fear.

"Have you ever stuck your finger with a pin or a needle?"

"Uh huh," Becky answered nervously.

"Well, this won't hurt any more than that. Just one little teeny hurt for one teeny minute right here—" She touched the back of Becky's neck. "Okay? Let your mother hold your hand."

With great effort, Madeline leaned over and looked into the frightened brown eyes as she gripped the little hand. As her fingers encircled Becky's wrist, she could feel the tiny pulse pounding and her daughter's body stiffen.

"Ouch!" Becky's body jerked slightly, then she gritted her teeth and squeezed her eyes tightly, preparing for more.

Mrs. Carter patted her. "Now, that wasn't so bad, was it?"

"Is it done?"

"That's it, kiddo."

Becky's eyes opened, bright with relief. "I didn't cry, Mama."

"You were a brave girl." Madeline squeezed her hand and looked away.

For a few minutes the room was quiet while Mrs. Carter busied herself with several trays of equipment. Finally as she returned and touched the back of Becky's neck, Madeline spoke softly. "What are they going to do to her?"

Mrs. Carter glanced quickly toward the window through which Dr. Gould and another doctor could be seen. A nurse was helping them on with surgical gloves. "Dr. Gould will explain it all to you. I—" She stopped, looking down quickly. "I can't say anything more, Mrs. Lloyd. Except that I know how you feel. I want you to know, this isn't something I approve of, but I'm implanted too. I—" She shook her head, her eyes pleading.

"I understand."

"Dr. Gould is one of the original founders of Shalev. He and the Major developed the idea of implantation, and—" The door pushed open, and she busied herself checking Becky's head position.

"Mrs. Lloyd?" With the surgical mask in place, Dr. Gould's voice was slightly muffled. "This is Dr. Abernathy, our X-ray and computer specialist, and this is Miss Brighton, our head surgical nurse."

It was difficult to tell what they looked like behind their masks, except that Dr. Abernathy looked young and had kind eyes, and Madeline guessed that Miss Brighton was very attractive.

Dr. Abernathy moved over to a large machine. Part of it looked like a traditional X-ray machine, but it had additional machinery with dials, a digital readout, and numerous switches. He moved it back to the bed and positioned it over Becky's head.

Mrs. Carter bent down and peered into Becky's eyes. "You're all set now, young lady. I'll see you in your room, and I'll have that big dish of ice cream I promised you, okay?" She stood up, touched Madeline's arm briefly, then left the room.

"Mrs. Lloyd?"

"Yes?"

Dr. Gould put his hands together, the fingers interlocking as he pushed the surgical gloves on more tightly. "Your presence here is necessary, but you must understand that we cannot have you interfere with the operation in any way. You may speak to Becky to keep her calm, and that's all. Is that clear?"

Madeline met his gaze, her eyes flashing, but she finally nodded, then leaned down and looked at Becky. "My goodness, Becky," she cooed, "doesn't Dr. Gould have a wonderful bedside manner?"

Dr. Abernathy nearly choked, and Miss Brighton dropped a pair of scissors into a tray with a loud clang. Dr. Gould glared at Madeline for a moment, then stalked around the table and thrust his hand out toward the nurse. She slapped a scalpel into it with a sharp crack.

"Dr. Abernathy, are you ready?" he snapped.

"Yes, doctor."

As Dr. Gould bent over the back of Becky's head, Madeline took a deep breath and bit her lip. Dr. Abernathy adjusted the machine slightly, then bent down and looked into Becky's eyes. "How you doing, squirt?"

"Is it going to hurt?" she asked, the quiver in her voice betraying her anxiety.

He smiled. "Have you felt anything yet?"

She tried to shake her head as Dr. Gould's voice commanded softly, "Hemostat. Sponge." Madeline caught the sudden flash of bright red on the fingers of his gloves and felt her stomach turn.

"Well," Dr. Abernathy continued, "that's your answer. Dr. Gould has already started. And see, you haven't felt a thing." He straightened and noticed Madeline staring at Dr. Gould's hands. "Mrs. Lloyd."

If she heard him, she gave no response.

"Mrs. Lloyd!" he said, more sharply, wresting her eyes to his. "The operation involves an inch-long incision at the base of the skull, which is only about half an inch deep."

Dr. Gould shot his colleague a withering glance.

If Dr. Abernathy saw it, he ignored it. "At that point, this machine here—" he touched the gleaming surface, "which is a laser drill—"

"Dr. Abernathy!" Dr. Gould's voice crackled with anger. "I told Mrs. Lloyd I will explain all of that afterwards."

Dr. Abernathy turned slowly, his eyes glittering embers of challenge above his mask. "This is her daughter! She has a right to know what we are doing, and she has a right to know it *now*!"

Evidently not many people challenged Dr. Gould, for his eyes registered shocked surprise, as did the eyes of Miss Brighton. Without waiting for an answer, Dr. Abernathy turned back to Madeline. "Do you know what a laser is?"

"Yes."

"Well, with an almost microscopic laser beam, four very tiny holes will be drilled in Becky's skull. Please," he said gently, as her hand flew to her mouth, "this is not nearly as terrible as it sounds. The laser cauterizes as it goes, eliminating any bleeding and any chance of infection."

Somewhere far back in Madeline's numbed mind pain registered as she bit down against the edge of her clenched fist to stop the cry of horror. *Oh, dear Lord, make this be a dream. Make it not be real.*

"Mama! What's wrong?" Becky's eyes were round and anxious.

Dr. Gould's head jerked up and he glared at Madeline, then at Dr. Abernathy. With a feeling of cold death constricting her heart, Madeline forcibly drew her hand away from her mouth and managed a thin smile. "Nothing, Becky. I just had a little pain, sweetheart. I'm okay."

She looked up, her eyes like stone. "I'm sorry, Dr. Abernathy. Please go on."

He turned and took one step toward the tray of instruments in front of the nurse. When he turned back, he held a flat piece of black plastic about one-inch square. From it extended four incredibly thin wires.

"Inside this plastic is a silicon chip, a miniaturized computer, as it were. The chip will be implanted under the skin at the base of the skull. The electrodes will be inserted through the four laser holes and placed very precisely with the help of X rays and the computer into special areas of the brain."

Not *Becky's* skull—*the* skull. Not *Becky's* brain—*the* brain. Even kind Dr. Abernathy had to depersonalize her to talk about it. It wasn't a freckle-faced six-year-old lying face down on the table, it was a mannequin used in a physiology class, a paragraph from an anatomy book.

When he saw her eyes, he stopped and took a deep breath. "It sounds terrible, but the brain itself has no sensory nerves. The insertion of the electrodes causes no pain."

"But why?" she whispered.

He let his breath out in one long, drawn-out sound. "I am afraid that is the one question Dr. Gould will have to answer."

"Are you quite through, doctor?" Dr. Gould asked icily.

"Yes, Dr. Gould, I am."

"Then, with your permission, may we proceed?"

Dr. Abernathy nodded. He turned and inserted the computer chip into a special slot on the underside of the machine and began to lower it until the electrodes nearly touched Becky's neck.

"Mama!" Becky's lip trembled, and clearly she was on the verge of tears.

"It's all right, darling," Madeline said, reaching out for her hand as Dr. Gould shot her a warning glance. "Hold real still. This won't hurt."

"Then why are you crying, Mama?"

Madeline blinked rapidly and sniffed back the tears. "I—I'm just so proud of you, how brave you are. Just hold real still, and be my brave girl."

CHAPTER

7

Nicole Lambert stood up quickly as the Major entered the narrow, darkened observation room, but he waved her back into her chair. "Sit down, Nicole, please." He stepped forward and peered through the glass. "How is our boy today?"

She smiled. "Bored stiff and increasingly restless."

"Good. Do you think he's ready?"

"Definitely. These two days have driven him up the wall. He should be ready for just about anything."

"Good. What's your evaluation? Can we turn him?"

Nicole pursed her lips thoughtfully. "Well, it's hard to say without any direct interaction, but he's full of hate and frustration. He spotted the speaker and knows what it is. I also think he knows what the mirror is. He demands to know about his family and the village. He hasn't said much the last while because we never answer him."

He sat down next to Nicole. "Okay," he said, with evident pleasure at what was about to take place. "Let's give him a few pleasant surprises, see if we can't lower the hate level a little."

"Yes, sir." Nicole took a deep breath, flicked a switch, then turned to watch the figure stretched out on the cot. "Eric Lloyd," she said softly into the microphone.

He shot off the cot and looked quickly around the room, then at the speaker in the ceiling.

"Mr. Lloyd."

"Yes. I hear you. Who are you?"

"My name is Nicole Lambert."

"Are you behind the mirror?" He was staring almost directly at her.

"Yes."

"Are you the head zoo keeper or just the overseer of the monkey's cage."

Nicole flushed in spite of herself. The caustic bitterness in his eyes burned through the glass between them. She took another breath, aware of the Major's soft chuckle beside her. "May I talk with you a moment?" she asked, keeping her voice completely impersonal.

"I'll have to check my calendar. It's been a hectic summer."

"Okay," she snapped back, "have it your way." She punched off the mike switch, knowing it would create an audible pop in the speaker. Ignoring the Major's questioning glance, she watched with great satisfaction as Eric's arrogant posture gradually slackened, and the bitter eyes filled with uncertainty.

"All right," he said, only half erasing the defiance out of his voice. "Talk."

"Beautifully done," the Major murmured.

"Mr. Lloyd, you are presently being held in a detention cell in the city of Shalev, about five hundred miles north of where you used to live."

"Where is my family?"

"I will answer your questions in a moment, but first I would—"

"First nothing!" Eric shouted. "I don't know who you are or what this is all about. Why am I being held? Where is my family?"

"Yes," Nicole said slowly, "I suppose that does need to come first. We came to your village in peace and wished only—"

"We?" Eric demanded. "Were you there?"

"No, but I—"

"I was! So cut the fairy tales please. Just tell me where my father and mother are. Are they here too?"

Nicole bit her lower lip, seeking for words. Then, at a nod of encouragement from the Major, she plunged in. "Mr. Lloyd, it is with deep regret that I must tell you that your father was killed in the battle for the river crossing. I'm very sorry."

Eric visibly flinched, his face momentarily twisted with shock, but then he straightened, squared his shoulders. "And my mother?"

"Your mother and sisters are fine. In fact, your mother will be visiting you later today. But I've been given the assignment to help you get out of detention and be reunited with your family. I'm sure you have some questions about why you're here and what you have to do to get out."

She paused for a moment, half expecting another angry reaction, but the anger was gone now and his face was impassive, watchful, making her more wary than if he had been glaring at her.

"Do you have any questions, Mr. Lloyd? I'll try to answer them for you."

His head came up slowly. "I do have one."

"Yes, what is it?"

"Do you know Travis Oakes?"

Nicole felt a tiny shiver down her back as she looked into the gray eyes boring at her through the glass.

"Well, do you?"

"Uh—yes, yes I do."

"Is he here?"

"No," she answered quickly, almost blurting it out. Then she was angry at herself for letting him frighten her. "That is, he's not right here with me, but he is here in Shalev."

"Could you send for him? I'd love to see somebody from the village."

The Major sighed. "This boy is not going to forgive easily, is he."

"Well?" came the insistent voice through the speaker.

"Mr. Lloyd, I—" She shook her head, took a deep breath, and plunged in. "Travis Oakes didn't kill your father. In fact, he tried to stop it from happening, but he was too late. I think I can understand your bitterness and hatred for us, and your tremendous frustration at being imprisoned. But *you are here*. You *are* in detention, and whether I like it or not, or whether you like it or not, I have been given the assignment to help you so you can get out." Her voice suddenly softened. "I can't bring your father back, but I can help you now, if you'll let me."

"I suppose I ought to be deeply touched by your concern," he said sarcastically, "but why do I feel this nagging doubt about your honesty?"

"I know you have no reason to believe me, but I promise that I'll be totally honest with you. I'll not lie to you, ever." She stopped, waiting for a response, but he had put his hands under his head and closed his eyes, and he remained silent.

"I'd like you to believe that, but whether you do or not is quite irrelevant. The important thing is that we begin a program so you can be released and be with your family again."

Still nothing. She glanced at the Major, who shrugged. "Do you have any further questions, Mr. Lloyd?"

His eyes opened slowly but he didn't turn toward the mirror. "Yes," he said finally.

"Okay, if I can answer it, I will."

"Are you pretty?"

Nicole stared at him, too surprised to answer.

"Well?"

"I don't see what my appearance has to do with anything," she stammered.

"So much for total honesty, Miss Lambert." The insolent challenge in his voice was unmistakable. "Or is it Mrs. Lambert?"

"No, it's Miss, but I—"

The Major flicked the switch on his own mike and leaned over to speak into it, but Nicole gave him a quick shake of her head. He leaned back, watching her curiously.

"All right," she said, watching the figure on the cot closely. "I don't see why it matters, but—I'm five feet, three inches tall, of generally slender build. I have medium-length, brown hair, green eyes, and I'm twenty-four years old."

"Quite normal looking then?"

Nicole smiled. "Quite. Why do you ask?" She again had the uneasy feeling that his gaze was piercing the mirror.

"You sound quite nice."

"Why, thank you." Nicole was baffled by the complete shift of mood.

"It would be more logical," he continued, half musing, "if the Creator had made people look and sound to match up with what they are really like inside. That way people would at least have some defense."

Nicole's smile froze in place, then slowly died as his words scalded their way into her consciousness. Her hands clenched tightly; then she reached up and clicked off the switch, cutting off the temptation to scream back at this infuriating presence through the glass. With great effort she fought to keep her breathing even, not daring for a moment to look at the Major. When she finally did, he was staring at Eric.

"Oh, don't sign off yet," the voice called through the speaker with bitter mockery. "I thought you were going to help me."

Nicole turned to the Major and forced a strained smile. "I don't think he likes us very much."

"He's a very angry young man," the Major agreed. He reached out and patted her arm. "But you handled yourself superbly, Nicole. Just superbly."

"I don't know. I've never had one so bitter, so utterly caustic before. What if we can't turn him?"

The Major reached up and stroked his mustache absently. When he dropped his hand, his expression brightened. "Then we'll implant him and send him to Serenity to farm. No one is that indispensable. But we haven't lost yet."

"Sir, I don't know if we ought to continue any more today, considering his present mood."

"Most definitely not. But bring his mother in as you had scheduled tomorrow morning. And remind Mrs. Lloyd not to say anything about being implanted, or we'll terminate her visit. Travis has already warned her to wear a blouse with a high neck to cover the bandage. If she doesn't say anything, Eric will never notice anything."

Nicole nodded. "She's set to come at eight o'clock. I'll brief her before she goes in."

"Good. Limit the visit to ten minutes. Then we'll play our next card at nine o'clock. Travis and I will meet you here a little before then. Okay?"

"Of course."

He stood up and smoothed his suit. "All right, we'll see you then."

CHAPTER

8

"Oh, Mama!"

Becky's eyes were wide as she stopped suddenly at the sight of the playground. Lori, always a pragmatist, didn't bother with exclamations of awe. With a shrill "Yippee!" she dropped her mother's hand and shot across the grass, heading for the slippery slide that was spewing children out of its mouth even as she ran.

Becky tugged on Madeline's hand. "Come on, Mother! Oh, this is neat!"

Madeline smiled, the first time in four days, and released her youngest daughter. "Go. Don't wait for me."

She walked to the low cement wall that separated the lawn from the sand of the playground and watched her two daughters in amusement. They would barely get started up the slide or on the swing when they'd spot a new attraction and off they'd dart, too excited to stay in one place for more than a few seconds.

They had come to the park after her visit to Eric, a visit that had left her greatly relieved and yet full of uneasiness and dismay. Why were they holding her son when everyone else was free? Why were they so adamant about not mentioning implantation?

She shrugged off the questions, still too confused by the events of the past week to sort it all out, and looked at her daughters.

Once again Madeline felt that curious intertwining of poignant longing and overwhelming revulsion. She knew the source of her longing. Shalev was all that they had lost—electric stoves, supermarkets, automatic washers, parks and slippery slides, ice cream sodas, movies, symphony orchestras, a university, clothes with a variety of styles, colors, and materials. Maybe the AFC didn't have everything, but compared to the village it was a dazzling array of plenty.

Then, as her hand raised slowly to touch the bandage at the back of her neck, she knew with equal clarity the source of the revulsion. Even now, as it welled up in her, she felt a quick clutch of fear. The revulsion always brought anger, and anger brought the pain.

"Watch, Mama! Watch me!" Lori was at the top of the slide.

"I'm watching, honey," she called, glad for the interruption in her thoughts. Lori squealed happily as she shot downward.

"Very good!" Madeline called. Then slowly she turned and walked over to a bench.

"Mr. Lloyd?"

Mastering the impulse to glance up at the mirror, Eric lay motionless on the cot.

"Mr. Lloyd!"

He noted with satisfaction the edge of exasperation in the cool voice.

"You have a visitor waiting outside."

In spite of himself, Eric opened his eyes. "Who is it?"

"If you would step to the back of your cell, please."

For nearly thirty seconds Eric lay there defiantly, irritated by the impersonal voice coming from the speaker, but then his desire to see who his visitor was overpowered his pride, and he swung his legs off the cot and stood up and moved to the far corner. The door opened and a tall figure stepped through. For a long moment Eric stared, completely dumbfounded. Then he exploded with joy. "Cliff!"

"Hello, Eric." Cliff Cameron stepped forward and clapped his hands on Eric's shoulders.

"Cliff! But I thought—I saw you—" He stopped, words failing him.

"I know." His leathery face broke into a wide smile. "Sorry to disappoint you."

"Why didn't Mom tell me? She was here just a little while ago."

"I've only seen her briefly. They've pretty much kept me away from the other villagers."

Eric shook his head, still stunned by the sight of this man. He was the same old Cliff, a little more tired looking but relaxed, poised, and confident. And yet he was different. Then Eric realized it was his clothes. The buckskin and homespun were gone, and he was dressed in tan slacks and an open-necked shirt. Eric stepped back to look at him, still unable to believe his eyes. "I was sure you were dead, or I would never have left you. I saw you go down."

"Well, I went down all right. These people have developed a weapon that uses ultrahigh-frequency sound waves. They call it a stun gun—an appropriate name. It focuses sound waves much as a laser beam does light waves, making it highly concentrated and powerful. It's like getting hit with a giant, invisible fist. On full power it can kill a man, but fortunately they only had it on stun capacity. It knocked me out instantly. When I woke up, I was tied up in the back of a truck."

Eric bit his lip. "You know about Dad?"

"Yes, and the others too. With nearly a hundred men, our few villagers didn't stand a chance."

"But at least you are alive. I can't believe it. I was so sure that you were dead."

Cliff motioned to the cot, then pulled up the stool so he could face Eric.

"Have you seen the rest of the family?" Eric asked.

"Yes. They seem fine."

"Are they? Did Mom tell you about some kind of operation they have forced her and the others to go through?"

Cliff's mouth noticeably sagged. "She didn't have to." He bent his head over and gently pulled the hair back. The bright red, inch-long incision was still held together with black stitches. "I took my bandage off this morning."

"What is it? What happened? Mom could only whisper a word or two when she kissed me goodbye after her visit."

Eric watched anxiously as Cliff paled slightly, and a brief flicker of pain touched his face.

"I've been implanted. I believe that is the correct terminology."

"Implanted? What's that supposed to mean?"

"It means I have a microminiaturized computer chip planted at the base of my skull. From it four microelectrodes protrude into the hypothalamus."

The woman next to her on the bench glanced quickly at the white bandage on the back of Madeline's head. Then she looked away again quickly, obviously embarrassed. She was silent for a moment, then said, "Are you new?"

Madeline nodded.

"And those must be your children."

To keep their hair off the bandages, Madeline had pulled it up into ponytails, and the patches of white were clearly visible.

"Yes, those are my girls."

"Do you have others?"

"A daughter, twenty-one, and a son—" She took a quick breath. "A son, twenty-four."

"Four children! Even without the bandages, that would give you away."

"Oh?"

"Yes. Most people here have one, sometimes two. I have six."

That won her a surprised look, for she looked young. She laughed at Madeline's expression. "I'm an outsider too. We were part of a small group of about fifty in eastern Oregon. They brought us in four years ago."

"Against your will?"

"Oh, we *came* willingly enough, wide-eyed to think we had found civilization. Then we woke up with bandages on our necks. But, of course, it was all for our own good."

Again Madeline nodded, warming to this woman who understood the bitterness and revulsion. "Which are yours?"

"The two boys there on the merry-go-round. The one in the blue shirt is nine; the one in yellow is eleven. I have two younger girls and two teen-aged boys."

"What does your husband do?" The instant she asked, Madeline regretted the question.

"He's an accountant for a chain of clothing stores. How about yours? Have they told him what they'll have him do yet?"

Madeline bit her lip. "He was killed trying to defend our village."

The woman touched Madeline's arm. "I'm terribly sorry."

"It's all right. I'm gradually getting used to the reality of it now." She looked away quickly. *Why do you lie? Tell her you cry yourself to sleep every night, that never in your life, not even the first time you lost your husband, have you ever felt so terribly alone.* But when she turned back she said only, "At least Shalev is a pretty place."

"Yes, and you adjust to—" The woman's eyes flicked up to the bandage again. "You adjust quickly. Even the children."

"How quickly?"

The woman looked away. "It was especially hard on my boys. They were never mean or malicious, it was just that they could never pass one another without one poking or shoving at the other. It was terrible for them at first." Her voice caught, and she had to finish in a whisper. "I used to get so angry with them for it. Now I'd give anything to have those days back again."

Eric stared at Cliff, his face blank, uncomprehending. "Hypothalamus? Microelectrodes? What are you talking about?"

Suddenly Cliff's eyes widened. "You mean, you haven't been implanted?"

"Of course not." Then Eric shot to his feet. "Wait a minute. I was drugged for several days." His hands went up to the back of his neck.

"Let me see." Cliff stood up and probed carefully at the base of Eric's skull. "No." He peered more closely. "No," he repeated in surprise, "you haven't been." He stepped back and gave Eric a long, searching look.

Eric returned his gaze as he rubbed the back of his head thoughtfully. "So that's what Mother meant?"

"Yes," Cliff said. "Every one of us from the village have been implanted except for infants under a year old." Again that searching look probed Eric. "Except you. Why not you?"

Eric sat back down on the cot heavily, and Cliff joined him. "Don't ask me. I've been sitting in this stupid cell slowly going mad trying to find out what's going on. Until Mom came, I didn't even know if anyone else from the village was here, or even alive."

"That's another puzzling thing. Why are you being held here? The rest of us are free."

"I don't know! Don't ask me what's going on. Tell me more about this thing. What does it mean to be implanted?"

Cliff opened his hands, his eyes defeated. "It is, very simply, the perfect human-control device."

"Control device?"

Cliff sighed wearily. "Let me back up and start at the first." The frustration pulled down the corners of his mouth. "I don't know the whole story yet. The man in charge is someone they call the Major. Evidently locating settlements like ours and hauling in people from all kinds of places is standard procedure, but newcomers aren't the only ones implanted. Every person in Shalev and the Alliance gets one of these little numbers."

"You mean everyone—" He left the sentence unfinished as the enormity of the thought hit him.

"Everyone, as near as I can find out. Over two hundred thousand in this so-called Alliance of Four Cities and every one of us penned up like sheep—only the fences are invisible, electronic ones."

He stopped suddenly, breathing deeply.

69

"Are you okay?" Eric asked.

Cliff nodded, but he continued to take deep gulps of air until his color started to return. "Okay," he sighed, "it's going now."

"What? What is it?"

"You have just witnessed the little black box in full operation. I've got to learn to be more careful. Whenever I start thinking about what this whole thing means, I start seething inside. That's all it takes."

Eric shook his head. "I don't understand."

"It's really very simple. I got angry and the little black box slapped me down for it."

"But how? How can it do that?"

Cliff took a deep breath. "Do you remember when you were in high school and I gave a lecture on operant conditioning to your social studies class? Pavlov and his dog and all that?"

Eric nodded. "Ring the bell when you bring the dog dinner, and he salivates. Pretty soon all you have to do is ring the bell to make him salivate."

"Right. That's conditioning in its simplest form. Well, I won't bore you with all the technical details, but this Major, whoever he is, has developed the ultimate conditioning device. Compared to this, Pavlov is a piece of academic trivia. These guys are light years ahead of him."

Eric shook his head. "You've lost me."

Cliff took a deep breath. "Early in this century, brain research was crude and very experimental. But then with the development of space-age technology—computers, electronic probes with tips a thousand times smaller than a needle's, electronic devices that measure the tiniest impulses from the brain—our knowledge was catapulted forward. In the fifties, they proved that all emotions—joy, anger, fear, ecstasy—all emotions begin as electrical impulses in the brain. They trigger physiological reactions such as rapid heartbeat, sweaty palms, and so on, but to begin with, they are only electrical impulses in the hypothalamus."

Eric nodded, beginning to understand. "And you said it was the hypothalamus where this implantation is put."

"Yes. In addition to the hypothalamus being the seat of emo-

70

tions, scientists found a thin stream of cells in that part of the brain, the source of all sensations of pain. They also found that if you stimulate those pain cells with an electrical impulse—a few hundred thousandths of a volt—it will 'tell' the body it is experiencing pain—*even though there is no outside pain.*"

He stopped again, raising his hands for emphasis. "Do you understand that, Eric? Pain may be artificially induced by electrically stimulating the brain. However, it is not artificial pain. It's as real, as trauma producing, as terrible as a blow to the body or a bad burn."

He stood up, moved to the washbasin, filled Eric's cup, and drained it swiftly. "Next came the development of what is called a stimoceiver."

"A what?"

"A stimoceiver, from the words *stimulus* and *receiver*. It's a tiny miniaturized radio receiver with microelectrodes attached to it that can read, or better receive, the impulses of the brain. An electrical impulse can also be sent down those electrodes to stimulate certain areas of the brain. Thus it both *stimulates* and *receives*, and thus its name—stimoceiver."

Eric stopped his pacing. "And that's what they mean by implantation?".

Cliff hesitated, then took a quick breath and sat down again. "Yes. The concept is brilliantly—no, hellishly simple. What they've done is to combine a stimoceiver with a miniature computer, or better, a computer chip. The electrodes are planted in the hypothalamus, and impulses, thousands of them every minute, are sent to the miniature computer, which sorts through them all. When a pattern associated with unacceptable behavior shows up—guilt, violence, anger, dishonesty, hatred—the computer reacts by sending a mild electrical charge down another electrode into the pain center."

His eyes were like dark pools in a muddy river as he turned and stared at Eric. "The result? A fiendishly effective teaching device. The perfect conditioning machine. You either salivate properly or you get burned. One step out of line and whammo!"

· · · · · · · · · · ·

71

"Faster, Becky!" Lori shouted joyfully. "Let's go faster." She pushed up hard on the teeter-totter and shot up to the apex of the board's path.

But as Becky came down to the bottom, she spied the nearby jungle gym. "Oh, that looks fun!" In one swing of her short little legs, she was off the teeter-totter and darting away. Lori plummeted like a boulder dropped over a precipice. The teeter-totter slammed to the ground with a bone-jarring thud, bouncing her off and sending her sprawling on her face into the sand.

For one or two seconds she was too startled to react; then tears of pain sprang to her eyes, and she burst out crying.

Madeline was off the bench and to her side in a moment, the other woman close behind. "What happened?" she said as she helped Lori up and put her arm around her.

"Becky made me fall!" She rubbed at her backside.

As her mother soothed her, Lori looked up and saw that the other children had gathered around her, wide-eyed and curious. One of the boys shook his head in disgust. "Girls!" he muttered. With an effort Lori bit back the tears, deeply shamed to be viewed with such contempt. Then she spied Becky, approaching slowly, head ducked in shame.

"Becky, you dummy!" she cried angrily. "Why did you—"

A sharp cry cut off her words, and she doubled over as though hit in the stomach with a huge fist. She stumbled forward, pulling out of her mother's grasp, and fell to her face. One long, agonizing scream rent the air as she rolled back and forth, clutching at her stomach.

CHAPTER
9

"Is there any way to take it out?" Eric asked, a sense of horror crawling in his stomach.

The grizzled head shook once. "No. Technically, putting the chip in is a very difficult operation, because even though pinpoint precision is impossible, the electrodes still have to be placed with great accuracy. But physiologically, it's a relatively minor operation. And getting the chip out is a snap. Just cut the surface of the skin and pull it out, electrodes and all."

"But you said there was no way to—"

Cliff slowly lifted his left arm. "See this?"

"The wrist computer?"

"Yes. Have you tried to remove it?"

"Oh, yes."

Cliff pointed to the spot where the band joined the watch itself. "In addition to being waterproof and shockproof, the band is connected to the face with pressure-sensitive relays, so you can't take it off. A good, hard pull triggers what they so elegantly call the 'punishment mode.' Also, I don't understand how yet, but the implantation and the wrist computer are somehow linked together with the main computers in Central Control. If you try and remove either one, it automatically triggers the maximum punishment response in the other. Either way it's lethal."

"There's got to be some way to get this thing out."

"Did you hear me, Eric? I said *lethal*. That means it kills you."

"There's got to be some way," he said stubbornly.

Cliff leaped up. "Will you listen to me? You aren't up against a bunch of amateur toy designers, Eric. They haven't built an empire of two hundred thousand people by overlooking the obvious. It's programmed to kill anyone who tries. They aren't doing this for fun."

He stopped, the pain suddenly twisting his features, and his voice fell to a whisper. "Eric, I haven't just been sitting around these last few days. I have asked everyone. *There is no way out of this thing.* None!" He sat down heavily on the cot. "None, Eric. Welcome to Utopia."

Eric's jaw was rigid, and his eyes had narrowed to tiny pinpoints. "I can't accept that. There must be—"

"Eric Lloyd!"

The blaring speaker caused them both to jump, and Eric spun around to the mirror. Cliff's reappearance from the dead, and then the horror of his revelations, had totally driven Nicole Lambert and the mirror from Eric's mind.

"Mr. Lloyd, we would like to talk to you and Dr. Cameron. We're coming in." As Nicole stepped through the door ahead of the Major, she watched Eric's eyes closely, anxious to read his reactions. They flicked once to her, then to the Major. They were a hunter's eyes, scanning quickly, missing nothing. Nicole was fascinated. The gray depths betrayed absolutely no expression as they probed. If the Major was bothered, he gave no sign, just waited patiently, as if amused.

Finally the eyes turned back to her. She caught what she thought was a flash of anger as he noted her orange and blue uniform, but it was gone so quickly that she couldn't be sure. When the gaze returned to lock into her own, a faint smile of derision toyed at the corners of Eric's lips, and she knew that he had deduced who she was.

The Major stepped forward and thrust out his hand toward the older man. "Dr. Cameron? How do you do. My name is Major Denison."

The doctor's eyes widened slightly as he accepted the proffered hand. "Dr. Major Denison? Curtis Major Denison?"

Eric's head jerked around to stare at Cliff, but he was no more surprised than Nicole or the Major. "Yes. Do we know each other?"

"No, I just know of you. What neurosurgeon hasn't heard of the pioneering brain research of Curtis Major Denison and the U.S. Air Force Cybernetics Team?"

"Well, thank you," the Major said, obviously pleased. "For you to remember that, after eighteen years, I take as a special compliment."

"When the others kept referring to 'the Major,' I assumed it was a title, a military rank."

The Major smiled, revealing even white teeth. "I don't know exactly how that came about. It just kind of happened over the years. Now everyone calls me 'the Major.'" He chuckled. "I've never had the heart to tell them, but actually I was a brigadier general in the Air Force."

Nicole's expression caused him to laugh. "See, even my staff doesn't realize they've demoted me."

He turned slightly and again put out his hand. "You're Eric Lloyd. I'm very pleased to meet you." He held his hand in midair for a moment, then shrugged, unperturbed by the other's implacable gaze. "Dr. Cameron knows me by reputation," he said easily, "and I knew of your father in the same way, Eric. Though I realize it's little consolation to you now, I deeply regret that he was killed. I admired his courage and integrity very much."

Nicole expected that to trigger an outburst, but Eric just watched, his face an unreadable mask.

The Major turned and took Nicole by the arm. "May I present Nicole Lambert, one of our staff officers in the Monitoring Control Center."

Dr. Cameron merely nodded, but Eric spoke for the first time. "We've met," he said dryly.

Nicole nodded, holding his gaze until he looked away.

"Sit down," the Major invited, motioning the two men to the cot. Not waiting for them to obey, he stepped over and picked up the wooden stool, flicked off a minute speck of dust, then sat it down for Nicole, placing it where she would be facing both men. As he straightened, he saw that neither of them had moved.

"Dr. Cameron, just before Nicole and I entered, you and Eric were speculating on his present condition, I believe."

The doctor nodded, almost imperceptibly.

"I can understand your suspicions and your reluctance to trust me, or anyone else in Shalev, for that matter, but I assure you, our only desire is to get Eric out of detention as soon as possible. Now, if you'd sit down, both of you, we'll not prolong this any longer than necessary."

Dr. Cameron complied, followed a moment later by Eric. As he sat on the cot, the doctor's eyes never left the Major's face. "So," he finally said, half to himself, "Dr. Curtis M. Denison. That explains a great deal. I heard you'd gone into top-secret brain research. Rumors kept cropping up, but . . ." He let the words trail off.

"Yes," the Major responded, leaning easily against the wall. "Actually I proposed a project for the military and was given control of it. We called it 'Benevolent Pacification.' Our basic task was to explore ways of taking a hostile civilian population conquered in war and render them harmless and obedient without resorting to violence, threat, incarceration, or military occupation."

"Benevolent pacification?" Eric said bitterly. "Is that what our village got? You make it sound so beautiful."

"No," the Major responded, "that's what we called our research for the Joint Chiefs of Staff. It was crude and ill-conceived. I'm not really very proud of those years, as a matter of fact. However, it did provide the foundation for what was to come."

"Obviously," Eric said. "And what does your Bureau of Beautiful Names call what you have done here? 'Brain Bending for Fun and Profit?' Or how about 'Self-Discipline Made Easy'?"

Nicole glanced at the Major, remembering how Eric's rapier-tongued comments could raise his ire, but if the Major had heard, he gave no sign. He was looking at Dr. Cameron and ignored Eric completely.

"Like Colonel Karl Lloyd, I sensed that the world's insanity was plunging us toward the brink of annihilation. And like Eric's father, I started to prepare." He paused for a moment, his eyes wide and thoughtful behind his glasses. "However, instead of retiring from the military, I used the tremendous resources at our disposal. It was so closely related to the Benevolent Pacification program that, in those last hectic couple of years, no one took any real notice of our change in direction. We had tens of millions of dollars at our disposal."

He smoothed his mustache with his thumb and forefinger, absently, as he thought back. "We chose this site very carefully. We figured Kalispell would not attract any direct strikes, which it didn't. It has the natural resources we needed to survive afterwards—a relatively mild climate for as far north as we are, rich farmland, unlimited water and timber, a major hydroelectric plant nearby—it was the ideal location. We spent millions purchasing equipment—not just the supplies we needed to survive, but manufacturing tools, whole factories, and laboratories. And more importantly, we identified and gathered experts from a dozen fields we considered would be critical after the war was over. It took more than two years of intensive and extensive preparations, and we still weren't ready when it came."

"How did you escape the war?" Dr. Cameron was obviously interested in what the Major was saying, in spite of his outward coolness.

"We convinced the Pentagon we were setting up a model community in which to fully test our program. We stockpiled enough food and supplies to last a year, and then, like your group, rode it out. Once it was over, we began collecting survivors."

The Major straightened, throwing off the somberness of the memories. "But the second way in which I differed from Eric's father is that I wanted to do more than *survive* the war. I wanted civilization to survive—with the assurance that such a war would never happen again."

He stretched out both hands in front of him, as though offering Cliff Cameron the concept in visible, tangible form for him to examine. "A moment ago, you and Eric spoke of Utopia. The ideal society. Civilization perfected. Do you know the one thing that has always stopped us from achieving that dream?"

"I'm at a total loss."

The Major obviously missed Cliff's faintly laconic sarcasm, for he nearly shouted the answer in his excitement. "People!"

"People," the doctor repeated like a dutiful student.

"Yes, people. Even the most brilliant of plans, the most carefully structured organization can be totally destroyed by one unpredictable, wild-eyed rebel, or brought into the dust by the groveling, self-centered mindlessness of the very people who would most benefit from it. Many have tried to overcome the incredible inertia of the human factor and failed. They have tried everything—religion, coercion, government regulation, laws, philosophy, bribery, terror." He punched out each word like a small explosion. "And all of them failed."

It was obvious from the expression on his face that the Major was not completely heartbroken at the dismal record. "And do you know why they failed? Do you know why?"

Dr. Cameron's slow, soft tone was like a dash of cold water in the face of that mesmerizing voice. "Let me guess. Because they couldn't get at the mind?"

"Exactly!" the Major exulted. "Exactly right, Dr. Cameron! Even the most fiendish, diabolical torture cannot change the way a man thinks. Oh, it will bring him into line temporarily, but once the threat is removed, he will revert back to old patterns immediately."

Eric had obviously taken a cue from the older man's example. When he spoke, his voice was soft but musing. "So instead of fiendish, diabolical torture, you use gentle, sophisticated electronic massage." His eyes came up and met Nicole's. "And get lovely young ladies to push the buttons to make it all seem very elegant."

Nicole flushed and fought the impulse to look away, to escape his gaze, but she couldn't hold her eyes up to that brutal, probing stare.

78

"Sneer if you wish, my insolent young friend," the Major snapped, for the first time stung by Eric's response. "You were brought up in a tiny village isolated from the world. You've never seen the results of man's uncontrolled nature. Rape, child molestation, terrorism, war, mass murder, genocide—ah, yes, Eric, you little know the effects of man's uncontrolled nature. And nothing in history—not religion, not government, not torture, not executions—nothing has ever cured man's animal tendencies. But we have! For the first time in history, we have taught man to suppress the evil in him and let only the good surface."

"Through implantation?" Dr. Cameron asked scornfully, his eyes full of contempt. Then even as she watched, Nicole saw the first flickers of pain tug at the corners of his mouth. She looked down quickly, as he visibly struggled with his emotions.

"Yes, through implantation," the Major said, his voice lowering again as he watched the doctor's reaction with an understanding nod. "At this very moment you're seeing it work. By punishing these negative tendencies in their earliest stages—with a very mild punishment, I might add—we teach an individual to give way only to his best impulses. We don't change him by force, only teach the better part of his nature to surface."

"It's obvious," Cameron said, wiping at the sweat on his forehead, "that your definition of force is very different from mine."

But it was like putting out one's hand to stop an avalanche. The Major rolled on without any detectable deflection from his course. He turned to Nicole, his eyes shining with excitement. "Just ask Miss Lambert. She's spent nearly all her life in Shalev. Is it so monstrous, Nicole?"

"Monstrous?" she responded, meeting and holding Eric's disdainful glare. "What is monstrous to me is what people tolerated before Termination. When I read what it was like then, or see the old movies, I find it difficult to comprehend that people could say that was an acceptable way to live."

Dr. Cameron's eyes held no condemnation like Eric's, only sorrow. "How old were you at Termination, Nicole?"

"Six."

"And your parents? Did they find life before so terrible?"

She lifted her head, her green eyes flashing fire. "My father, a Seattle policeman, was killed by six hoodlums when he tried to help an old woman they were beating up. My mother was eight months pregnant at the time. The shock caused her to go into labor. She died giving birth to me."

Dr. Cameron's face was suddenly very old and very tired. "I see."

"Do you, Dr. Cameron?" the Major broke in. "Do you really see what we have accomplished here?"

"Yes, I see very clearly. I lived in Los Angeles for thirty years. I've walked the streets at night and feared for my life. I've read in the papers and watched on television the incredible evil of man's dealings with his fellowman. And I watched as the world took the ultimate plunge and destroyed the work of a thousand years."

His head came up, and he stared directly into the Major's eyes. "But I don't think I have ever felt deeper horror, that I have ever been more thoroughly terrified, than I am at this moment."

The Major flinched as though he had been struck, and Nicole noted the almost instant flush of anger, but when he spoke, his voice betrayed nothing. "I'm sorry you feel that way, Dr. Cameron. I'm confident that as time goes on, your feelings will change. You expect some kind of chamber of horrors out there, but you'll quickly see that just the opposite is true."

He took a deep breath and turned to Eric. "But enough of this. I didn't come to try and convert you. Shalev will convert you soon enough. We've come to make Eric a special offer."

Only Eric's eyes betrayed the fact that he had heard the Major.

"It's obvious," the Major went on smoothly, "that you detest the idea of implantation. I'm offering you an opportunity to avoid it."

That broke through the mask momentarily, and Nicole smiled inwardly at the sudden start of surprise that flashed across Eric's face. The Major was a master at this, using the bait and the prod simultaneously.

"Why?" Eric finally asked.

"We have an organization called the Guardians. Within the cities, they function only to help and protect people. They serve as our firemen, traffic officers, paramedics, and so on. They have no crime to fight, no riots to suppress, no disorders to worry about. So they're not police, merely guardians. But that's not our real challenge. We have an outer perimeter of over a thousand miles, much of it forest wilderness. Eighty percent of the total Guardian forces patrol that perimeter and keep out intruders—roving bands of savages who prey on the labor of others. I believe Travis said you called them the Marauders."

Cliff nodded.

"An appropriate name. But anyway, we need someone of Eric's experience in the mountains in that perimeter watch force."

"You still haven't answered the real why," Cliff spoke up. "I can see why you'd have use for a man like Eric. But why not implant him too?"

"Good point," the Major conceded. "The answer is that the nature of the work may sometimes require him to do things, such as engage in combat with the Marauders. The implantation would never allow him to do that. He must be free to act quickly and without fear of pain in such cases."

"You are still begging the question, Dr. Denison. Why not simply take someone who has grown up in Shalev and make him a Guardian by removing his implantation?"

"A very perceptive question," the Major responded with grudging approval. "I must admit that once someone has grown up under implantation, he becomes thoroughly conditioned to it. Simply removing it makes little difference. He continues to act as though implanted."

"Yes, I understand that perfectly," Cliff answered with disgust edging his voice again. "It says mountains about the effectiveness of your system."

Eric broke in before the Major could respond. "Why should I be interested in joining you?"

The Major half turned. "Nicole, would you like to answer that for Eric?"

She nodded. "Obviously the most important and immediate benefit to you would be to avoid implantation yourself. But there are other benefits. The salary is very attractive. You'd be furnished with both a car and an apartment or a small home. But probably the second most important advantage is that your family would be brought up to a Stage One implantation as soon as you'd convince us you're sincere about becoming a Guardian."

"What does that mean—Stage One?"

"Implantations are not all the same. There are three levels of intensity. Stage Three is the most tightly controlled. This is rarely used. The majority of people in Shalev are at Stage Two. This is what Dr. Cameron and your family are under now. Dr. Cameron has described quite accurately how that works. Stage One implantation is minimal, protecting only against the grosser kinds of behavior. The assumption is that people will be motivated to control themselves if they know they may lose their Stage One status."

"I'm sorry if I keep shaking my head," Eric said, "but I'm still trying to adjust to this. You talk about it as if you were sticking a fork in a piece of meat to see if it's done or not. These are people you're talking about. People! Not halves of beef!"

Nicole flushed but went on firmly. "Once you have fully proven yourself as a Guardian, your immediate family members will have their implantations completely removed. I suggest that if you're so horrified by it all, you seriously consider the Major's offer."

When Eric gave no response, the Major spoke up. "So you see, Eric, if you agree to join us, we benefit, you benefit, and your family benefits. It's an opportunity that not many young men are offered."

"I'm deeply touched."

The Major ignored the sarcasm in Eric's voice. "We'll let you think about it for twenty-four hours. Nicole will be your controlling officer should you choose to accept. You may call her anytime before then. She'll be happy to answer any questions you may have. If she isn't in the observation room when you need her, they'll get her."

Nicole stood up, sensing the meeting had ended.

"Consider it carefully, Eric," the Major said earnestly. "I know you're full of hate and bitterness now. But be realistic. And think of your family as well as yourself." He turned. "Dr. Cameron, I'm afraid you'll have to leave with us now."

Without answering, Eric turned to Cliff and gripped his hand. "At least you're alive. That's something."

The older man nodded, his eyes probing deeply into Eric's. "Eric," he finally said, "Dr. Denison is right. Don't let your emotions take the reins now. Think very carefully about his offer. I see no other options. If your father were here, he'd say the same thing. *There are no other options.* Do you understand that?"

Eric finally nodded, his mouth a hard line. "Yes, I think I do."

CHAPTER

10

"Miss Lambert?"

His voice startled her, for he hadn't stirred at all from the cot.

"Are you there?"

"Yes, I'm here."

"When is the Major coming for my decision?"

She glanced at her wrist. "At nine o'clock, about an hour from now."

"I have a request."

"Okay."

"I'd like to ask you some questions before he comes."

"All right, ask them. If I can answer them, I will."

"No, not this way. I want you to come in here."

Her eyebrows arched upward, and, as though he sensed her reaction, he sat up and turned to stare into the mirror. "Well?" he demanded.

"Why? I can hear you very well from here."

"Yes, and you can see me too. Which gives you the definite advantage. I want to be able to see you. Then I'll have a better idea if you try to lie to me."

She sighed, then leaned over the mike, as though her nearness would more accurately convey her earnestness. "Mr. Lloyd, I told you that I'd always be totally honest with you. I know you have no reason to believe that, but—"

"Well, ironically enough I do believe it." He smiled at her through the glass, the first time she'd seen a real smile from him. "At least I want to. But I need to be sure, and I can't do that through a microphone."

"I—I'm not sure I can."

"Are you afraid of me?"

"No," she answered quickly, a little surprised that that hadn't occurred to her.

"I'll sit clear across the cell, if you'd like."

"I'm not afraid that you'll hurt me, Mr. Lloyd. It's just that I'll have to get permission from the Major."

"I don't have any other engagements pending at the moment," he said dryly. "Get it. I'll wait right here."

"All right, I'll ask. Just a minute."

As she stepped through the sliding door into his cell, Eric got quickly to his feet and made a tiny bow. "Well," he said, "I'd about decided I'd scared you off."

"No," she said, giving him a cool smile, "you didn't."

"Sit down." He motioned to the cot, waited until she sat down, then pulled the wooden stool up for himself.

"Who's minding the store?" He motioned toward the mirror.

"Travis and the Major."

"Figured so. Well, shall we begin?"

"Yes." She put her hands in her lap and tried to appear completely relaxed.

"Mother said you're moving my family out of Shalev. Is that true?"

"Yes, they'll be leaving in the morning."

"Why?"

"All of your village are being transferred to Serenity—near where Great Falls, Montana, used to be. We have a great need for skilled farmers."

"If I agree to cooperate, can they stay?"

"No. I'm sorry, but their transfer has nothing to do with you and your status. Serenity is our newest city. It received a direct nuclear strike during the war. The region was not fit for habitation until just a few years ago. It's become a major source of food for the Alliance, but we don't have sufficient people to run the farms."

As she watched the hardness of his jaw, she continued quietly. "After your preliminary training, you'll be allowed to visit Serenity and see them often."

Without so much as a nod, he changed directions. "Why does the Alliance want to capture new populations? We were obviously no threat to you. We didn't even know you existed. Why go to such great effort to seek us out?"

"Actually we have two reasons. First, we survived Termination as well as any group we know of. We still have civilization, technology, medical facilities, schools. We hope to share that with as many others as possible."

Eric nodded. "You just don't find that kind of generosity any more."

She ignored his sarcasm and continued. "Secondly, the Alliance needs people—farmers, laborers, skilled professionals like Dr. Cameron."

"That's a little surprising. You talk about having limited food resources. You'd think natural growth would tax your abilities to keep up. Why such a vigorous program to bring in new people?"

Nicole hesitated, suddenly aware that the Major and Travis were waiting for her answer too. Then she remembered the Major's counsel to be straight with him. "Because the growth rate is negative," she said.

Eric's gray eyes widened a little. "Negative?"

"Yes. The birthrate is not keeping up with the death rate. No one is exactly sure why, but the infusion of outside people is necessary to balance the population."

"Well, well. Everyone in this little paradise just loves it to pieces—they just don't want to bring children into it."

"That's a simplistic conclusion not justified by the data we have."

86

The sudden sharpness in her tone only made him smile. "And you're not married. Is that typical for twenty-four-year-olds in Shalev?"

Nicole felt her cheeks go instantly hot and was furious that her face betrayed her reaction. "It's not unusual," she said evenly, though it cost her a great deal of effort.

"Well, that's clearly part of your population problem. Hardly a girl in the village is still single past eighteen. By twenty-four they have three or four children."

"And how old are you, Mr. Lloyd?"

He gave one short bark of laughter and then shook his head. "Point well taken. I apologize for making reference to your personal life."

"I accept your apology," she said, her voice still stiff. "Is there anything else?"

He watched her for a long moment, his eyes wide and thoughtful. "Hey," he finally said softly, "I really am sorry. I'm afraid that the last week in here has soured my manners. My mother would be appalled."

"I understand. Do you have other questions?"

"Yes, I do."

"Okay."

"Are you implanted?"

She was instantly on guard again. "No. As we told you, Guardians are exempt. Why?"

"Oh." He fell silent.

"Why do you ask if I'm implanted?" she finally asked.

"Oh, I just wondered what button to push to get you to smile."

Her eyes flashed and her mouth snapped into a tight, hard line.

"Whoops," he said, with a rueful expression. "Obviously not that one."

She momentarily fought it, but she couldn't contain it, and she laughed out loud.

"Well, that's better. And while we're at it, how about knocking off this 'Mr. Lloyd' business? Nobody in my life has ever called me Mr. Lloyd. Okay?"

Nicole nodded. "If you wish. I'm Nicole."

"Does anyone ever call you Nicky?"

"No, thank heavens."

"That's too bad. My sisters call me Ricky. Ricky and Nicky, controller and controllee. It has a special ring to it."

She pulled a face. "Ricky and Nicky? That's awful." She was amazed at the change in him. Suddenly he was a gracious host charming a visiting guest.

He nodded; then slowly the smile left his eyes. "And if you decide I'm not responding as the Major wishes?"

"I will so report."

"And?"

"You'll be implanted and sent to Serenity to be a farmer for the rest of your life."

Eric leaned forward, studying her face so intently that she finally looked down. "And you could really do that?"

Her head came up and she met his stare unflinchingly. "Yes, I could."

He leaned back, his face thoughtful, and once again he shifted direction, catching her off guard. "What stops people from running?"

"Running?"

"Yes. Going through the Outer Perimeter."

"They're happy here."

"Sorry. You'll have to do better than that."

"It's true!"

"Are *you* happy?"

Her head snapped up so sharply, her hair bounced lightly on her shoulders. "Of course."

"How do you manage to hide it so well?"

The emerald eyes had suddenly become twin volcanoes belching fire. "I'm sorry if my basic nature doesn't fit your picture of the giggly, happy-go-lucky female, Mr. Lloyd, but *I am happy.* Sorry. Try again."

Undeterred by her anger, he bored in, his own voice rising. "Are you telling me that happiness is the *only* thing that keeps people in the Alliance?"

She was taken back by that and hesitated for a moment. He sensed his advantage and pressed in relentlessly.

"Or has the Major invented another one of his little electronic gimmicks to see that no one crosses over the line?"

"I—"

"Yes, I'm listening," he said sarcastically. "They aren't totally free, are they?"

"No, Mr. Lloyd," she said, the anger at his attack suddenly giving her the control she needed. "The wrist computer is monitored by the central computers. If a person crosses the Outer Perimeter, it automatically triggers the Punishment Mode. Intense agony would result."

"How intense?"

She bit her lower lip.

"Well?" he demanded.

"It would probably be fatal."

"That's what I figured. So much for happiness."

"But, no one ever—"

"I'm sure of that. Now, I have one other condition for acceptance."

"Somehow I thought the Major was setting the conditions," she said dryly, "but go ahead. It's your little show."

"I want Dr. Cameron put on the same status as my family. As soon as I prove myself, he goes up to Stage One implantation, then has it removed when they do. Agreed?"

She shook her head. "The policy is strictly limited to immediate family members, and I can't change that."

Eric turned to the mirror. "Major? That's my condition."

The silence in the cell stretched out for a long moment. Then the overhead speaker popped.

"Nicole is right, Eric. That's a very strict Guardian policy."

"If it weren't for your Guardian policy," Eric shot back angrily, "my father would be alive right now. Since he's not, Cliff is the closest thing to it. I want him counted as my father now. I figure you owe me that."

Nicole watched his reflection in the mirror, a little awed that one minute he could absolutely infuriate her, and the next moment move her emotionally to his side, hoping that the Major would grant his request.

Finally the speaker blared again. "It's against my better judgment, but Travis thinks we ought to make an exception in this case. Nicole? What do you think?"

Eric turned around and watched her, but she detected no pleading in his eyes, no submission on his face, just a patient scrutiny of her inner depths.

"Yes," she finally said, looking past him. "I think the special circumstances warrant the exception."

"All right," the Major said after a moment. "You have your agreement, Eric. Does that mean you accept?"

Eric nodded. "How soon do I get out of here?"

The Major laughed. "Well, we didn't expect your decision for another half hour. It will take that long to get ready. But I took the liberty of sending for your entire family. Your sisters are very anxious to see you. I'll send them in now, and that will help pass the time."

"All right. Thank you."

As Nicole stood up and the door opened, Eric stepped back and bowed slightly, then lifted his hand in salute. "Well, Nicky," he said with mock solemnity, "here's to a great partnership."

CHAPTER

11

Becky shot through the door first, with Lori close on her heels, and they nearly bowled Eric over as they leaped into his outstretched arms. He swung them both around once, like sacks of flour under each arm, then dumped them on the bed, making them squeal with delight. In two quick steps he was to Stephanie and swung her off the floor too.

"Eric," she laughed, "put me down." He did, but only so he could encircle his mother with his other arm and squeeze them both.

"Hello, son," Madeline Lloyd said with a huskiness in her voice. "Travis told us the news about your release. That's wonderful."

"Yeah, I suppose."

Stephanie spoke up. "Travis said you'll be trained for four weeks, and then you'll get leave. We'll be anxious to see you."

He nodded, then turned and squatted down. "So what have my two favorite young ladies been up to?"

The girls came to him and put their arms around his neck, one sitting on each knee. "Oh, Ricky," Lori said, "it's so neat here. We went to the park yesterday, and they have swings—real swings, not just ropes and boards—and a slide, and teeter-totters, and a merry-go-round." Her face wrinkled up with joy. "It's so neat!"

"I got dizzy on the merry-go-round," Becky said, holding her head and rolling her eyes around.

"Oh you did, did you?" Eric laughed.

"Yeah, and guess what, Ricky." Her eyes were like two luminous brown saucers.

"What?"

"You can get ice cream here any time you want. Even in summer."

"Really?" he said, giving her a look of serious doubt.

"Yes, *real* ice cream."

Lori leaped off his knee and opened the blue metal door in the wall. "Oh look, Becky, Ricky has his own bathroom. And a shower too." Becky jumped off his knee and followed her sister.

Eric stood up and turned to his mother. "Do they know about their implantation?"

"Yes, I've tried to explain it to them. I thought I'd better."

"And?"

She looked down and bit her lower lip. "Yesterday, Becky jumped off the teeter-totter and let Lori clunk on the ground pretty hard. She flashed out at Becky, like any normal child would, and one second later she was writhing on the ground in pain."

"Tell him about last night," Stephanie said quietly, noting the fury in Eric's eyes.

Madeline took a deep breath, then sighed. "About midnight, Lori woke up vomiting. At first I thought it was something she had eaten. But as nearly as we can figure, she had a dream about Billy Maddox. He was teasing her, as he usually did at school. In her dream she got so angry, she hit him."

Eric stared at her. "You mean that even a dream can set this thing off?"

"Yes, if it's real enough."

"I can't believe it." He nearly turned to glare at the mirror, then caught himself.

92

"Becky!" Madeline had turned and was looking past Eric. "What are you doing?"

Becky had pushed the stool up to the washbasin and was looking at the things on the shelf above it. "What's up here, Ricky?"

"That's just my shaving stuff. Get down before that stool tips over."

"What's this?" She waved a brightly colored object.

Eric looked more closely, puzzled for a moment. "Oh, that's a candy bar from my dinner tray last night."

Becky jumped down, waving the bar. "Can I have it, Ricky? Can I?"

Eric started to nod, but before he could say yes, Lori's hand snaked out and snatched the bar. "No, I get it."

Becky's reaction was as swift as Lori's hand. "Give me that!" she yelped, and, doubling up her fists, she pounced on Lori's back. But even as she lit, she gasped, her body contorted wildly for one second, and she collapsed into a crumpled heap on the floor.

"Becky!"

Eric wasn't sure if his mother or Stephanie had screamed, but he beat both of them to the still form on the floor. He scooped her up, her legs, arms, and head dangling limply.

"Becky!" Madeline cupped the small head in her hands and lifted one eyelid with her thumb, but the eye was rolled clear back in the socket. She took the limp body from Eric's arms. "Get help, Eric. Quick!"

But even as Eric turned, the door whisked open and Travis darted into the room. "Bring her here," he commanded, shouldering Eric aside. "Stephanie! Lori! You come too. Let's go!"

As they hurried out, he straight-armed Eric back into the room. "You've got to stay here. We'll let you know as soon as we find out what's wrong."

Too stunned to resist, Eric stared at the door as it slid closed again.

"Eric?" It was Nicole's voice. He half turned to the mirror.

"I'll go down to the infirmary and find out how she is. I'll be back as soon as I can." The speaker crackled softly as she clicked off the mike.

It was nearly half an hour later before Nicole slipped into the observation room. The soft pop of the speaker jerked Eric around from his erratic pacing in the cell.

"Nicole?"

"Yes, it's me," she answered, still breathing hard from her swift pace back from the infirmary. "She's fine, Eric. Everything's okay."

His shoulders sagged visibly as the air whooshed out of him in a great sigh of relief. "What happened?"

"They aren't sure, but the doctor thinks the implantation may have been programmed too high."

"What?"

"She's small for her age. The stimulation triggered by her anger should have given her only a light dose of pain. Instead it was strong enough to knock her unconscious."

"And if it had been slightly higher than that?" His voice was low and caused a shiver to run up Nicole's spine.

"But it wasn't. She's fine now."

"She could have been killed, couldn't she?"

"Eric, *she is fine*. Stop torturing yourself."

"I want to see her."

"You can't right now."

"*I want to see her now!*" His face was murderous, and again she felt a sudden sweep of fear.

"That's impossible. They've taken her back to the hospital for surgery to correct the—" She broke off, realizing instantly that she had made a serious error.

"To correct what, Miss Lambert?"

Her hand came up to her mouth as she stared at the raging in his eyes, so evident even through the darkened glass.

"*To correct what?*" he thundered, making the speaker crackle with the overload of sound.

"They're going to reimplant her," she said in a half whisper. "Correct the error."

He swung around like a raging bull, looking for some kind of a weapon. In one swift motion he had the wooden stool by one leg and took a step toward her.

"Eric! Put the stool down." She jabbed at the alarm button and heard the buzzer out in the hall start to sound. "Put it down, or I'll have to trigger your Punishment Mode."

"Do your best, lady!" he shouted, hurling the stool with all the pent-up fury that had been building up in him. Nicole instinctively ducked even as she leaned on the red button on the console marked PM.

The stool smashed against the mirror, and Nicole heard the sharp crack of glass. An intricate spider's web instantly appeared. She stared through it in horrified fascination, as he staggered backwards, his whole left side twisting like an overwound spring.

"Is that the best you can do, Nicky?" he gasped, as he careened sideways, nearly losing his balance. But incredibly, he came up with the stool in his right hand. She could clearly hear him gasping in agony as the jolts from his wrist computer hit him again and again. Like a discus thrower in slow motion, he whirled once, and the stool came hurtling at her again.

Nicole threw up her arm as the glass shattered with a roar, spraying her with a stinging rain of a thousand tiny missiles. She spun around and dove for the stun gun in a rack near the door. For nearly thirty seconds she remained frozen, crouched in a firing position, but when no figure loomed to confront her, she straightened up slowly and peered through the shattered glass. Eric was lying in a twisted mass on the floor, not moving. Suddenly Nicole's knees were so weak they wouldn't support her, and she sat down quickly in her chair. Her heart was pounding so violently that she could feel it throbbing even in her fingertips.

A few moments later the door burst open, and Travis darted into the room. She started to give him a nonchalant wave, but then she realized her hand was trembling so violently that it would instantly give her away, and she stuck it down her lap. "Hi," she managed, forcing a smile. "Have you got a broom?"

"Are you okay, Nicole?" the Major demanded, as he joined them at the table in the cafeteria.

"Yes, I'm fine. I—"

95

He clenched his fist and smacked it into his palm. "I can't believe how stupid, how utterly stupid this boy is. Right on the verge of freedom, and he pulls this."

"Sir," Nicole said, "if it weren't for his sister, I don't think—"

"I know," he snapped impatiently, "but we can't have someone who goes berserk on us, even in a crisis."

Suddenly, to her amazement, Nicole wanted to defend Eric Lloyd, the sight of Becky collapsing into a heap on the floor still vivid in her mind. "Major," she said evenly, "I know that what he did is unacceptable, but I think what happened was very unusual provocation."

"Agreed," he conceded reluctantly. "Travis, I want to know who implanted his sister and why she was overprogrammed."

"I've already ordered an investigation."

"Good. Everything we do with this young man seems to be botched up. If we do turn him around, it'll be a wonder."

Nicole's head shot up. "You mean you're not rejecting him?"

"Oh, no. We'll give him one more shot at it. But starting right now, I want a twenty-four-hour monitor of his movements kept in Central Control. If he so much as tweaks his nose in the wrong direction, that will be it. We'll slap a Stage Three implantation on him."

Even Travis's eyes widened at that. Nicole knew personally of only five in Shalev who had ever received Stage Three—two vile-looking men caught trying to penetrate the Outer Perimeter, and three others declared to be incurable psychopaths.

"Nicole, I want you to oversee the monitoring of his movements. Check the tapes every day." The Major turned to Travis. "Who'll be his training officer? Have you decided yet?"

"Clayne Robertson."

"Ah, yes, a good choice. Have you told him yet?"

"I was briefing him when Eric went off his gourd."

"I want Clayne to actually move in with Lloyd until we're perfectly satisfied he's turned. We'll give him a month and then decide whether to lift the implantation."

"You're going to implant him?" Nicole blurted, feeling her stomach drop.

"Of course," the Major said, surprised at her question.

"But you said you were going to give him another chance."

"We are, but not without implantation. We can't risk any more outbursts."

"Oh." Nicole dropped her eyes under his probing gaze.

"Can we?"

"No, sir, of course not. I don't want to face any more flying stools."

"You seem bothered by that, Nicole. Why?"

She considered that, noting again that it was not images of Eric that she saw, but of his mother and sisters. "I think *surprised* is a better word," she said, looking up to meet his gaze. "When you said you were going to give him another chance, I assumed you meant with the same status."

"Stage One or Stage Two?" Travis broke in, winning a grateful look from Nicole.

"Stage Two." The Major glanced at his watch. "In fact, it should be done by now. That's why we've got to turn him in a hurry. If we wait very long, he'll be so conditioned to it that he'll lose his value to us. So get Clayne on it now. He'll be out of sedation within the hour."

Travis straightened, aware that the interview was over. "Yes, sir. Consider Eric Lloyd under control from this point on."

CHAPTER

12

Nicole watched wide-eyed as Clayne Robertson polished off his third piece of pie and washed it down with the last of a quart of milk. She turned to his wife and shook her head. "Adrienne, you must spend your whole life cooking."

Adrienne Robertson smiled, the well-formed, white teeth a startling contrast to her ebony-brown skin. She looked at her husband with obvious pride and fondness. She was lighter skinned than he, and as slender as he was muscular, with delicately shaped features and jet-black hair that was fluffed into a short but full Afro cut.

Clayne smiled back at his wife. They were in the comfortable, modern dining room of the Robertson apartment, lingering over the remains of dinner. He turned to Nicole. "If you don't put fuel in the boilers, you won't get any power in the turbines."

Nicole laughed. "Turbines are a good analogy. I'll bet you burn more fuel than an ocean-going liner."

He gave a deep chuckle and patted his stomach in easy contentment. An ocean-going liner wasn't too far off, Nicole decided. A former middle linebacker for the Pittsburgh Steelers, Clayne was built like a fifty-gallon oil drum. Central Supply had his uniforms specially tailored to cover the massive shoulders and thick legs. He had no neck, just a square block of a head precariously stuck on his shoulders. Football was not played anymore in the Alliance of Four Cities, because a player had been killed some years before. He had smacked helmets with another player with particular force, and the implantation had misfired into his brain. But Nicole had seen movies of football games, and it caused her to shudder slightly when she thought about running headlong into this bull of a man.

"Tell you what," he rumbled good-naturedly, "if you're so worried about Adrienne, tell the Major to pull me off this baby-sitting job and let me come back home before she gets out of practice."

"Oh, no," Adrienne said quickly, her dark eyes teasing. "I miss you. But I figure I've saved enough out of my food budget in the last four weeks to buy a new car. I say let the Guardians feed you another two weeks, and we'll be completely out of debt."

A deeply hurt expression flattened Clayne's features even more. Then suddenly he lunged forward, causing the dishes on the table to jump and Adrienne to squeal as he caught her arm. "So that's how it is, huh?" he growled.

"Clayne!" she wailed, as she tried to pull free. "Let me go!"

"Buy a new car, huh? Get out of debt, huh?"

"Clayne! You'll wake the children. Nicole! Help!"

But Nicole just waved her away, laughing too much to render even psychological assistance.

Suddenly Clayne sobered, and Adrienne instantly followed. She leaned forward and gazed into his eyes. The meat-cleaver hands came up and brushed at her cheeks gently, and Nicole looked away, embarrassed to witness such open and unabashed love between two people. She knew that she and Travis were moving in that direction, but they weren't there yet. Few people she knew were.

"Forget the car," Adrienne said softly. "Just come home again. Okay?"

"I will, soon as we get this young bronco tamed. You know that."

Slightly flustered at her own emotions, Adrienne put her hand over Clayne's and turned to Nicole. "How soon are you going to let this man of mine go?"

She shook her head. "Clayne can answer that better than I. The training period is over now, but until Eric has proven himself on the job, the Major wants Clayne to stay with him. I'd say another two weeks probably."

"Did they ever move his family up to Stage One?" Adrienne asked.

"No. Because of that little show with the stool, the Major insists that he totally prove himself first. Eric still has a Stage Two."

Clayne stood up and motioned to them. "Let's go in the living room to talk."

They moved into the next room and sat down, Clayne and Adrienne on the couch, Nicole in a comfortable chair facing them. "Well, I know he's a challenge," Adrienne said, once they were settled, "but I think he's nice. The kids just love him."

Without thinking, Nicole pulled a face.

Clayne laughed. "I don't think Nicole is quite as taken with Eric as you are, dear."

"Why?"

"He's insolent, arrogant, and totally self-centered," she shot back.

"Translated, that means he takes particular delight in needling his Monitoring Officer," Clayne explained. "And he has a peculiar talent for that. And as if that weren't enough, the first day on the job he nearly decked her fiancé."

"Your *fiancé?*" Adrienne cried.

"Yes—Travis. If I hadn't pulled him off—"

"You lunkhead," Adrienne said, smacking Clayne's leg with her fist. "You didn't tell me Nicole was engaged."

"Oh. I meant to when I called you last night."

"You," she said, doubling up her fist at him. Then she turned to Nicole. "When?"

"Night before last. We get the rings next week."

"That's wonderful. Had I known, we'd have made Travis come tonight in spite of his meeting. Have you set a date yet?"

Nicole shrugged. "No, not yet. Travis thinks we ought to be engaged for a little while before we make final plans."

"Ah, cold feet already," Clayne teased.

"Oh, Clayne," Adrienne said, slapping his leg again. "I'm so happy for you, Nicole."

"Thank you. I have to admit I'm pretty happy myself."

Then just as suddenly as she had dropped it, Adrienne picked up the conversation again. "Well, don't be too hard on Eric. He's going through a terrific adjustment."

"That's my Adrienne," Clayne chuckled. "Watcher of the downtrodden, protector of homeless boys, Mother Superior to the wayward—"

Adrienne elbowed him in the ribs. "Feeder of the hungry."

"Right on, babe," he agreed without rancor.

"So," Nicole spoke up, wanting to get off the subject of her feelings about Eric, "is he going to make it?"

"You're his Control Officer," Clayne shot back, good-naturedly. "What's your evaluation?"

"That he's biding his time, waiting for a chance to run. You're his training officer," she countered, "what's your evaluation?"

"Well, he's a very bright kid, the best all-around trainee I've ever seen. His training is over now. Tomorrow night we begin his first shift. It'll be interesting to watch him in action."

"Honey," Adrienne cooed, "you're evading the question."

"Oh," Clayne said in innocent surprise. "No question about it. Nicole's right. He's biding his time, looking for some way to beat the system. I think at first his plan was to hurry and get accepted, have the implantations for his family removed, then find some way to beat the Outer Perimeter."

"You say he thought that at first?" Adrienne asked. "But not now?"

"When he lost control in his cell and ended up implanted, it blew the whole plan for him. By the time he completely proves himself to the Major, his family will be conditioned to the implantation. He's asked me quite pointedly how long that takes. I've told him that if they are real careful not to trigger it too often, they'll be good for three months, maybe four at the most."

"And it'll be six, if he's lucky," Nicole broke in. "Perhaps even a year, before the Major frees his family."

"Exactly," Clayne said. "So he's got to find a quicker way."

"There isn't a way," Nicole said flatly.

"I know that," Clayne agreed with a note of regret, "and you know that, but he won't accept it. That's why I don't know if he's going to make it."

They were purring through the nearly deserted streets, the electric motor barely audible, as Clayne let the orange and blue squad car roll slowly along. An early evening rainstorm had buffed the night air crystal clear, with puddles here and there in the streets and a few droplets still clinging to the clear plastic bubble over their heads. Both windows of the Guardian car were down, and Eric took a deep breath, savoring the cool, moist air.

"Beautiful night," Clayne said lazily. It was the first they had spoken in over ten minutes, but the silence had been easy, comfortable, with no strain.

"Yes. It reminds me of nights in the valley."

"Travis said it was a beautiful place."

"It was."

"So is Shalev."

"True," Eric conceded. "It really is."

"We love it here."

Eric turned and gave Clayne a long, searching look. Again there was silence for almost a minute. Then Eric spoke again. "Was your application for the country club accepted?"

Clayne's head jerked around. "How did you know about that?"

Eric laughed softly. "My dad used to talk about scuttlebutt in the Army. I never really understood what he meant until I started training with the Guardians. Rumors and gossip fly everywhere in that place."

"Yeah, that's for sure," Clayne grumbled.

"So?"

Eric noticed Clayne's hands tighten on the wheel, but when

102

he spoke his voice was light and nonchalant. "No, our application was deferred. We've been put on a waiting list."

"Uh huh," Eric said gently. "And what about George Marshall?"

"What about him?" Clayne said, more quickly than he had intended.

"He applied after you, so they say. And he's been accepted."

"Who told you that?"

"What? That he applied after you, or that he's been accepted?"

"That he was accepted."

"Oh, George told us in the locker room a couple of days ago."

Clayne grunted, then turned back and stared out the window, concentrating on his driving.

"It's not the first time, is it."

"The first time for what?" Clayne snapped, obviously irritated.

"Racial discrimination."

"Buzz off, Lloyd," he said, really angry now. "You don't know what you're talking about."

"Sorry. I was just wondering."

"Look, Eric," Clayne said, pulling the car over to the curb. He shut off the motor, and half turned in his seat. "Why don't we cut the innocent, wide-eyed, child-wants-to-know routine? What're you driving at?"

"Me?"

"Yes, you. You're about as subtle as a pack of wolves running down a moose."

Eric laughed. "I get the feeling you'd be some kind of moose to bring down." Then, cutting off Clayne's retort, he added, "and I don't mean that in just the physical sense."

Clayne's dark face held its anger for a moment, then split in a wide grin. "I think physically, too."

"Yeah," Eric said ruefully. "Did they pick you as my training officer before or after I threw the stool through the window?"

"Before. Now stop the runaround. If you've got something to say, get it out."

"Okay, I will. Why is it everyone is so eager to talk about all the wondrous advantages of life in the Alliance, and yet every time I raise a question about some problems, defenses spring up like dandelions on a ditchbank?"

When Clayne didn't immediately answer, Eric pushed on. "Nicole tells me everyone here is ecstatically joyful, but she admits that an electronic fence keeps people in the Happiness Corral. The penalty for escape is merely death. Every time he turns around, the Major is pontificating on how they've eliminated all evil in men, and yet your family is experiencing one of the most ancient and persistent of all evils—racial discrimination. Everyone raves about what a thoroughly delightful place the AFC is, and yet the hospitals are clogged with neurotics and psychotics, and the birthrate is so low you have to drag people in by the hair to maintain a growth potential."

Eric raised his hands in a gesture of puzzlement. "I was just curious, that's all."

Clayne looked at him, his features expressionless, then finally shook his head. "Leave it alone, Eric."

"See. That's what I mean."

"Leave it alone, or it's going to break you. You're here. You're in it. Your only hope is to get it through that boyish head of yours that this is the way things are. They're not perfect. Nobody claims they are. But if you want to get any freedom at all, *leave the rest alone.*"

Eric started to smile, about to quip something cute and deflect Clayne's sober intensity, but then suddenly he became equally serious. "I don't think I can, Clayne. It's too terrible to leave be."

"I was afraid of that." Clayne turned back around and started the motor. As he eased off the clutch, he looked at Eric again. "I'm just telling you, it's going to break you. So—"

Suddenly the radio blared. "Baker Able Seven."

Clayne picked up the mike and pressed the button. "This is Baker Able Seven, over."

"Baker Able Seven," intoned the female voice in a bored monotone. "We are getting a three-six-six at the power substation on Overhill and Pepper Streets. Investigate and advise."

"Ten-four. We'll check it out and advise." Clayne hung the mike back onto its hook, started the car again, and accelerated smoothly.

"What's a three-sixty-six?" Eric said, raising his voice over the noise of the wind rushing through the windows. "I don't remember that one in the code list."

Clayne leaned the car into a curve, and then, as it straightened out, glanced quickly at Eric. "It's what we call an interference signal. Something's on the fence at the power substation."

"You mean an alarm?"

"Kind of. Several years ago, a young boy climbed a substation fence and was badly burned when he brushed against one of the transformers. Since then any place that constitutes a danger zone has been fenced off and wired with a pressure-sensitive switch. If something pushes against the fence, a mild electrical shock is given. If it continues, the shock steadily increases until it is a pretty stiff jolt. That's what we call a three sixty-six. It rarely happens, because the system works so well."

"So what could this be?" Eric asked. "An animal?"

"Not likely, unless it's stuck somehow. The first charge would drive it away. No, I'm afraid it's an MC."

"A what?"

"A masochist. We call them MCs." He swung around another corner. "Okay, here's Pepper Street. Less than a minute now."

"A masochist?"

"Yes. You know, the opposite of a sadist. A sadist likes to inflict pain on others. A masochist likes to have pain inflicted on him."

"I know what the word means. I just don't understand what—"

"Occasionally we find people who deliberately seek to create pain for themselves. They get some kind of sick satisfaction out of it. I haven't seen one for several years now." He flicked the lights on bright. "There's the substation, coming up."

He braked down hard, and the car slid a few feet on the wet pavement. The headlights illuminated a small fenced area and a heavy-set figure with his back to the light, arms outstretched and fingers interlocked into the fence. As Clayne flipped on the spotlight, the figure whirled around.

"Well, I'll be—" Clayne breathed. "It's Charlie Bird. I thought he was still in the psycho ward of the hospital."

He swung open the door. "Bring the stun gun," he commanded, "but don't use it unless I say."

Eric got out of the car, taking the long pistol off its rack underneath the dashboard.

The man was peering at them, blinded by the lights. He was young, probably less than twenty-five. His hair was wildly tousled, his eyes wide and glassy.

"All right, Charlie," Clayne called easily. "The fun's over. Come away from the fence."

The hands snaked backward and grasped the chain links. Eric saw the man's arms stiffen slightly and his eyes widen.

"Who is it?" the man cried. "Who knows Charlie Bird?"

"It's Clayne Robertson, Charlie." Then to Eric, more softly, he said, "Call Central Control. Tell them to cut the juice here."

As Eric obeyed, he saw Clayne move forward, talking softly. Eric called in quickly, then got out of the car and moved forward, the stun gun ready.

"Come on, Charlie," Clayne soothed, approaching slowly.

Suddenly Charlie gave a little cry of dismay and released his hold on the fence. "No! Don't turn it off. Don't!" It was almost a sob, as from a child deprived of a favorite toy. Then he leaped at Clayne like a clawing tiger. Eric ducked into a half crouch, looking for a clear shot with the stun gun, but Clayne saw him and shouted, even as he spun Charlie around and flung him off his shoulders. "No, Eric! Don't!"

Charlie bounced off the fence and lit on his feet, quick as a cat. He launched himself again, his fists flailing, but this time Clayne was waiting for him. He side-stepped the rush, then swept up Charlie from behind in his massive arms.

"Get the cuffs, Eric," he grunted, trying to hold himself clear from the kicking feet. "They're in the glove box."

In a moment they had Charlie's arms pinned behind him and the cuffs on. The fight went out of him, and he wept quietly.

"All right, Charlie," Clayne said gently, "it's all over." He brought him back to the car and gently pushed him into a half-sitting position on the fender. "Just stay right there for a minute, then we'll take you home."

He jerked his head at Eric. "Watch him for a minute. I think he'll be okay now." He slid into the driver's seat and picked up the mike.

Ten minutes later, as Eric watched the ambulance drive away with Charlie Bird, Clayne turned to him. "Well, Mr. Lloyd, that's more excitement than I've had on shift for months. Welcome to your first night as a Guardian."

"I don't understand," Eric said. "How can he attack you like that?"

"Oh, he was infuriated that we turned off his pain. He's not a bad kid, just a very sick one."

"No, that's not what I mean. How can he do that with implantation?"

"Oh, I see. The MCs have their implantation removed."

"They do?"

"Sure. Otherwise they could constantly create pain for themselves deliberately. With their problem, you want to avoid any and all pain. That's why I didn't want you to use the stun gun."

"And why you can't use the Punishment Mode in his wrist computer."

"Exactly. That's what makes them such a challenge to handle." Suddenly Clayne brightened. "Tell you what. Since I did all the work on this one, I'll let you buy me a malt to celebrate. Okay?"

Eric laughed. "All right, you're on." Then gradually the smile on his face died away, and he looked upward. The clouds were scattered and broken now, and the stars glittered with startling clarity through the gaps in them. Finally, he turned back to Clayne. "I'll only say this once, then I'll drop it."

Clayne sighed. "All right. Say it."

"Somehow, it seems as though everything in Shalev is covered with a highly polished veneer. But I suspect that if you pry up any corner of the box, the stench of something rotten would bowl you over."

CHAPTER

13

Eric signed the check-in forms and returned the warm smile the brunette clerk gave him. Clayne followed suit, then frowned at Eric. "How come I don't get the flashing white teeth and fluttery eyes when I step up to that counter?"

Eric grinned, his eyes full of innocence. "From Carol, you mean?"

"From Carol, you mean?" Clayne mimicked in a high voice.

"She's a nice girl."

"Not to me, she isn't. All I ever get is a polite, 'Sign here, Lieutenant Robertson.'"

"Well, if you didn't come up to her like a porcupine with a migraine headache, maybe she'd smile at you too."

"I treat her just like I do everybody else," he rumbled.

"Like I said . . ."

Eric jumped as the massive elbow nearly knocked him against the wall. "Keep it up, and you'll spend your day off in traction," Clayne retorted.

Eric just grinned and pushed open the locker room door, but Clayne stopped in the hall. "Nope, sorry. I've got a short staff meeting before I can call it a day."

"Oh? Do you want me to wait and give you a lift home?"

Clayne rolled his eyes in mock terror. "Are you kidding? I'd rather face the whole front line of the Dallas Cowboys." He pulled a face. "That's a football team, or was."

"Hey," Eric said, with a wounded look, "my driving isn't that bad. I'm learning fast, I think."

"True. I can see some real improvement. Now I don't worry *until* you start the motor." Then he touched Eric's arm. "No, really, Adrienne's coming for me."

"Okay. See you tomorrow. Tell Adrienne and the kids hello for me."

Five minutes later Eric came out of the locker room, waved to the men going on shift, and started for the parking lot. As he opened the door into the garage, Nicole Lambert came around the corner, her head down, and nearly collided with him.

"Oh!" she blurted, looking up. "Oh, hello, Eric."

"Hello, Nicky," he said, bowing slightly as he held the door for her. "And how is my illustrious Monitor today?"

"Weary of being called Nicky, actually."

He sighed, his face contrite. "That's right. You must forgive me. It just kind of slips out. Nicole it is. Or would you prefer Miss Lambert?"

"Nicole is fine." She tried to push past him.

"I hope you brought a book," he said, smiling at her stiffness.

"A book? Why?"

"Because I'm going to bed, and I'd hate for you to sit in front of Big Mama all day with nothing to do."

"You flatter yourself if you think I sit and watch the tracking screen and your every movement all day long."

"Tell me, is Big Mama sensitive enough that you can tell when I turn over in my bed?"

"Big Mama, as you so flippantly call it," she said acidly, her eyes snapping with anger, "can even tell me if you're having a bad dream." This was a slight exaggeration, but not much. She started away, then spun around. "And the sooner you start taking Central Monitoring and our abilities seriously, the sooner you'll get some serious consideration for release from implantation."

"Why, Miss Lambert," he drawled, "what ever made you think I don't take Big Mama seriously?" A sudden glint of hardness darkened his eyes. "I can't think of anything I have ever taken more seriously."

"Well," the Major said, looking around the table, "shall we begin? Clayne, you're on. By the way, is your wife glad to have you back?"

He chuckled. "It's been three days now. I think it's starting to wear on her."

"I'll bet," Nicole interjected. "I saw her down at the supermarket the other day with a flatbed truck getting ready for his return."

"I know, and that was only for my welcome home dinner. Well, anyway," he said, turning back to the Major, "I really don't have much to say. Eric is a model trainee. He learns fast and is quick to take the initiative. If it weren't for the other question, I'd recommend that he be transferred to the Perimeter Forces."

"But unfortunately," Travis spoke up, "there is the other question."

The Major tapped his pencil on the table thoughtfully. "He was in training for four weeks and has been on regular duty for two more. Has he at any time acted in a way that is erratic or unacceptable?"

Clayne glanced at Travis. "Other than that first day when he lost his temper and nearly decked Travis? No. His behavior has been exemplary."

The Major turned to Nicole. "How many times has he triggered the Punishment Mode from his wrist computer?"

Nicole pursed her lips as she scanned the computer printouts quickly. "Five. The worst was that day he started to attack Travis. Other than that, they've been relatively mild responses. Nothing unusual in any way. Two at night during dreams."

"I've warned him," Clayne said. "I told him if he triggers pain responses too often, he'll start conditioning himself so heavily that he'll lose his usefulness to us."

110

"So what's the bottom line, Clayne?" the Major pursued. "His behavior is above reproach. Does that mean we have really turned him, or is he just biding his time?"

Clayne traced circular patterns on his napkin for a long moment. "I have nothing to base it on except for a gut feeling, but no, I don't think we *have* turned him. I don't even think we've bought a serious glance in our direction as yet."

"Exactly!" Nicole flashed. "It's a game with him, a front. He's laughing at us behind our backs, just waiting for a chance to make us look like fools."

"Travis?" the Major said without looking up. "Do you agree with that?"

His dark eyebrows pulled together as Travis considered the question. "Yes and no." He smiled at Nicole to soften his disagreement with her. "I think Nicole and Clayne are right in that he's merely waiting. But I don't think it's a game with him. Whatever he's up to, he's deadly serious about it."

"Absolutely," Clayne agreed. "His Mister Innocent routine is a deliberate, calculated attempt to keep us all off balance. But he and his family are threatened. It's a matter of survival now. What you said, Travis, is exactly right. He's deadly serious about this whole thing."

"Isn't that just a bit overdramatic?" Nicole asked dubiously.

Clayne shrugged, and for a moment he hesitated. He liked Eric—very much, in fact, and he knew that his report could drastically alter what happened to him. But on the other hand, if they didn't stop Eric soon, he was going to do something very foolish, and a Stage Three implantation would be the result.

"Well?" the Major probed, taking off his glasses to watch Clayne steadily. He seemed content for the moment to collect all the data from his staff before making a decision.

"I don't think you fully understand how deeply this whole thing has affected him," Clayne answered. "He's far too shrewd to throw any more stools through the window. He realizes he made a serious mistake in getting himself implanted. It cut him off from the easiest way out of here."

"Meaning going through the Outer Perimeter?" Nicole asked.

"Yes, so now he's fighting with the only weapon we have left to him—his mind. So he treats each of us in exactly the right way to get the reaction he needs. It's a carefully calculated strategy with him." He turned to Nicole. "If he was gushy sweet to you, what would you think?"

She answered instantly. "That it was a snow job."

"Exactly. So he needles at you constantly to keep you half angry, but not enough to bring you to the point where you say he's beyond hope."

Before Nicole could protest, he swung around to face Travis and the Major. "He knows I'm the second most important factor in determining what happens to him, but with me he's the model trainee. And with you, Travis? How has he been?"

Travis leaned forward and rubbed his chin thoughtfully. "Since that first day, fine. Cool and reserved, but polite."

"Do you think he's forgiven you for betraying the village and getting his father killed?"

"Well, I suppose *forgive* is a little strong, but he does seem to have accepted it."

"I rest my case," Clayne said, leaning back in his chair. "I don't think he's accepted that for one minute, but each one of us gets exactly the response that serves his purposes best."

"So what's he waiting for?" the Major asked quietly.

"You're the ones who keep using the term 'biding his time,'" Clayne said. "Me, I don't think he *is* waiting."

"What do you mean by that?" the Major said, putting his glasses back on to peer more closely at Clayne.

"Remember this is just a hunch, a linebacker's intuition, okay? I might be reading the play all wrong."

"Go ahead."

"Eric has had one goal, and one goal only, since the first day when he came out of sedation. He has never wavered in pursuit of that goal, and that is freedom for him and his family."

"But," Travis reminded him, "we are offering him that freedom, for him and his family."

"Not freedom by his definition. He's been stymied by the system, and that's the only reason he hasn't made his move.

But . . ." He took a deep breath and let it out slowly.

"But what?" Nicole demanded.

"This is where my instincts come in, all right?" They nodded and he plunged on. "But now he's worked it out. Just in the last week or so, he's worked it out."

"Worked what out?" Travis asked.

"His escape."

He savored the look on their faces, his own expression one of benign satisfaction.

"Escape?" the Major said, for the first time looking skeptical. "How? How could he possibly escape?"

"That I don't know," Clayne admitted. "But he's worked it out in his mind, that much I'm sure of. And he's moving forward on it, whatever it is, as swiftly as he can. I'd bet my breakfast on that."

"Then I believe you," Nicole laughed. But almost instantly she was sober again. "If that's true, then—"

"When did it turn?" the Major cut in. "Can you remember which day you first sensed the change?"

Clayne wrinkled his brow in thought. "Definitely by last Monday, maybe a day or so sooner. I wasn't sure at first what it was, but that's when it started."

"All right," the Major responded. "Clayne, I know you've been on shift all night, so you go home and get some rest. Travis, I want you and Nicole to go back two weeks. Make a careful analysis of his movements every minute since then. Cross-check every item that forms a pattern, every action that seems even the tiniest bit out of the ordinary. Use the computer to check anything that catches your eye."

He stood up. "We'll meet in my office at six tonight and decide then what to do about this difficult young man."

CHAPTER

14

The office of the Major was a direct extension of himself, Nicole decided as she looked around. It was her first entry into the inner suite of offices that housed the chief executive officers of the Guardians, and she was a little awed by it. The rich, lustrous walnut paneling on two of the walls was so highly polished that she could see her own reflection in it. Bookshelves completely filled with books lined two of the walls clear to the ceiling, and they were arranged so that each shelf had books of the same height.

She glanced at her wrist computer. It was two minutes after six, which surprised her a little. The Major was renowned for being punctual almost to the second. She shrugged and turned to examine the desk, whose top gleamed like polished glass. The only things on the entire expanse were a gold desk set and a picture of the Major's family—his wife, four children, their husbands and wives, and his twelve grandchildren. The twin pens of the desk set framed a small, gold plaque on which were engraved three lines, and Nicole leaned forward and read it upside down:

To Curtis Major Denison
For service beyond our highest expectations
The United States Air Force Cybernetics Research Team

Nicole sat back just as the door opened, and she jumped guiltily, but it was only his secretary, an older woman with her hair pulled up into a bun at the crown of her head.

"The Major just called, Miss Lambert," she said. "He and Captain Oakes are on their way up. They'll be here in a moment."

"Thank you." Nicole opened her file and began studying the computer readout again.

The door opened again, and she stood up swiftly as the Major swept into the room with Travis close behind.

"Oh, don't get up, Nicole," the Major said with a wave of his hand as he moved behind the desk.

"Hi, hon." Travis moved to her side and gave her a quick kiss on the cheek.

"I see," the Major said with a smile. "It wasn't me for whom you stood." Before either of them could respond, his mind had left preliminary amenities. "No Clayne yet?" he asked.

As if on cue, a soft knock sounded on the door, and Clayne Robertson entered. "Good evening," he rumbled.

"Ah, Clayne, you're just in time." The Major waved them all to chairs. "Let's get started, shall we?"

He turned to Nicole. "Travis has shared your preliminary findings with me, but go over them quickly again for Clayne's benefit. Travis and I have been checking a couple of items the computer search turned up, and we can add some information as you go along."

He sat back and formed a steeple with his hands, a typical pose when he was thinking. Nicole opened her file and turned to Clayne. "Only four things seem out of the ordinary, really. There are typical patterns, such as visits with Dr. Cameron, walks in the park, movies—"

"He's like a kid about movies," Clayne broke in. "That and ice cream."

"Well," Nicole went on, "I checked the last two weeks, and four unusual things caught my eye. Or better, two patterns and two one-only items—a trip to the Nielsen Building and Lumber Company, and a trip with Clayne's family to Glacier Park and Hungry Horse Dam."

Clayne spoke up. "Both of those were with me. He said he wanted to see the park and the dam, so we made it a family outing. He seemed to really enjoy it, but he didn't do anything strange. And I was with him when he went to the lumberyard. He bought a large redwood burl and a two-foot length of two-by-twelve board."

"A redwood burl?" Nicole said.

"Yes. A burl is a knot in the wood. In redwood trees, some of them get huge. He paid a bundle for it, because the lumberyard can get them only occasionally from traders coming in from the West Coast."

"What does he want with a knothole?" Nicole said.

"Not a knothole," Travis said with a smile. "It's the knot itself, a twisted, gnarled piece of wood where the branch once tied into the main trunk."

"He wants to carve it," Clayne added. "Once they're shaped and polished, they're very beautiful. In fact, he's already working on it."

The Major leaned forward. "What is he carving it with?"

"A set of woodcarving tools," Travis answered. "I authorized Clayne to let him buy them."

"Are they dangerous tools?"

Travis shook his head. "Not really. I mean, they're sharp but not like a dagger or a butcher knife or something. He asked for permission to get them, and I agreed. He carved all the time in the village. He's really quite good."

That seemed to satisfy the Major, and he leaned back again. "Okay, Nicole, what about the two unusual patterns of behavior?"

"In the last two weeks he has suddenly started visiting the university library and also the Museum of Remembrance."

"Travis and I were just checking those two things," the Major said. "It's very interesting. Travis, tell them what we found."

"Well, he made his first visit to the library a week ago yesterday. He's made four additional visits since, averaging about an hour to an hour and a half each."

"Eric's mentioned some novels he's reading," Clayne said

"True. He's checked out six books, all of them novels, but—"

Travis paused to give emphasis to his next sentence. "While he's at the library, he has not been in the fiction section. According to the librarian, he spends most of his time in the psychology section, asking for books on the physiology of the brain."

"Maybe it's not significant that all of a sudden he has a great interest in the human mind." The Major pulled a face. "But we find the coincidence of interest."

"Okay," Travis continued. "The Museum of Remembrance. He first visited it on his day off three weeks ago. His tracking report shows he wandered throughout the various rooms, spending roughly the same amount of time in each. A very normal first visit. But he returned last Monday. He spent over twenty minutes in the World War Two Room. He returned on Tuesday, on Friday, and again yesterday. In each instance he goes quickly through a room or two, probably to maintain the appearance of a normal visitor, then makes a beeline for the World War Two Room, where he spends up to half an hour."

He let the words sink in for a moment. Then, obviously saving the best for last, he added, "And in every visit since the first, he has spent almost the entire time in front of one large display case."

"Ah," Clayne breathed softly. "And what does that case contain?"

"We were just there. Numerous items, but the most significant would be an M-1 rifle, a Thompson submachine gun, a bazooka, and three or four hand grenades."

"But surely none of that stuff is still useful," Nicole said with a frown. "I mean, are the hand grenades still live?"

"No, of course not," said the Major, "but have you forgotten? Eric's father was a leading chemist. They made their own explosives in the village."

"And loaded their own ammunition," Travis added.

"Oh," she said, her eyes widening.

"But he's implanted," Clayne said, his brow furrowing as he worked through the information Travis had given them. "Even if he gets it, he can't possibly use it against us. And why *steal* a rifle? He can get a hunting rifle at any sporting goods store. Or for that matter, why not take a stun gun from supply?"

"He can't do either of those," Travis responded, "because he knows we're tracking his every movement. A visit to the museum is innocent enough, but if he walks into a store and buys a rifle, we've got him immediately."

Clayne's expression was still dubious. "I don't know. It doesn't quite fit. He's smarter than that."

"I'm not so sure of that," the Major said. "If he's so obsessed with breaking loose, who knows what twisted logic he's laboring under."

Silence prevailed in the office as each of them considered Eric Lloyd. Finally Travis spoke up. "So what now?"

"Good question," the Major said. "Do we let him play it out and learn his lesson, or do we just assume now that we have failed with him, drop him to a Stage Three implantation, and send him to Serenity?"

"No," Nicole blurted, and then flushed slightly at her vehemence. "Stage Three is so—" she paused, groping for a sufficient word. "So final." She didn't like Eric and his mocking arrogance, but to make him little more than a functioning vegetable? The thought made her shudder. "If we can't use him in the Guardians, can't he just be left at Stage Two?"

The Major was watching her, his eyes thoughtful.

"No, Nicole," Travis said gently. "He's at Stage Two now, and here we sit worrying about what he's up to. Stage Two is obviously not enough for Eric."

"Aren't we jumping the gun a little?" Clayne mused, half to himself. "We're basically acting on my hunch that he's going to go for it, and it is only a hunch at this point. Let's play it out. Knowing Eric, he may have to test the system once to really believe he has no options."

"I agree," said Travis. "We have got to prove to him that our option is the only way to escape implantation. Let's allow him to bump his nose once, then if he doesn't change . . ."

The Major nodded slowly, then turned to Nicole. "You're his Monitor. What do you say?"

"I agree. If he weren't implanted . . . But obviously he can't do anything too drastic."

118

"All right. That seems to be a consensus." The Major leaned forward, his expression hardening. "But that doesn't mean we just sit back and let him have a free hand. Nicole, I want a 'tickle' notice put into the tracking computer. Anytime he heads for either the library or the museum, I want that computer to start buzzing. Also if he heads for anyplace that has chemicals. Tell all the Monitors to call you immediately, day or night. Put a blow-up floor plan of both buildings in the tracking center so we can see exactly where he is when he's inside either one."

He turned to Travis. "Also, I want a TV camera put in the World War Two Room and a link-up to the screen in the Monitoring Center. Make it as inconspicuous as possible, but I want a clear shot of that one case."

Clayne straightened and spoke. "Is access to the inside of the case difficult?"

"Well, yes and no," Travis responded. "Since it's a permanent display, the back is hinged across the bottom but clamped shut at the top. You'd need a screwdriver and about five minutes to undo the clamps."

"Good. Mount the camera so we can see the back of the case. Travis, I want a twenty-four-hour monitor on his family. Anything suspicious there and I want to know instantly."

"Yes, sir."

"And Travis, call our electronics specialist. I want a tap put on his telephone and a microphone in his apartment."

Travis stared at the Major, as did Clayne and Nicole.

"But sir," Clayne blurted, "under the laws of Shalev, that's illegal!"

"Except in a case of national emergency," the Major said. "If Eric somehow escapes, he could threaten our whole system. Put one on Dr. Cameron's phone and in his apartment too. If Eric is up to something, you can bet Cameron is also in on it."

Travis took a deep breath. "Yes, sir."

The Major looked from one to the other. "All right. Is there anything else? What are we overlooking?"

Clayne stirred as if about to speak, then shook his head. When neither Travis or Nicole said anything, the Major stood

119

up. "Then that does it. We'll meet at nine o'clock every morning until the status changes one way or the other. Thank you."

As the three of them moved out into the hall and down to the elevator, Travis put his arm around Nicole and smiled at her. Then, as he pushed the button for the elevator, he turned to Clayne. "Well, what do you think?"

"I don't know. Something still doesn't add up."

"Do you really think the fox can outsmart this hound?"

Clayne considered that, then shook his head. "No. We've got him covered. There's no way he can pull it off."

"The real problem," Nicole said, "is that the fox isn't aware of just how smart the old hound on his tail really is."

The elevator door opened and Travis and Nicole stepped in. For a moment Clayne stood and looked at Nicole without really seeing her. Then he too lumbered in, and the elevator dropped slightly with the additional weight. As the door closed, he turned and stared at the door.

"I think you've just hit on it, Nicole."

"What?"

"That's what's troubling me. I think the fox knows exactly how smart we are, and it doesn't seem to bother him at all. He's too shrewd not to know we suspect him, but it doesn't stop him. That's the real question. Why doesn't it?"

CHAPTER

15

"Let's stop here," Cliff said, slowing their leisurely pace along the pebbled path through the park and pointing to a bench. It was a beautiful summer's evening, with the last of twilight lingering far past its expected stay.

As they sat down, Eric picked up a small pebble from the path and flipped it into the water.

"Okay," Cliff said, "let's hear it. And I'm warning you, I'll be playing the part of a very skeptical critic. We're not the first ones to ever try beating this, you know. I've now documented thirteen cases—and there are probably many more—where people have tried to break free of the Major's little Utopia. Four are burned-out hulks—living bodies with no minds—and the rest are dead."

"I know," Eric said, "but I've got it all worked out." Then he shook his head ruefully. "Except for one question."

"All right, let's hear your solution first, then the question."

Eric took a deep breath, determined not to let his excitement show through. "We have two problems, as I see it. First, we have to get the implantation out, and second, we have to get the wrist computer off. Right?"

"*Three* problems," Cliff corrected. "Have you forgotten that the wrist computer and the implantation chip are electronically interdependent? *If* you could break the band of the wrist computer—which you cannot do, because any pull automatically triggers the Punishment Mode. But *if* you could—"

"I can."

"How?"

"I'm not going to break it. I'm going to cut it."

Cliff's head jerked up, and he stared at Eric. "It can't be done. As I told you before, the band is made of specially hardened steel. You'd need a saw with a very hard blade—which would probably be very hard on your arm—or special cutters. And we've already checked those. All are carefully controlled. You need a special permit to even touch one. With the Major monitoring your every movement, you won't get within a mile of one."

"I'll get it off," Eric said. "I'll tell you how in a minute. So go on with my third problem."

"We went through all this before. The wrist computer, if cut, triggers the implantation. The implantation, if removed, triggers the Punishment Mode in the wrist computer. Either or both are fatal." He sighed. "Eric, the third problem is *the* problem. The other two are irrelevant until you solve it. Every one of the nine who were killed was killed in one of those two ways. No, you've got to give the Major and Dr. Gould credit. They have devised a very effective, interlocking system."

"True, and that's what's been absolutely stumping me. But I've worked it out."

"How?"

"Remove both of them at precisely the same instant."

Cliff stared at him, disbelieving.

"If you have heavy-duty bolt cutters, you can do it. Have the incision in the neck already made, and don't even touch the chip until the cutters are in place. Then simply yank the implantation out at the exact moment you cut the other, and all you have is a very clever interlocking system sizzling in thin air. Right?"

Cliff shook his head slowly. "Your timing would have to be absolutely precise. A second or two off and . . . It's very dangerous."

122

"Dangerous yes, but impossible? No!"

Cliff's eyes were narrowed in deep concentration, and for a moment he started to nod, then suddenly he shook his head. "It's a brilliant plan, except for one tiny item."

"What?"

"Who's going to perform these two simultaneous maneuvers with such perfect timing?"

Eric smiled, fully enjoying the fact that he had already anticipated this question. "If you'll teach me a few fundamentals of minor surgery, I'll take yours out, you take mine. Fair enough?"

Cliff sighed, the disappointment drawing the corners of his mouth down sharply. "And have you forgotten that we are implanted? Illegal removal of an implantation is a capital offense. As much as I hate this thing—" he touched the back of his neck in disgust, "how steady do you think my hands will be with the chip sending jolts of electricity into my brain every time I think about what we're doing?"

He stood up, angry that he had let his hopes rise. "Steady hands! I'll be lucky to stay on my feet. Sorry, Eric, but I've never operated from a prone position before."

"Okay. Now you've come to my question."

"Great!" Cliff grunted irritably, "and since the whole plan depends on that one question, why don't we just wait until then to work it out."

"I know, I know. But I know there's a solution. I'm on the verge of it, but I need your help to break through." He reached into his shirt pocket and pulled out a folded piece of paper. "Let me read something to you. This is from a book on positive thinking."

"Come on, Eric! Face reality. We need more than positive thinking to come out of this."

"Will you just listen?" Eric said patiently, smoothing the paper out across his knee.

Cliff sat back down on the bench wearily. "Why not?"

Eric took a breath and plunged in. "'Man's brain and nervous system is a remarkably engineered, interwoven system. Man is the only known creature with an imagination. A person's imagination has a very direct and visible effect on his nervous system. Outside reality is not nearly as important in determining man's reaction to things as what he *thinks* about that reality. A human being acts not so much according to what reality is as he does on the basis of how he *perceives* that reality. Or, to put it another way, his body reacts according to what he *believes* reality is.'"

Eric looked up, but Cliff's expression was impassive, unmoved. So he hurried on. "'For example, in a horror movie, consciously the person knows that reality is simply moving images projected on a screen. He knows that what he is seeing is not real, but his imagination quickly begins to accept it as real, *and his central nervous system reacts as though it was reality.* He starts to sweat, his heart races, he grips the edge of his chair. *It becomes real to him.*'"

Eric looked up, then rushed on. "Note this," he said eagerly. "'Your nervous system does not distinguish between a *real* and an *imagined* experience. What person has not awakened in the middle of the night with pounding heart or cold with fear? A dream is a totally fictional experience, but if the mind *believes* it is real, the body will react accordingly.'"

He stopped, pleased to see that he had now captured Cliff's attention and erased the skeptical look from his face. "Hasn't that happened to you, where you had a dream trigger a pain response?"

When Cliff nodded slowly, Eric raced on.

"So have I! That has got to be a key. If somehow we could make your mind believe—just even for five minutes—that operating on me is not wrong. Then once mine was out, I could do yours with no problem."

Cliff was staring at the water, deep in concentration.

"But how? That's where I'm stumped."

Suddenly Cliff jerked up. "Hypnosis!" He nearly shouted it, then quickly looked around and lowered his voice to an excited whisper. "Hypnosis would have the same effect."

"Hypnosis?"

"Yes, that's it! Of course that's it!" He grabbed Eric's arm. "Listen. When people are placed under a hypnotic trance, they react in remarkable ways, do incredible things. It's nothing mysterious or supernatural, it's merely that the hypnotist is able to convince the person to believe differently about himself. He leads the subject to believe whatever the hypnotist says is true!"

Eric leaped to his feet. "Do you mean—"

But Cliff was too excited for interruptions. "I took a hypnosis class in medical school. We watched a dentist do a root canal without anesthesia. The patient was conscious the whole time and felt no pain or discomfort. Why? Because his mind *believed* there was no pain."

"That's it! That's our answer. Can you teach me how to hypnotize you?"

For a long moment, Cliff was silent. Then finally he shook his head. "I don't know. Somehow the whole subject left me a little nervous. I always felt we were toying with powers we didn't fully understand, so I never used it in my practice. It's been decades since I've tried to do it. But . . ." Again he was deep in thought. "We don't need some deep and total trance, just enough to let me take your implantation out without feeling guilt."

"Once mine is out, we'll have to work fast, because our Guardian angels will know it immediately. But we can do it! I know we can!"

"Let's walk." Cliff stood and put his hand on Eric's elbow. For several minutes they strolled quietly through the thinning crowds in the park while he challenged Eric with questions, and in turn he listened while Eric challenged his objections. Finally he fell silent, deep in thought.

"How soon?" he suddenly demanded.

"As soon as you can train me."

"We'll need three or four training sessions to be sure. Also, I've got to show you how to make the incision and stitch it up again."

"That's fine. I think it will take me about a week to get what I need to cut the wrist computers."

"What?"

"A set of bolt cutters used by Navy frogmen in World War Two. There's a set in the Museum of Remembrance that I can get to."

125

There was another long silence. Then, "Are they still tracking your movements?"

"Yes. Twenty-four hours a day. But at least Clayne is no longer living with me. That gives me some breathing room."

"How can you get the cutters without them knowing?"

"I can't."

Cliff's head spun around, as Eric went on.

"Remember Sam Gillespie's magic show that he always did for Halloween?"

"Yes."

"Well, as a teenager I asked him one day how he did it. He would never tell me, but he finally said, 'The art of the magician is to make the eye look where you want it to look.' That's what I plan to do. I'm carving a duplicate set of cutters to put back in the case. The tricky part will be getting the guards to look where I want them to while I make the change."

"That's no problem," Cliff grumbled, "it's the *only* tricky phase of the whole operation. Everything else is a piece of cake."

"Agreed," Eric said. "Can you get the necessary instruments and stuff?"

"Yes. No problem. Do you want some help?"

Eric looked up in surprise. "Help?"

Cliff nodded.

"Who?"

"Dr. Chester Abernathy. He is one of the surgeons on the implantation team with Dr. Gould. As a matter of fact, he assisted with your family."

"And you want *him*?"

"I think he'll come if we ask him. He absolutely loathes the whole system, and after doing this last batch of implantations from the village, he refused to do any more. Gould blackballed him out of surgery because of it, and he works in the emergency room now, stitching up minor cuts and dispensing aspirin."

Eric's face softened, but his expression was still dubious. "It would be taking a tremendous risk just to ask him."

"I don't think so. I'm ninety-nine percent sure of him. I'm not talking about doing it at the same time as we do you and me. But if we pull it off, we'd do him next. Once we're free, we could use a drug on the others to avoid triggering their guilt responses. Sodium Pentothal would be perfect. Relieve their anxieties enough to perform the surgery."

"How long after us would you do it? We'll have to move fast to get to Mom and the girls. And would he come with us back to the valley?"

Cliff stopped and turned to face Eric. "I've been thinking a great deal about afterwards. I don't think we ought to head for Serenity the minute we are free."

"What?"

"I mean, I don't think we ought to get your family and go back to the valley."

Now it was Eric's turn to stare. It was nearly full dark now, and they had moved just out of the circle of light from an overhead lamp post. Cliff's eyes were hidden in the shadows, but Eric could see that his mouth was drawn into a hard line. "Eric," he finally said, so softly that Eric stepped closer to hear him, "we can't just walk away from all this. It isn't enough for us to get free, or even to get your family free."

"What do you mean, it isn't enough. What isn't enough?"

Cliff had never been much of a frivolous man or given to a great deal of levity, but Eric had never felt the depth of gravity that he sensed now, as Cliff reached out and gripped his arm.

"Eric, your father was a deeply religious man. He believed in God, and he tried to bring his life into conformance with that belief. As you know, when he began forming a group to survive the coming war, he selected men who were like him in that respect. They were good men, honest men, and for the most part, religious men like himself."

"Yes, I know."

"Many people wondered why he chose me." He shook his head. "*I* wondered why he chose me."

"But you've always gone to church, Cliff."

"Once we were in the valley that was true, but before then I didn't have much patience with organized religion. There was too much promise, too much rhetoric, too much running after the

127

ways of the world trying to keep people happy, with little or no attention paid to true religion. I went to several churches when I was younger, but finally gave it up. But anyway, it surprised me that your father would choose me under those conditions."

He released Eric's arm, and dropped his hand to his side. "But I think I know now why he did."

"Why?"

"Because I think he sensed that while I was not outwardly religious, I do feel deeply about good and evil."

He shrugged, obviously embarrassed to be talking about himself so openly, then looked up at the stars for a long moment. "Ironically enough, though it would surprise some of my former associates to hear me say so, I believe in God. And I also believe in a devil. Oh, not in the sense of some horrible demon who peeks into windows to frighten little children, who wears a red suit and has a forked tail. No, I picture him to be much like us, only brilliant, cunning, enormously talented, and totally dedicated to evil. I guess I'm like C. S. Lewis in that regard. Maybe Satan is a fallen angel who now, knowing that he can never succeed in dethroning God, devotes every thought, turns every purpose to frustrating God's will for us."

Once again he stopped, peering into Eric's face with intense earnestness. "So what has Satan and evil got to do with all this in Shalev? Normally we think of good men and bad men in classical, almost Hollywood terms. The good guys wear badges or calvary uniforms or Superman capes, while the bad guys are dark, with twisted faces, hiding a perpetual sneer behind a bandana or a gun.

"But let me tell you something I've learned from seventy years in this old life. Most of the truly evil men in the world do not wear masks or carry guns and knives or slink through the back alleys of the world. They wear custom-made business suits and fifty-dollar ties and meet around polished conference tables."

"Like C. Major Denison?" Eric asked softly, beginning to understand.

"Precisely! And the fact that he has created much that is good and eliminated much that is bad in no way lessens the fact that he's a deeply evil man. Even God, with all his incredibly majestic

128

power and infinite knowledge, chooses not to force men to be good. And the reason is clear. When man has no choice but to do good, there's no point in calling him moral. Men cannot be good without making that choice themselves. They can be made to act in good ways, but they cannot *be* good."

He shook his head wearily. "The Major can spout on forever with his high-sounding motives, but this society is as evil as any that has ever stood upon the face of the earth. And we can't just walk away and leave it intact, to prey upon others. We must try and bring it down."

"And you really think *we* can do that, Cliff?"

"I don't know. I think a lot of other people in this city are just like Chester Abernathy. Most have accepted what is because the alternative carries too much risk. But a lot of people would join us in a moment if we can show them we've beaten the system. We'll have to pick them carefully at first—not only to protect ourselves, but to find those who can be of the greatest help to us."

"But we've got to get my family free."

"Your family is the family of man, and you can't just abandon that larger family."

"But what about Mother and Stephanie and—"

"They must be freed too, but—" Cliff's hand came up and rubbed at his eyes. "But Eric, while they may be more important to you and me, in the greater perspective they are no more nor no less important than the seventy thousand slaves living around us." He waved his hand. "Or the hundred and thirty thousand others living out their lives of programmed existence in the Alliance of Four Cities."

The iron quietness in Cliff's voice shook Eric deeply. "Do you know what you're asking of me?" he whispered, his eyes stricken.

Cliff sighed. "And of me. Your father and your family are the only family I've ever had. But Eric, if we free the others, we'll free Madeline and the children. If we don't free them, freeing the four who mean the most to us will never justify us before God or our fellow beings."

"The longer the implantations are in, the more permanent the conditioning will be," Eric said. "I can't just forget them."

"We won't forget them. But we can't just forget the others either."

For almost a full minute, Eric stared out into the darkness, his fist clenching and unclenching. "Can we do it, Cliff? Can we pull all of this off?"

"I don't know. We face terrible risks, tremendous obstacles. But the greater question is, can we not try and ever face ourselves as men again?"

CHAPTER

16

Nicole picked up the phone, expecting that her dinner engagement with Travis was about to be cancelled. "Yes, this is Nicole."

It was Shirley Ferguson, the afternoon tracking monitor who had taken over for Nicole at four o'clock.

"Nicole, cancel the alert. Eric isn't headed for the Museum of Remembrance."

"Are you sure?"

"Positive. When he entered Alliance Square, we assumed that was his destination, but actually he's coming here."

She frowned. "To Central Control?"

"Yes. He'll be inside the building in another minute or two. Which surprises me a little. Isn't this his day off?"

"Yes, it is. Maybe he left something he needs." Nicole was too relieved to really care. As long as he wasn't headed for the museum, he could roller-skate down the hallways of Central Control for all she cared. "Thanks, Shirley. Keep an eye on him just in case."

As she dropped the phone back onto its cradle, she thought about Eric for a moment. Then she returned to her paperwork.

A few minutes later a knock sounded at the door, and she looked up, a little surprised. She and Travis were supposed to work until five, and it was still only twelve minutes to.

She brushed at her hair quickly with her hands and swept the papers into the top drawer of her desk. "Come in," she called.

The smile of welcome froze on her face as the door opened and Eric stepped inside. He was dressed casually, in jeans, an open-necked knit sports shirt, and tennis shoes. A large, odd-shaped package wrapped in brown paper was tucked under one arm.

"Hello, Nicole."

She managed to recover and keep her composure. "Hello, Eric. This is a surprise."

He closed the door, moved to the chair in front of her desk, and sat down. "You mean nobody is watching me on Big Mama?" he said, teasing her gently.

"Well, I—I mean I'm surprised that you're here to see me. What can I do for you?"

He lifted the package and set it carefully on her desk. "Well, believe it or not, I'm here on a mission of peace."

"Oh?"

"During the past weeks I've decided something about you."

"What?"

"You don't particularly enjoy this, do you."

She started at that, and gave him a long, searching look. "I enjoy my work," she finally said.

"Oh, I know that. But being my electronic supervisor—you don't particularly enjoy that, do you. Or the thought of having to recommend me for Stage Three implantation if I don't make it?"

She dropped her eyes, unable, in her surprise, to meet his. The Major's threat of Stage Three implantation was supposed to be a secret. How had he found out?

"You even find the whole idea of implantation distasteful, don't you."

"I . . ."

"You promised me once that you'd always be totally honest with me," he said softly. "Remember?"

"I—yes, I'll have to admit, I don't like some things about this particular assignment. And I've never been overly thrilled with implantation."

"I thought so."

"But make no mistake, Eric Lloyd. If you aren't smart enough to accept the way things are, I'll recommend whatever is necessary. Please believe me on that."

"Oh, I do. And I suppose in some ways that still raises my hackles a little. But not as much as it would if you enjoyed doing it."

Her face softened. "No, I don't relish the task. I can honestly say that. Not for you or anyone else. So give in," she pleaded, leaning forward. "You can't win. Don't make me recommend anything but removal of the implantation."

His eyes narrowed slightly, and she thought she sensed sudden rebellion in them, but they were as fathomless as the gray mists that shroud Flathead Lake during a winter storm. Then suddenly they were filled with wide innocence. "Give in? What makes you think I haven't already?"

Before she could answer, he leaned forward quickly and pushed the package toward her. "I've been working on a project in my free time. I'd like you to have it."

Nicole stared at him, completely disarmed by the surprise move.

"Go ahead," he said. "It's not a bomb."

She waved that aside, embarrassed. "I know that, it's just that—" She stopped and looked at the package.

"I thought about giving it to Clayne, but decided this would be a way to tell you I'm sorry I happened to come along and put you in a situation you'd rather not be in." He stood up, suddenly anxious to go. "I suppose also that I have a bit of a selfish motive as well. I hope it'll help you understand why I've made it so difficult for you."

He stepped to the door and opened it.

"Eric, wait! Let me see what it is."

He shook his head. "I've got to get some things out of my locker. Good-bye, Nicky. Take care." He flashed her a quick smile, tinged with sadness, and then he was gone.

For a long moment she stared at the door. Then she turned to the package. Opening the drawer of her desk, she took out a pair of scissors and snipped the twine. The brown wrapping paper slipped partially off, and she pulled it away. She stared for a moment, then slowly set the scissors down.

Travis had said Eric was good at woodcarving, which made him a master of understatement. From the redwood burl, using its natural shape and grain, Eric had carved an American bald eagle, suspended in flight, its wings nearly forming a V. For a moment she thought he had caught it in the moment of descent, just before it landed on the tree limb that formed the base for the sculpture. But the balance was off. The bird was almost tumbling over backwards, its neck bowed grotesquely.

Puzzled, she leaned forward and turned the piece slightly. And then she saw why. The eagle was not landing but taking off—or more correctly, trying to take off—in flight. But one leg was shackled to the limb with a heavy chain, and the eagle was clawing at the air with wings and talons, trying to break free. Eric had left the detail rough and the surface unpolished, which only added to the riveting force of the piece.

Something happened inside her as she stared at the carving. A deep revulsion welled up, a revulsion focused on the chain that bound this wild creature, born to ride the wind. A small, rectangular area smoothed into the rough wood, with numbers on it, caught her eye. She pulled it closer, not understanding. Six numbers had been left raised in the smoother area. Then suddenly she knew. Four-four-five-five-one-two. It was Eric's computer file number.

For some unaccountable reason, Nicole was deeply stirred. She was looking not just at the artist's signature, but at the title of the piece. And for the first time, she understood Eric Lloyd and what was driving him.

Several minutes later, a soft knock on the door interrupted her thoughts, forcing her attention away from the carving on her desk. "Come in," she called.

"Hi, honey," Travis said, as he stepped through the door. "Are you ready?" He stopped as he saw her uniform. Then his eyes dropped to the desk. "Hey, what's this?"

Nicole glanced quickly at the statue, then looked up. "Eric brought it to me a few minutes ago."

"Well, well," Travis said, moving closer. He picked it up and turned it over slowly in his hands. "It's beautiful."

"He's going, Travis."

"Is that what he said?"

"Yes. In his own way."

"Well, we figured that."

"*Tonight*, Travis."

He set the carving down slowly. "Tonight? Are you sure?"

"Yes, I'm sure. You'd better call the Major."

He looked dubious, torn for a moment, and then the phone rang. Nicole picked it up, then nodded. "Yes, he's right here."

"This is Captain Oakes."

The dubious look disappeared instantly as a wave first of surprise, then of anger, clouded Travis's face. "Yes, thank you. We'll be right down."

He slammed the phone down. "It's Eric. He just went inside the Museum of Remembrance."

From his vantage point near the windows on the second floor of the Museum of Remembrance, Eric spotted Clayne Robertson's huge figure hurrying across the quad toward him. Eric smiled grimly. If he hadn't been watching, he'd never have seen him. And it made his throat constrict for a moment. If Clayne came in after him, it would be blown. But Clayne didn't come into the museum. He slipped in behind a large blue spruce tree near the front entrance, and Eric saw him take out a walkie-talkie and speak into it quickly.

He turned away from the window, a look of triumph on his face. *They've taken the bait!*

Glancing at his wrist computer, Eric patted the hard object tucked in underneath his belt. It was 5:27. The loose-fitting shirt had been chosen specifically to hide his second and far more important piece of sculpture. He moved past the War Rooms at a leisurely pace, checking to make sure he was alone. Once he was sure, he ducked into the custodial closet and pulled the door closed behind him. Reaching high up on the top shelf, he groped in the dark behind the cans and bottles, then gave a little grunt of satisfaction as his fingers closed on the screwdriver he had hidden there three days earlier. Burrowing behind a stack of dirty linen, just in case the museum's caretaker felt impelled to check every room, he settled down to wait, trying to ignore the dull pain now hammering steadily in his stomach. With a conscious effort he pulled his mind away from the next few minutes and what he had to do, for he knew that was betraying him, and would only cause the pain to increase until it wracked his whole body. He began to whistle softly, thinking of summer days spent in the mountains around the valley. Today was August first, he suddenly remembered. A good day for starting something new.

"Central Control?"

Clayne's voice was almost a whisper as it came through the speaker in the Monitoring Room. Travis, the Major, and Nicole all looked up, but it was Travis who answered. "Yes?"

"The caretaker of the museum is just now leaving. He's locked the door."

"Roger," Travis responded, lowering his own voice. He glanced at the monitoring screen. "Eric is still sitting tight in the janitor's closet." He glanced up at the clock. "But he'll have to move pretty soon. The cleaning crew starts arriving by 6:30. That gives him only forty-five minutes."

"There he goes," Nicole called.

"He's moving, Clayne. Just to be sure, from this point on we'll communicate with you via your wrist computer. A window may be open, and he'll be in the front of the building directly over you."

"Ten-four."

Travis turned to Shirley Ferguson. "Okay, Shirley. Don't wait for our command. Just keep Clayne posted with a running commentary into his wrist computer. And for heaven's sake, don't make it buzz first."

"Yes, sir."

"He's moving toward the War Rooms," Nicole said, watching the blip of light on the enlarged plan of the museum's second floor.

"Okay," the Major commanded. "Activate the camera."

The large screen sprang into life as Nicole flipped a switch. She recognized the World War Two room almost immediately. The back wall, covered with a huge enlargement of Pearl Harbor and the battleship *Arizona* billowing clouds of dark smoke filled the screen. She pushed some buttons and zoomed the lens in on the nearest display case.

"Can he see the camera?" the Major asked.

"No, not unless he looks closely," Travis responded. "It's hidden in a heating vent, but we had to make a small hole for the lens."

"He's been in that room twice since it was installed," Nicole added. "He hasn't ever given any hint that he's seen it."

"Here he comes," Shirley called, watching the board. Then she typed rapidly on her terminal to keep Clayne informed.

"Look," Travis said, pointing. "He's got a screwdriver in his hand."

"Well, you were exactly right, Nicole," the Major said with a trace of sadness. "I was half hoping you weren't."

"So was I," she answered softly.

"Keep me posted on the readings from his implantation," he commanded, then turned to watch.

On the screen they saw Eric pause for a moment at the entrance to the War Room, then move swiftly to the case.

"Pain response at the point-zero-four level," Nicole called.

"Ah," Travis said, "so he's already starting to feel it. And he hasn't even started on the case yet."

"Pain response at point-zero-eight-five," Nicole intoned as Eric knelt down next to the case and took a screwdriver from his pocket. "Going up—point-zero-nine-six."

"Zero-nine-six!" the Major echoed. "How can he stand it?"

"Look!" Travis was nearly shouting as he pointed at the screen. "You can see him trembling. Look at his hands."

Nicole looked, then glanced away quickly. "Pain level holding steady," she said, staring at the computer console.

Suddenly Eric leaped to his feet, took one lurching step away from the case, then doubled over, retching violently.

"That's more like it," the Major exulted. "Did he really think he could ignore his implantation?"

"Pain response dropping, point-zero-six-two." She watched as Eric slowly straightened. *Give it up!* she urged him silently, but he turned slowly and lifted the screwdriver again. "Pain level climbing again."

"If he can override those feelings," the Major said, a little awed by the sight of the figure kneeling down again at the back of the display case, "then we've got to implant him at a Stage Three level immediately."

"Well," Travis said, "he's not giving up. There goes the last clamp. In a moment we'll know what he's got his eye on."

"He just jumped to point-two-five milliamps," Nicole said.

"That's incredible!" the Major exclaimed. "Look at him. He can barely work the screwdriver, he's shaking so badly."

"He's got the back free!" Shirley cried, momentarily forgetting that she was Clayne's eyes and ears.

"Pain level climbing sharply," Nicole said. "Point-six-two. Point-eight-eight. Now it's steadying."

"He's fighting for control." Travis's voice was tinged with awe. "I can't believe he can endure that and just stand there."

Nicole thought of an eagle clawing the air for its freedom, and dropped her eyes to the monitor, unable to watch any longer. The tension was as tangible as a steel cable stretched to the breaking point.

"He's reaching inside the case."

"What's he going for?"

"I can't tell with his back to us."

"Point-eight-four," Nicole said in a hoarse whisper. "Point-nine-two. *One-point-four!*"

"That's impossible!" Travis shouted. "How can he still be on his feet?"

"Blackout!" Nicole cried. She looked up just in time to see Eric's knees buckle as he toppled forward across the case. His fingers clutched desperately at the top of the glass, but he couldn't find a grip, and he slipped slowly to the floor.

"Look!" Travis said. "It was the M-1 rifle he was after." The muzzle of the rifle projected out of the back of the case about six inches.

"Well, he didn't get it," the Major murmured, obviously pleased.

"What now?" Nicole asked. "Shall we send Clayne in to get him?"

"No," the Major said quickly. "No, he should come out of it in a moment or two. Let's see what happens."

When Eric finally stirred and got slowly to his feet, he looked like a toy robot whose battery had run down. His head hung down, and his movements were jerky and trancelike. The four of them watched in silence as he made an attempt to push the rifle back into place, then gave up and let the screwdriver slip out of his hand and bounce noisily on the floor.

He turned so he was half facing the camera, then shuffled slowly out of the room.

"Tell Clayne he's coming out," Travis said to Shirley. He turned to watch the flashing light on Nicole's monitoring screen as she flipped a switch, and the screen that had carried the television signal went dark. The Major also turned in his chair to watch Eric's slow progress toward the front door of the museum.

"Do you want me to have Clayne pick him up?" Travis asked.

"Wait a minute," Nicole said. "He's stopped again."

"He's near the front door." Travis pointed to the floor plan superimposed on her screen.

"That's a pay phone there," Nicole said, touching a small square on the grid plan. "He's stopped at the telephone."

"Patch us into Dr. Cameron's phone," the Major commanded. "Quickly!"

Nicole typed a command on her keyboard, then leaned over

to the control panel and flipped a switch. For a brief moment a dull hum came over the speaker, and then a click sounded, followed by a sharp buzz and then another.

"You guessed it," Travis whispered, as though he could be heard over the phone line. "He's calling Dr. Cameron."

"Shhh!" the Major commanded.

Another click popped, and then a deep voice spoke. "Hello."

"Cliff?"

"Eric? Is that you?"

"I couldn't do it, Cliff." His voice held an infinite weariness.

"I was afraid of that. I tried to tell you."

"I got into the case, but I couldn't get the rifle."

"Eric, it's okay."

"I couldn't get it out, Cliff."

"Did you put everything back?"

"I didn't get it."

"I know, Eric," the deep voice said patiently. "But did you leave things like they were, so they won't know?"

"I—I can't remember. It doesn't matter. I didn't get it."

"Eric, go home. You sound terrible."

"It was terrible, Cliff. So much pain—"

"Look," Cliff said, "why don't you come over here for a while. We'll watch some television."

"No. I'll just walk."

"Eric!" The voice grew sharp. "Stay there. I'll be right over for you."

A deep sigh sounded over the line, then finally Eric replied. "All right."

"Stay at the front entrance." He paused, then, "Eric, it's not the end of everything. I told you we couldn't beat the system."

"Yeah, I know. I didn't believe you."

"Okay, stay put, and I'll be there in five minutes."

The speaker clicked, and the hum sounded again. Travis switched it off.

The Major looked at Shirley. "Tell Clayne to wait until they're gone. I want to let Eric go with Dr. Cameron, see what they say. Tell Clayne to go in and check the case to make sure

140

nothing is missing once Eric is clear. If it checks out, tell him to come back here."

He stood up. "Nicole, you and Shirley continue to monitor Eric. If they don't go to Cameron's place, or there is anything out of the ordinary—*anything*—call me immediately. Otherwise, I want you to patch the bugging device in Cameron's apartment into my office. Travis and I will listen to it there."

"Yes, sir."

"And Nicole—"

"Yes, sir?"

"A job well done, Nicole. Thanks to you, we caught him in time."

"So what now?" she asked, suddenly feeling as weary as Eric.

He shook his head sadly. "We don't have any choice. He's an incredibly brave young man, but he's too resourceful, too dangerous. We're not ever going to feel safe with him running around uncontrolled."

"But he's already implanted."

"Yes, and obviously Stage Two is not sufficient. We'll let him and Dr. Cameron have their little talk, see what they plan next. Then we'll pick them up and take them in for Stage Three."

He sighed deeply. "Such a waste. Such a tragic waste."

Nicole nodded, staring numbly at the monitoring screen as a point of light moved slowly across the streets of Shalev.

CHAPTER

17

When Cliff's car drove up the circular driveway, Eric stood up, threw one last pebble in the Fountain of Peace that stood in front of the museum, and moved slowly to the curb, his head down.

Cliff leaned over and opened Eric's door, then laid his hand on his shoulder as he got in. Eric let his head drop until it almost touched his chest. Nor did he raise it again when he spoke. "Clayne's in the shrubbery directly off to our right."

"Okay," Cliff murmured.

"Let's wait a moment or two before we leave," Eric said in a low voice, "but he can't hear us over the noise of the fountain." He stifled a grin. "Give me some solicitous comfort to help me deal with my disastrous failure."

Cliff leaned forward, his face earnest. "So you got them?"

"I got them!"

"You sounded so convincing on the phone, I was afraid you really had failed."

Eric shook his head and pushed Cliff's hand away from his shoulder, as though in anger, but his eyes were bright with excitement. "I wasn't faking the shakiness in my voice."

Straightening back into his own seat, Cliff started the car moving. "Do you think Clayne'll follow us?"

"I don't think so. He walked here across the quad from Central Control, but let's take it slow and easy to your place just in case."

They drove in silence until they were clear of Alliance Square. Eric glanced quickly out the back window, then unbuttoned his shirt and extracted the set of heavy bolt cutters he had stuffed in his belt.

"So there they are," Cliff said.

"Those are the babies. Used by Navy frogmen to cut through submarine netting, shore defenses—you name it."

"Tell me about it."

"Well, I had some minimal pain going in and while I was waiting, but I forced myself to think of other things. But once I started on the case, it was pretty bad. When I had the back off and made the switch, I could feel myself going. I fought it desperately, keeping my back to them while I got these under my shirt. But suddenly I lost control. The last thing I remember as I blacked out was saying to myself, 'Fall on your stomach! Fall on your stomach!' I could picture me lying there on my back in front of that hidden camera with this conspicuous bulge under my shirt."

"Are you sure they didn't see you take them?"

"No, I'm not positive, but nearly so. But if they had seen me take them, I think Clayne would've confronted me as I came out. Remember the magician's trick—make them look where you want them to? I pulled the M-1 rifle partly out so they could see it once I turned around."

"I hate to sound like the worried mother, but how much chance is there they'll spot the phony cutters?"

Eric shrugged. "I've never carved anything with so much care before in my life. And I think the job I did with the modeling paints was pretty fair too. If this set and the phony cutters were side by side, you'd spot the difference in a minute, but they aren't. I was very careful to place the phony cutters in the exact position as these were in."

"Good."

And then suddenly Eric's excitement boiled over. "We're going to pull it off, Cliff!" he shouted exuberantly.

Cliff nodded. "I think you're right, but we've got a hairy hour yet to go."

"Yes, I know." And with that they both fell silent for the rest of the way.

Eric stopped outside the apartment door, glanced quickly up and down the hallway, then turned to Cliff. "Dr. Cameron?"

"Yes." His voice was dull, his eyes disinterested, his shoulders slightly stooped.

"From this point on, you will obey only written commands. Do you understand that?"

"Yes."

"You will take only written commands until you are told to wake up. At that time you will be totally awake. You will not remember what you have done. Is that clear?"

"Yes."

Eric took a deep breath, pushing aside the pain that was back again now, his heart pounding. If they were waiting for them inside— He breathed a great sigh as he opened the door and saw that the apartment was empty. Cliff had been in such a high state of excitement when they reached the carport behind his apartment building that it had taken Eric nearly five minutes longer than they had planned to settle him down enough to go under. Eric was keenly aware that even though they had "failed," the Major and Travis couldn't let this go. Now time was everything.

He shut and locked the door, stepped quickly to the coffee table, and picked up the note pad Cliff had left there. Cliff had printed out all of the commands in large block letters.

Eric turned around and shoved the first one under Cliff's nose. Cliff began to speak loudly, reading as he was told. "Eric, sit down. I'll turn on the television. I'll get some dinner. You sit here and relax."

Eric winced. Cliff had spoken slowly, loudly, and in a monotone, like a first grader painfully sounding out each word. If

Cliff's apartment had been bugged, as they suspected, Eric's only hope was that they would assume Cliff was speaking to him like a child because of his condition.

In three quick steps, Eric moved to the television set and turned it on, letting the sound blare out through the apartment. Then, taking Cliff by the hand, he led him into the kitchen, opened a cupboard door, took out a pan, and banged it on the stove. He took the cutters out of his shirt and set them on the table where Cliff had laid out the surgical gloves, scalpel, suturing thread and needles, and syringes. His mind leaped ahead as he saw the things Cliff had pilfered from the hospital, and suddenly he was on his knees, gasping as ribbons of pain sliced through him like fire. Cliff watched him, curious but unmoved.

"Oh baby!" he whispered as it gradually subsided. "One more of those mistakes, and you'll have the Major and his boys running here on the double. Think of the valley. Think of Becky. Think of anything!"

Breathing heavily, he picked up the nearest syringe and handed it to Cliff, then tore off the top page of the note pad and showed him the second message. YOU WILL GIVE ME THIS SHOT AT THE POINT WHERE MY FINGER IS TOUCHING. Eric lowered his head, touching the back of his neck.

Dutifully Cliff lifted his arms. Eric felt a sharp sting as the local anesthetic was injected under the skin. The pain in his chest and abdomen surged upward again, and he clutched at the chair as he tore off that sheet and held up the next command.

I AM GOING TO GIVE YOU A SHOT IN THE BACK OF YOUR NECK. YOU WILL NOT FEEL ANY PAIN.

Cliff offered not so much as a shrug. And he had no reaction at all when Eric stuck him with the needle.

But Eric was not impervious, and he had to drop onto one of the kitchen chairs, gasping for breath, his face a sheen of cold sweat. He had thought the preliminaries would be easy. What if he blacked out as he was supposed to cut the band? Cliff would go right ahead and yank out the implantation, and that would be it.

Eric shook his head impatiently. Adding worry to guilt would certainly not ease the pain. "It is *not* wrong," he muttered fervently. "Implantation is wrong. It's good to take it out. What you are doing is not wrong!"

It helped a little, and he stood up again, feeling the time factor squeezing in on them. And all the time, Cliff stood beside him, watching him with a curious detachment while the television blared some inane musical variety show.

Eric took a deep breath, tapped the back of his neck, and grunted in satisfaction when he felt nothing. "Okay, I'm ready if you are," he said to himself, and shoved the next note in front of the dull eyes. DR. CAMERON. THE OFFICIALS OF SHALEV HAVE DETERMINED THAT ERIC LLOYD'S IMPLANTATION IS TO BE RE-MOVED. PLEASE MAKE THE INCISION AND PREPARE TO RE-MOVE THE PLASTIC CHIP. DO NOT—WE REPEAT, DO NOT—RE-MOVE THE CHIP UNTIL YOU ARE INSTRUCTED TO DO SO.

Climbing quickly up on the table, Eric lay face down, grateful that he no longer had to stand, for his legs were trembling violently. Cliff put on the surgical gloves with maddening slowness, then moved slightly and leaned over his head. The scalpel flashed briefly, and then, a moment later, Cliff stepped back, and Eric saw the bright red of his fingers. He snatched up the note pad and tore off the next page.

DR. CAMERON. PREPARE TO TAKE OUT THE IMPLANTA-TION. YOU MUST YANK IT OUT SWIFTLY WHEN ERIC SAYS THE WORD THREE. DO NOT TAKE IT OUT UNTIL YOU HEAR HIM SAY THE WORD THREE.

Cliff nodded and stepped forward again.

As Eric picked up the bolt cutters, the ribbons of pain became rivers of molten lava coursing through his body. He jerked once in agony, almost knocking Cliff's hands away. Clenching his teeth against the pain, he inserted the band of the wrist computer into the jaws of the bolt cutter, ignoring the sudden warning buzz. Yellow flashes of light edged in around his vision, and he felt himself slipping away, blackness rushing toward him.

"One!" It was a hoarse gasp. "Two!"

He rose up and slammed down his full weight on the handles of the bolt cutters. "*Three!*" he shouted.

He heard a sharp snap and a brief, odd sensation at the back of

146

his neck, but those impressions were instantly swept away with the sudden, total cessation of the pain, which left him gasping in amazement and relief. With one great sob of release, Eric collapsed back on the table, drawing breaths of air like a threshing machine gobbling up harvest wheat.

Finally he looked up. "We did it, Cliff!" he whispered exultantly. Cliff watched him steadily, holding the bloody black plastic chip in his fingers.

Eric tore off the next sheet on the pad and held it up. STITCH UP THE INCISION AS QUICKLY AS POSSIBLE. WHEN YOU ARE FINISHED, LIE FACE DOWN ON THE TABLE.

Cliff nodded, unconcerned, stepped forward, and picked up the needle and some suturing thread.

"We did it!" Eric whispered again, hardly able to fathom the total absence of pain. It provided a pleasure more exquisite than anything he had ever known. He slapped the table with his fist, careful not to move his head. "We did it!" he said again in a joyous whisper of triumph.

Nicole gave a sideward glance at the monitoring screen, stared for a long moment at the blinking white light and the small sentence across the bottom of the screen, TRACKING ERIC KARL LLOYD, #445512, then leaned back and closed her eyes. The aspirin she had taken immediately after Travis and the Major had left had not yet taken hold, and she massaged her temples with her fingertips, ignoring the questioning look Shirley Ferguson shot in her direction.

She felt angry—angry at herself for letting her emotions override her good sense, angry at Clifford Cameron for not stopping Eric's foolhardy recklessness, and most of all, angry at Eric. She had tried to warn him. Travis had tried to warn him. Clayne had put it to him straight again and again. But by tomorrow at this time, he would have a Stage Three implantation in the back of his neck. And it would be his own stupid fault.

A soft knock came at the door behind her, and Nicole and Shirley both turned as Clayne Robertson entered, gave them a quick wave, and moved over to stand behind Nicole and stare at the monitoring screen. "They're still at Cameron's place?" he asked.

"Yes. The doctor is cooking them some dinner. Eric's in the living room." She made a face at the noise coming from the speaker. "That's the television you hear."

Clayne shook his head as he leaned forward and peered at the placement of the blinking light on the simple floor plan of Clifford Cameron's apartment. "He's not in the living room," he corrected. "That's the kitchen."

Nicole turned to look at him. "Are you sure? I got the impression Dr. Cameron left him on the couch."

Clayne shook his head, and his finger touched the screen. "I've been in there two or three times. That's the kitchen. This is the living room here. He's probably gone in to be with Cliff."

"No," Shirley said. "He hasn't moved out of that room since Cliff—Dr. Cameron—told him to sit down."

Clayne shrugged, not really caring one way or the other. "Sorry, but he's in the kitchen. Any word from the Major yet?"

Nicole shook her head. "He's going to have them picked up tonight, and then he'll put them both on Stage Three." Before Clayne could respond, she returned to the other question. "Are you sure that's the kitchen?" She didn't like the fact that she had so clearly pictured him in the living room, only to find him in the kitchen.

"Yes, I am. Can you bring both Eric and Cliff on the screen at the same time? Bet you a malt they're in the same room."

Nicole punched the keys, and a second light came on the screen so close to the first as to almost form one point of brightness. The line of print beneath the two blinking lights expanded to read: TRACKING ERIC KARL LLOYD, #445512 AND CLIFFORD CLARK CAMERON, #446823.

"See," Clayne said, pleased with himself, "they aren't moving, and they're right next to each other. I'd guess they're eating dinner together. Eric can't be too emotionally crushed if he's eating already."

"I could have sworn—" Nicole didn't get to finish her sen-

148

tence, because suddenly the monitoring alarm clanged wildly. The two points of light disappeared and bright red letters flowed across the screen. WARNING! WARNING! WRIST COMPUTER, #445512, ERIC KARL LLOYD HAS BEEN SEVERED. TERMINAL VOLTAGE SEQUENCE NOW INITIATED.

"What!" Nicole exclaimed, unable to believe her eyes.

Then just as suddenly as it had begun, the alarm shut off, and a dull buzz took over. ERIC KARL LLOYD, #445512, HAS NOW BEEN TERMINATED. SUBJECT CAN NO LONGER BE MONITORED.

Nicole's hand flew to her mouth. "No!" she whispered.

"Terminated!" Clayne cried. "How can he be terminated?"

Shirley snatched up the phone on her console and punched two buttons. "Get the Major!" she shouted. "Eric Lloyd has been terminated."

Nicole shot one stricken look at Clayne, then spun back around to gape at the screen again.

"What is it?" Clayne roared.

"He must have cut his band," she whispered hoarsely. "That triggers the automatic termination voltage sequence in the computers."

"Cut it?" Clayne cried again, shaking her gently, trying to pull her out of her shock. "How could he cut a wrist computer band? That's impossible."

"They did, Clayne! Look at the screen. He's dead. Eric's dead!"

"Something's wrong. Maybe a computer error."

"No," Shirley answered firmly, "in that sequence there are three back-up systems. Only one thing can bring this up on the screen. They have somehow cut his band."

Suddenly the buzzing stopped, the flashing red letters faded away, and a single point of light reappeared. Across the bottom came the white explanation. TRACKING CLIFFORD CLARK CAMERON, #446823.

"That's Cameron. He's still there, standing in the same place as before." Then suddenly his eyebrows shot up in surprise. "He must have cut Eric's band."

He spun around and started for the door. "Tell the Major I'm headed for Cameron's apartment. I want to see what's going on over there."

As the door shut behind him, the two women stared at the screen for several long seconds before Shirley finally said, "He was so depressed. Maybe he did it deliberately."

Nicole turned and gave her an empty stare, then finally her eyes focused, and she shook her head. "No, he wouldn't do that. They were trying to get it off. Didn't they know what would happen?"

Before Shirley could answer, the door crashed open and the Major strode in with Travis at his heels. "What's going on?" he shouted. He crossed the room in three steps and leaned forward to stare at the monitoring screen.

"It's Eric. They've cut his wrist computer. He's dead."

"Dead? He can't be dead!"

"They didn't give up," Nicole said, the tightness in her throat making her voice harsh. "They were in the kitchen together. I was getting some pain readings from Eric, but I assumed he was simply remembering what he had done at the museum. Dr. Cameron must have cut his band, not knowing what would happen."

"Not knowing?" Travis interjected. "Of course he knew what would happen. He explained the whole system to Eric back in the detention cell, remember."

That brought the Major upright. "That's right. So why would he do it?"

"Maybe Eric did it," Shirley volunteered. "He was very depressed when he came back."

"Eric wouldn't commit suicide," Travis snapped, his mind racing. "Somehow they thought they could beat the system."

"Is that Cameron now?" the Major demanded, jabbing his finger at the screen.

"Yes. He hasn't moved since it happened."

"That's odd. Is he all right? What's his reading?"

Nicole turned to her terminal and quickly punched in the code numbers. The readouts appeared almost instantly, causing her eyebrows to lift in surprise. "He's lying down, and his brain scan shows a comatose state."

"Comatose?" the Major said, his eyes narrowing. "Eric's just been terminated, and he's comatose? What's going on there?"

"Lieutenant Robertson is on his way there now," Shirley said.

"Was Eric lying down when this happened?"

"I can check." Again her fingers flew over the terminal keys. Then, even more surprised, she nodded. "Yes, in exactly the same place. And look, just before termination, his pain level jumped sharply. That's when Clayne came in, and we were checking on Dr. Cameron's position, so I didn't see that."

The Major's fist crashed down against the top of the table so hard that Nicole jumped. "They're operating on each other!"

"What?" Nicole and Travis had blurted it out together.

"Eric's not dead. If he were, would Cameron be lying there like a sick ox?"

"But how could they take out the implantations without triggering the wrist computer?"

"Because they've cut off the wrist computer!" he roared, his face a mottled patchwork of red and gray. "Somehow they've done it simultaneously. The computer shows Eric terminated, but if the silicon chip was out of his head when the terminal voltage was sent, it would be completely harmless."

Travis shook his head, his expression dubious. "I don't think—"

Suddenly the Major's face contorted in shock as his mind carried his conclusion one step further. "Nicole, hit Cameron's PMT button!" he shouted.

Nicole's head jerked around as though he'd yanked on it with a rope. "What?" she cried out in stunned surprise.

"They've got Eric's out and now they're operating on Dr. Cameron! Hit the PMT button! We've got to stop them!"

Stupefied, Nicole just stared. The *Punishment Mode—Terminal* button was on every console, bright red, in the far upper left corner. She had never used it, had even avoided looking at it because of what it did to her when she pictured what would result if she touched it.

"*Terminate him!*" the Major thundered. "*Now!*"

Nicole's hand raised, hung for a moment over the keyboard,

then she snatched it back as if it had been burned. "I can't," she whispered.

In a rage, the Major grabbed her chair and whirled her away from the terminal. He turned to Shirley, but she was white-faced and shook her head in shock.

"Travis! Which button is it?"

Travis too was rigid, staring at the Major's hand hovering over the keyboard.

"Travis!" His voice was an explosion echoing inside the small room.

Travis jumped to the Major's side. "Hit this blue release button first. Then the PMT button is here."

Nicole bit her lip to stifle a cry as she saw the Major's finger stab down twice and heard the electronic beep. The flashing light on the screen flared into a bright point twice its normal size, then slowly faded. Then the red letters began to unfold onto the screen. WRIST COMPUTER #446823, CLIFFORD CLARK CAMERON. PUNISHMENT MODE-TERMINAL VOLTAGE INITIATED. SUBJECT TERMINATED. UNABLE TO READ FURTHER MOVEMENT.

The Major turned back around, shot Nicole one quick, withering look, then turned to Shirley. "Send a message to Lieutenant Robertson via his wrist computer. Tell him that Eric is free and dangerous. We're on our way."

He leaped up and started for the door. "All right, Travis! Let's go!"

CHAPTER
18

Nicole sighed and stood up, averting her glance from the odd-shaped brown package on the coffee table. She made herself think of how good a hot shower and then cool sheets would feel, tempting as it was to collapse now on the couch and give in to a stupefying weariness. She had come into the living room to put the redwood sculpture down, and staying here with it would only keep the turmoil and shock churning. Tomorrow she would put it away somewhere or perhaps give it to someone. The eagle had broken free, but it had cost an honorable, decent man his life doing it.

Pushing away the sudden guilt, Nicole clicked off the light and started for the bedroom, realizing how totally wrung out she was. As she opened the bedroom door, the soft chime of the doorbell stopped her. She glanced at the clock on her dresser. 12:47. Who would be calling at this hour of the night? Without turning on the lights, she slipped to the door and moved back the curtain a crack.

"Oh!" she said in surprise, then flipped on the lights and opened the door. "Travis, what are you doing here?"

"Hello, Nicole." He came inside as she stepped back. He was in street clothes now, a pair of jeans and a soft pullover shirt that emphasized his broad shoulders and lean waist. "They said you'd left just a few minutes before I came back to Central Control, so I thought I'd take a chance on catching you. I saw your light go off just as I was getting out of the car."

"Did you find him?"

"No, not yet. But we will. Every Guardian has been called out, and we're combing the city. I'm going to grab a few hours of sleep and be back at seven."

"How's Clayne?"

"Fine. His pride is hurt more than anything."

"It shouldn't be. Eric must have seen him drive up and been waiting for him inside the main entrance."

"That's what I told him, but it still hurts him a little to think Eric could get his stun gun away from him that easily. And then to use it on him after he carried Dr. Cameron's body out to the car, that—"

"Carried Dr. Cameron's body?" Nicole blurted. "That wasn't in your reports coming in."

"Yes. Eric was in a rage. Said he wouldn't leave Cliff as a trophy for us to parade. He made Clayne carry him out to the car, then used the stun gun on him. Clayne was just coming to when the Major and I pulled up."

"I heard the report that you found Clayne's squad car about nine."

"Yes, in the Cherry Heights section. We spent a fruitless hour searching the area from house to house before a lady came running out to tell us her car was missing. We found it just a few minutes ago over on Spruce Street. But he could go on stealing cars all night. Half the people in Shalev leave their keys in their cars."

"He'll head out of the city, probably hole up in the mountains for a day or two, and then head for Serenity and his family."

"That's exactly what we figured, so we've put up roadblocks on all the roads out of town, and a twenty-four-hour surveillance on his family. But I think he's still in town. We figure he took some time to find a place to bury Cameron and then went back for Dr. Abernathy. He wasn't operated on until almost ten o'clock, so they couldn't have gone very far since then."

"That was a real surprise," Nicole admitted. "Cameron must have brought Abernathy in on this from the beginning."

"That's been puzzling me, too. If Abernathy was in with them, why wasn't he at the apartment helping them? If he wasn't, how did Eric know he could trust him?" Travis passed his hand across the stubble darkening his chin. "I don't know. Who can tell what's going on in Eric's mind?"

"I can't answer that," she answered softly, "but whatever it is, it's been there from the beginning."

"They almost made it, you know."

"What do you mean by that?"

"We found Cameron's wrist computer in the apartment along with Eric's. And *both* computer chips. They must have been within seconds of getting Cameron's out when the Major hit the PMT button."

"You mean that Eric cut Dr. Cameron's wrist computer off anyway?"

"I guess so. Cameron's wrist computer was completely burned out from the Terminal voltage, and Clayne said he noticed a charred spot on the back of his wrist as he picked up the body."

"Don't!" Nicole whispered, averting her face.

"I'm sorry."

They both fell silent for almost a full minute. Then Nicole looked up. "Is the Major angry with me?"

Travis shook his head quickly. "He understands."

"Travis, I don't want to be a Monitor anymore."

"Hey!" he said in surprise. Then his voice gentled. "You've had a rough day. Things will even out again once we get Eric."

"I mean it, Travis. I'll do anything else, but I can't do that again."

He held up his hands. "That's fine. But you don't have to decide that tonight. We're both exhausted. Let's get some rest and talk about it tomorrow."

Quickly she ducked her head to hide the tears that welled up and spilled over onto her cheeks. "You're right. It's just that all I can think about tonight is an old man lying face down on a table, being terminated long distance by computer."

He took her face in both hands and tenderly brushed the tears back. "I understand, honey, that *was* awful tonight."

But you showed him which buttons to push! To her surprise, Travis continued to smile gently down at her, and she realized she had only shouted the words in her mind. She took a deep breath. "I'll be better tomorrow."

Suddenly the door into the kitchen slammed open, causing both her and Travis to jump. "Don't count on it!" Eric said, stepping into the living room, a stun gun held easily in his hands.

Nicole and Travis whirled around to stare at the figure facing them. "Eric!" Nicole cried, as Travis pulled her behind him and stepped forward to face him.

"Easy, Travis." Eric's voice held a mocking dare, like the soft rattle of a snake. It froze Travis in midstep.

Even as she gaped at him, Nicole's mind registered that Eric had changed his clothes. His short-sleeved sports shirt and light cotton pants and tennis shoes had been exchanged for heavy hiking boots, work pants, and a long-sleeved, flannel shirt. He stood easily, half leaning against the doorway, but his eyes gave him away. As they stared at her and Travis, they were like the gray ashes in a campfire through which one could glimpse the smouldering, red-hot coals beneath.

"This is an unexpected bonus, Travis," Eric said. "I thought I'd have to leave a note. Now I can tell you directly."

"Tell me what?" Travis snapped, recovering his balance quickly.

"I'm taking Nicole with me."

Nicole's mouth dropped open, but if Eric heard her sharp gasp, he ignored it. "You'll receive word from us day after tomorrow sometime in the afternoon. The exchange will be made a day or two after that. We'll tell you where."

"The exchange?"

"Yes. You will have my mother and three sisters with you by then. Their wrist computers and their implantations will have been removed."

Travis laughed, a short, derisive bark, touched with nervousness. "Oh? Just like that?"

156

"Yes, just like that."

"And if we do, then—"

"You get Nicky here back in one piece—still pretty, still healthy, and perhaps even a little wiser. Otherwise, you won't see her again."

Travis's fists clenched and half raised. "You wouldn't dare harm her, or I'll—"

"I didn't ask for commentary," Eric said as he squeezed the trigger of the stun gun.

Nicole screamed as Travis slammed back into her, spun around once, then crashed heavily to the floor. In one bound she knelt at his side and cradled his head in her lap. "What have you done to him?" she cried.

Eric crossed the room swiftly, ignoring her and the icy shock in her eyes. He bent over Travis, patted his pants pockets, then extracted the keys to his car and tossed them behind the couch. As he bent over, Nicole's eyes caught sight of the crude bandage taped to the back of his neck. Smears of dark brown were clearly evident beneath the edges, and she shuddered involuntarily.

"All right, Nicky," he said, taking her elbow. "On your feet."

Nicole jerked away, swinging at Eric's head with her free fist. He caught her arm roughly and dragged her to her feet, causing Travis's head to fall heavily on the floor. He spun her around. "My father taught me to treat women and old folks with respect," he said, "but after tonight, my manners are wearing a bit thin."

Nicole tried to yank free, kicking at him, but with ridiculous ease, his arm circled her throat. He jammed the muzzle of the stun gun in the small of her back. "You listen," he hissed in her ear, "and you listen good. You're coming with me. And it doesn't much matter whether you come under your own power or over my shoulder like a sack of dried beans. Now, which will it be?"

Nicole made a croaking sound, as if she were choking. Surprised, Eric loosened his grip slightly, and she dropped through his arm like a block of granite. She hit the floor, rolled once, leaped over the coffee table, and darted into the bedroom, slamming the door behind her. But before she could move, the bedroom door exploded inward, blasted off its hinges, and crashed to the floor.

157

"Now," Eric said, standing in the shattered frame, "I'll ask you once more. Vertically or horizontally? It's your choice."

Her shoulders sagged, and suddenly the fight was gone. "All right."

"Okay. Get some warm clothes—a jacket of some kind, some warm pants, warm socks. It'll be chilly." He gave her light summer clothing a quick glance. "There isn't time to change now, just get whatever you need. Toilet articles. Whatever. Do you have hiking shoes?"

"No."

"Tennis shoes, sneakers? Anything you can walk in?"

"Yes, I've got tennis shoes."

"All right, get them. You've got exactly one minute."

As they came back out into the living room, she glanced at the still figure on the floor. "What about Travis? You can't just leave him. What if he's badly hurt?"

He took her elbow and pushed her toward the telephone on the desk. "Since he strayed into this, we may as well make him useful." He held up the stun gun so she could see the power dial on the side, then twisted the pointer into the red zone. "They tell me the red zone signifies a lethal stunning force. Never having used it, I'll have to take their word for it."

She stared at the dial, her heart dropping like a stone.

"Now, I'm only going to say this once, okay? No commentary."

Her tongue darted out quickly as she wet her lips.

"You're going to pick up the phone," he said softly, "and call Central Control." He swung the muzzle of the weapon around so it pointed down at Travis's head. "Now here's what you're going to say, nothing more, nothing less, or else Travis terminates. Isn't that the charming little phrase you people use?"

Nicole's eyes were wide with shock, and her mouth opened slightly as she glanced quickly at Travis on the floor.

"If you're wondering if I'd really do it, just remember, I watched a seventy-two-year-old man electrocuted tonight. Understood?"

"Yes." Her voice was barely a whisper.

"All right. Tell them Travis just phoned you. He tried to call in to them but couldn't get through. Something is wrong with his radio. He called you to relay the message."

He paused, and she nodded quickly. "I understand."

"Good. Here's Travis's message. I was waiting at Travis's house when he came home. He attacked me, but I escaped. Travis has me trapped in the neighborhood but needs every unit—*every unit*—sent to his home, Code Three. Have you got that?"

"They'll never believe that. It's too flimsy."

"Sure it is, once they stop to think about it. But they're too eager for the kill now to stop and evaluate." His eyes were suddenly very frightening. "But Nicole, if you want Travis still sleeping peacefully on the floor when we leave, you'd better be convincing."

She swallowed once, aware of the sudden dryness in her throat, and picked up the phone. For almost a minute she spoke quietly but urgently, then hung up with a curious mixture of sinking despair and vast relief. They had accepted her story without blinking. She had barely finished when in the distance a siren suddenly wailed, then another and another.

He grunted in satisfaction. "Okay, now let's get out of here."

Once they cleared the town limits, Eric pushed the car up to its maximum speed, still leaving the lights off. They headed north, on the highway leading to Glacier Park. Nicole was forced to grab wildly for the dashboard several times as the onrushing ribbon of road suddenly veered away from them and Eric had to brake hard and lean the car into a curve.

The ruse with Travis had worked perfectly. They encountered no roadblocks, no Guardian checkpoints. By ten miles out, any hope Nicole had of interception melted away.

She glanced at Eric, seeing only the hard line of his jaw and his rigid grip on the wheel in the semidarkness. Her physical exhaustion combined with the numbing shock of being kidnapped to act like a hallucinogenic drug, giving the whole experience a sense of eerie unreality. Feeling the first tentacles of madness squeezing at her mind, she spoke quickly to bring her back to sanity.

"Where are you taking me?"

"Up."

"Where?"

"Away from the tender clutches of C. Major Denison."

"Why me?"

Silence. It stretched on for several minutes before she spoke again. "Eric?"

Silence.

"I—I didn't push the buttons to terminate Dr. Cameron. They wanted me to, but I—" She sighed, giving up in the face of the hostility hanging like a barrier between them.

Silence. He could have been miles away. Angry now, she bit her lip and rolled down the window, staring into the night. She jumped and gave a startled cry as a cold nose pushed over the seat and touched her bare arm. "Lay back down, Cricket!" she commanded sharply, pushing the dog away.

As Eric had led her to the back alley behind her house, Nicole's German Shepherd had bounded up happily, wagging her tail. In Shalev, watchdogs were unnecessary, but a bark or two? Was that too much to ask? Even a curled lip and low growl would have been appreciated, but Cricket had never lost her puppylike friendliness, and she bounded up to everyone in welcome. When Eric had opened the door of the stolen car and motioned for Nicole to climb in, the dog had beat her to it, slipping into the back seat quickly. To Nicole's surprise, Eric had given in when she pleaded that the German Shepherd would starve with no one to care for her. She had been glad then, but now, irrationally, her anger boiled over, and she jerked away from Cricket's nuzzling. "Lie down!" she snapped, knowing even as she did so that it wasn't really Cricket she wanted to lash out at.

The dog whined, then pulled away and lay back down in the rear seat. Suddenly chilly, Nicole rolled up the window and stared out at the moon-bathed trees whipping by.

"So who did?"

"What?" For a moment she wasn't even sure he had spoken.

160

"Who *did* push the buttons?"

She hesitated, thinking of Travis, how he had jumped guiltily when the Major shouted at him.

"At your house, Travis said the Major did. Is that right?"

"Yes."

Silence.

"He told me to, but I couldn't."

"I thought *we* had done something wrong." He spoke as if from another world. "I thought we'd missed our timing. Mine came out without a hitch, then suddenly, just as we were about finished—" He lapsed into silence again for almost a full minute. Then finally he added, almost laconically, "It must be a real source of pride to work for an organization with so much compassion for people."

"I—" She bit her lip. "I am terribly sorry about Dr. Cameron."

Silence. She looked away again, too tired to care anymore.

A few minutes later, Eric slowed suddenly and veered to the other side of the road. After a moment, he gave a little grunt of satisfaction, stopped, and clicked on the headlights for a brief moment. A small sign with hand-lettered lines was nailed to a tree. "Kurt's Circle K Ranch. Riding—Backpacking—Wilderness Guides." He turned in, and after a hundred yards the pines thinned out into a small clearing. He stopped and turned off the motor.

"Come on," he said gently, anger no longer tightening his voice. "I can't offer you a lot of comfort tonight, but I think I can give you one pleasant little surprise."

He got out of the car and came around and opened her door, but she was frozen in place, staring at the two figures who had emerged from the trees and were approaching them. As they came out of the deep shadows of the trees and into the full moonlight, her mouth dropped open. The first man was tall, angular, with wavy gray hair.

"Dr. Cameron!" she whispered, stunned.

Eric nodded, watching her reaction. "Let me introduce you to a couple of friends of mine."

Nicole got out slowly, dazed, certain that the madness had broken through the walls of her mind.

"Hello, Nicole," Clifford Cameron said.

"Dr. Cameron! But you—how could you be . . ."

"It's the real me," he said, chuckling softly. "In the flesh."

"Nicole's a little taken back, Cliff," Eric said. "She thought you were dead."

"So did we," Chet Abernathy said, stepping forward.

"Nicole," Cliff said, "this is Dr. Chester Abernathy. You probably heard about him in Central Control tonight. Chet, this is Nicole Lambert, Eric's Monitor." He laughed quickly. "Only now I think it's the other way around."

"Nicole explained what happened," Eric spoke up. "Our timing was fine. The Major was on to us—figured out what was happening and pressed your termination button."

Even in the moonlight, Nicole could see the lines around his eyes deepen. "Oh?"

"Yes, it was even closer than we thought." Eric turned to Nicole to explain. "We had a system worked out once the incision was made. On the count of three, I was to cut the band and Cliff would yank out the computer chip. Cliff had a hold on the chip and I had just said 'one' when suddenly he jerked violently. Fortunately, his hand pulled the chip out. That must have been when the Major hit the button. Cliff was writhing on the table, screaming with the pain, and it took me another second or two to cut the band. By then he was unconscious. I thought he was dead. I even listened for a heartbeat, but I must have been in too much of a hurry."

"I think it *was* stopped," Cliff said. "Eric gave me mouth-to-mouth resuscitation. I think he saved my life."

"Then I heard a car drive up," Eric continued. "It was Clayne."

"Thank heavens you didn't just leave me there," Cliff said.

"I did that once before. Not again."

"Did you have any trouble clearing the roadblocks?" Chet asked.

"No. Travis was at Nicole's when I came in the house. He gave us a helpful, though somewhat unwilling, hand and pulled all the units into Shalev. We left him sleeping peacefully on

Nicole's living-room floor. In fact, if you hurry, it may help you get back in with less trouble."

Back in? Nicole was still reeling from seeing Dr. Cameron alive and had been having trouble following anything coherently for the last two minutes.

"Good," Cliff said. "Come on, the horses are over here in the trees."

"Did the ranch owner suspect anything?" Eric asked.

"No. We just told him we were off to a very early start, headed for the high country. We've got two good riding horses and a pack horse. Everything is loaded, all set to go. Use those pain pills and antibiotics in the pack. The ultimate irony would be to get infection in that incision and die."

Eric laughed shortly. "Right." He took Nicole's elbow and firmly guided her as Chet and Cliff walked to where the three horses were tethered.

"Have you got the cutters?" Eric asked.

Chet reached into the saddlebags of the nearest horse and retrieved a heavy set of bolt cutters.

So that's how they got the wrist computers off. Nicole stared as Chet turned back around and stepped next to her and Eric. She tried to jerk away, but he was too fast for her, and his fingers dug into her flesh. "Just relax, Nicky," he said easily. "All we want to do is make you free."

She gave a short, bitter laugh. "Then let me go."

"All in due time." He turned her arm over, and Chet inserted the band into the jaws of the cutter.

"The minute this is cut, they'll have a fix on us," Cliff said, even as the computer started its shrill buzzing, "so we're going to have to move out of here fast."

The cutters snapped sharply, and the wrist computer dropped into Eric's hand. He released Nicole's arm, spun around, and flung the buzzing object smashing into a tree. "There. Now you're free from the Major's all-seeing eye. Let's get Cricket and get out of here."

She rubbed her wrist, and the bitterness made her voice almost a whisper. "It isn't the Major who's taken away my freedom."

CHAPTER

19

Eric reined up his horse and looked around. They were at the edge of the thick stand of pines that clung to the north side of the slope. His eyes methodically scanned the open area and then the sky. Finally he clucked softly and nudged the horse with his heels. The mare flicked her ears once, then reluctantly moved forward into the bright sunshine. Nicole's horse followed without urging. Cricket raced forward ahead of them and disappeared over the ridge into a clump of heavy brush.

Nicole drew in a quick breath and stared, the numbing weariness momentarily forgotten as her eyes drank in the panorama before them. Spread out as far as the eye could see to the north and west was a lush carpet of deep green, rolling over gentle hills, surrounding a turquoise jewel of a lake, then racing up steep mountainsides and spilling over the top. A glint of the afternoon sunshine caught her eye, and she could see a thin ribbon of silver at least a mile below them. It was the North Fork of the Flathead River, which they had forded shortly after dawn.

Above them, towering monolithic peaks propped up a sky so incredibly blue as to hurt the eyes. Jagged spots of glaring white signaled the location of several small glaciers clinging to the twisted, convoluted cliffs as they tried to stave off the steady, hungry embrace of the August sunshine.

For almost a full minute they both sat transfixed, and then Eric spoke. "I always thought our valley was about the prettiest place on the earth, but I think this tops it."

Nicole didn't answer, his voice bringing her sharply back to the where and why of reality. Then Eric turned and gave her an appraising look. "How are you doing? Are you about ready to stop?"

Pride is a seductive master. By dawn, after only three hours in the saddle, she had felt as though her backside had been pounded steadily with a heavy wooden paddle. By ten she had decided that the horse knew that every inch of her from the hips down was one combined mass of searing agony and was deliberately walking stifflegged to add to her misery. By noon she was praying fervently that lightning, or some other act of God, would strike either her or Eric or the horse—preferably in that order. But when she heard Eric's question, her head came up, her jaw jutted out, and her eyes were defiant. "I'm fine. Don't stop for me."

"You're sure?"

"Of course. I'm doing fine."

"Good." He squinted up into the sky. "I figure we should make it to our base camp by late tonight, another six or seven hours maybe."

Nicole barely stifled a groan. "Whatever you say." Her chin came up defiantly as she sensed his probing gaze.

He chuckled softly to himself. "On the other hand, we could drop back to that little spring we passed about a quarter of a mile back and call it a day."

She couldn't help it. The rest of her body rebelled against her reckless tongue, and she had such a look of longing, hope, and relief on her face that he laughed out loud. "Maybe you can go on all day," he said, "but after two months without riding a horse, I'm getting just a mite tender. So unless you feel strongly about it, I vote we stop."

She nodded, knowing that he had read her precisely, but too sore and tired to care. Tomorrow she could be proud and angry again. Now she just wanted to detach herself from this hated horse and its conspiracy to pound the lower half of her into a shapeless, unrecognizable pulp.

The spring gurgled out of the ground in a small clearing, forming a tiny creek less than a foot wide. The tall pines were so thickly clustered that only a tiny portion of sunlight filtered down to the ground. The sounds of the horses' hooves, soft and muffled in the thick carpet of forest needles and leaves, barely interrupted the gentle sighing of the wind through the upper branches.

Eric swung down and tethered his horse and the packhorse to a tree branch, then turned and watched as Nicole gingerly dismounted. Reaching up, he fumbled in his saddlebags briefly, then extracted a dark brown bottle. "Here," he said, tossing it to her.

She grabbed quickly and caught it. "What is it?"

"Some liniment Cliff put in. He knew we'd both be needing it." He moved to the packhorse and began untying the ropes. "We can't do anything about the stiffness—that will just have to wear off—but I imagine the skin on the inside of your legs is pretty chafed, right?"

She nodded, keeping her face impassive. Never, to her knowledge, had she heard such an understatement.

"Well, this will help it heal and toughen up more quickly." He took down the bag she had packed her things in and walked over to her. "Here. I'd suggest you change into something warm. It'll be very cool tonight."

Her eyebrows shot up, but before she could speak, he went on. "You and I are going to be living together for the next few days, so we need some ground rules. I have every intention of respecting your privacy."

"Thank you," she murmured, as she felt her cheeks color slightly.

"However, I can't have you slipping away from me either. So whenever you want to be alone, just stay within shouting distance. Call to me every minute or two, and I'll stay clear of you."

"I understand."

166

"But," he added firmly, "don't forget to call, or I'll come charging down, ready or not. Now go change, and don't be afraid to rub that liniment on liberally. We've got another two full days of riding."

When she returned ten minutes later, dressed in tennis shoes, jeans, a long-sleeved shirt, and a hooded sweatshirt, he was squatting down in front of a small fire. Two forked sticks had been thrust into the ground on either side of it, and an iron kettle hung suspended over the flames from a cross bar between them. He was slicing something into the pot with a hunting knife.

He looked up. "Hungry?"

The pot was steaming slightly and giving off a delightful aroma. "Yes," she admitted, realizing that *famished* would be a better word. "What is it?"

"Stew."

Nicole sat down gingerly next to the fire and leaned back on one elbow, feeling the weariness and yet strangely content for the moment to forget the harsh realities of the situation. She was a hostage, he a fugitive. But sitting here in a shaded mountain glen, with the delicious aroma of food tickling her nose, it was hard to believe that.

A few minutes later Eric sipped a spoonful of the stew, murmured his approval, and then served them with a flourish. Cricket was first and had gulped her portion down before Eric could even finish getting Nicole's in the plate. To her surprise, once he had served her, he walked over to the spring, bent down for a moment, and came back, a bunch of small pink flowers in his hand. He bowed slightly as he handed it to her, ignoring her astonished look. "I know you'd rather be dining somewhere else tonight, so I hope this will make up for it a little."

Too surprised for words, Nicole reached out and took the flowers. Then suddenly, she was angry—at him and at herself. "Is this supposed to make me glad I'm here?"

His expression had been friendly, offering a temporary truce. Slowly that faded. "Look, Nicole, I just wanted you to know that I—well, I don't like this any better than you, and I—"

"You don't like this any better than I!" she cried. "How dare

167

you stand there and make a condescendingly stupid statement like that? You break into my home in the middle of the night at the point of a gun, you nearly kill my fiancé, you threaten his life and mine, you drag me up into the mountains against my will, then you have the unmitigated gall to stand there and say you don't like it any more than I." She flung the flowers into the flames. "Your arrogance is incredible, Mr. Lloyd. You think one tiny bunch of flowers makes all of that all right?"

His eyes narrowed into gray slits, which sent a chill up her spine. "*You* are the wonder, Miss Lambert. Because of your precious fiancé, six good men lie buried in the black dirt of a riverbank. Six! And *you're* upset because I left him lying peacefully on the floor of your living room? You say you're outraged that I dragged you up here against your will? Then tell me, Miss Lambert, where was your outrage when a whole village was trucked like cattle to a place five hundred miles from their homes? Why wasn't your voice trembling with fury then?"

She rocked back, as though he had struck her, her face drained of color.

"You talk about gall to me?" he said, spitting out the words like red-hot slivers of steel. "When I stick probes into the brain of a six-year-old and send her crumpling to the floor because she was accidently 'overprogrammed,' then you can talk to me about gall. And on the day I push the buttons to execute an old man for the highly treasonable act of wanting to be free, then you can fill your voice with horror and talk about my arrogance."

"I didn't push the buttons," Nicole whispered.

"You were there!" he thundered. "Did you try to stop them?"

The blood drained from her face. "I—"

His voice was suddenly deathly quiet. "Did you even so much as protest?"

She looked down quickly and stared at her knuckles, white now as they gripped the plate.

"Did you?"

She shook her head almost imperceptibly.

"Well, so much for offended conscience and flowers in the fire."

CHAPTER

20

For several moments Nicole stared at the flickering shadows on the pine needles directly over her head before her mind registered where she was. After the blowup at dinner, Eric had worked swiftly to construct a small but snug shelter of pine boughs stacked against an A-frame. He had then laid nearly six inches of additional branches on the ground and rolled out her sleeping bag on top of them. When she had crawled in, she found it surprisingly soft and comfortable and had dropped instantly into a deep sleep.

Now it was full dark, though moonlight filtered through the trees and mixed with the faint light from the campfire. As she lifted up on one elbow, she saw Eric's dark shape across the fire, dragging a large rectangular-shaped object, and realized that that was what had awakened her. As she watched, he sat down on a rock, leaned over the dark shape, then began to speak.

"Home Base, Home Base, this is Eagle One. Do you read me?"

Nicole sat up, bringing a thumping welcome from Cricket, who was stretched out at her feet. The air had taken on a definite chill now, and for a moment she debated about snuggling back into the pleasant warmth of the bag. But she had seen the radio strapped on the packhorse and wanted to hear what was going on.

After a burst of static, Cliff Cameron's voice answered, clearly recognizable even through the distortion of the speaker. "Eagle One, this is Home Base. We read you loud and clear. Over."

Nicole moved with infinite slowness, every muscle in her legs and hips screaming in protest, as she put on her tennis shoes, then walked stiffly to sit down next to the fire. A twig snapped under her feet, and Eric's head jerked around. He watched her for a moment, then turned back to the radio. "You're coming in fine, Eagle One. How's everything going? How's Nicole holding up?"

Eric half turned again. "She's sitting right here. Why don't you ask her?"

"Nicole?" Cliff called. "Is Eric treating you okay?"

Eric held up the mike in her direction.

"Hardly!" she muttered.

"I didn't catch her answer."

Eric watched her across the fire as he put the mike back to his mouth. "She said, 'Superbly.' How are things in Shalev?"

There was a deep chuckle. "Alert. I think that would be the best word."

"Are you out of the city now?"

"Yes. We're all clear."

"Have you done the other operations yet?"

Nicole's head jerked up. *Operations?*

"Yes, they're all complete."

"Any problems?"

"Not really. It's too bad we couldn't use Sodium Pentothal on you. Once we gave them a shot of that, just enough to put them in a state of relaxed euphoria, they didn't have a moment's problem."

"Good. Who all have you done?"

"We did Dick Andreason and his wife and their two children first. He's the radioman Chet told us about. In fact, these are his radios we're using now. We cleaned out a bit of his equipment before he closed up his shop. Also, he'll have walkie-talkies, set on an unused frequency, for each of us once we reach the dam."

Nicole leaned forward to hear better. Dam? That could only be Hungry Horse Dam, a few miles northeast of Shalev. The only

170

other dam in the area was Libby Dam, but that was almost ninety miles west of the city.

"Good," Eric was saying. "Who else?"

"We also did Dick's friend, a man by the name of Rod Loopes."

Nicole leaped to her feet. "Rod Loopes!"

"Hold it, Cliff," Eric said, turning to stare at her. "I think you just got Nicole's attention."

Cliff's chuckle was distinctly evident, even over the speaker. "He wanted to see Nicole's face when she heard. He's the one I told you about. He was, until this afternoon, the head of computer services at Central Control."

"I don't believe you," Nicole cried.

"She says she can't believe that," Eric dutifully repeated.

"You think Nicole is shook—you should've heard the Major on the news broadcast tonight. He was absolutely livid."

Nicole sat back down slowly, dazed by what she had heard.

"So we have four men?" Eric asked.

"Five counting you, and each one is good to very good with a rifle."

"But can they use them? Or have they been so conditioned to implantation that they'll freeze up in a crisis?"

"I don't think so. Chet and I have talked about that with them. They may have to make a conscious effort to overcome their conditioning, but they all feel very strongly that what we're doing is right. We think they'll be fine. We'll have a few surprises of our own for Travis on Saturday if he decides not to play it straight."

"You made contact with him all right?"

"Yes."

"Do you think we can trust them to hold to the bargain?"

"Not for a minute. I expect the Major will come early to lay a trap, but we're camped up above the dam now, and the exchange is not for two more days. We'll see whatever he does and be ready for him."

Nicole turned, suddenly tired beyond measure, the two more days before she would be free stretching out before her. But as

171

she got up, she froze in position. Eric had built himself a lean-to shelter a few feet away from hers, and sticking out from beneath his sleeping bag, glinting dully in the faint light of the moon, was the barrel of his deer rifle. He had carried it in the scabbard on the saddle all day long, and she had eyed it longingly several times, hoping he would step away from it for just a moment or two. Now it lay there, invitingly.

She glanced up quickly at Eric, but his back was to her again, the bandage on his neck glowing like a target in the moonlight. With her heart pounding wildly, she began inching slowly toward the weapon, silently praying that Eric would not turn around and that Cricket would stay put. With a leap she covered the last few feet, yanked the rifle out, and spun around, levering a shell into the chamber.

"Eric!" Her voice cracked like a bullwhip.

He jerked around and stared for a moment, his eyes widening. Then he slowly stood up, his arms lifting into the air, bringing the microphone up with them.

"Get away from the radio, Eric."

For what seemed like an eternity he stared at her, his expression lost in the darkness; then he brought the microphone back down to his mouth. "Cliff," he said, "we'd better quit for now. I've got a slight problem here. I'll call you again tomorrow night at the same time." He clipped the mike back in place without waiting for a response, then straightened slowly.

"Well, well," he mused.

"Stay where you are, Eric. I'm not bluffing." She jumped slightly as Cricket brushed against her leg, looking up at her curiously.

"I know the accommodations are not first class, Miss Lambert," Eric drawled, "but I'd hoped the rates would kinda make up for that."

"I mean it, Eric. Move away from the radio. I'm going to call Central Control."

She could see him smile in the dim light as he dropped his hands. The smile infuriated her. "*Now*, Eric!" she shouted. "Move away from the radio."

"But you told me to stay where I was." He took a step toward her. "You're not nervous, are you, Nicky?"

"Eric, stay back!" she commanded, raising the muzzle higher.

"Make up your mind. Do you want me to stay back, stay where I am, or move away from the radio?"

When she spoke, her voice was steady and cool. "It's not funny, Eric. I don't want to hurt you, but I will if I must."

He cocked his head to one side. "Oh, really? I have a hard time believing that." He took another step toward her.

The rifle bucked in her hands with a deafening roar, and Eric jumped to the side as the bullet cut the air a foot wide of his head.

"I may seem to you to be a foolish, frightened female," she said, levering a new shell into the chamber, "but I know how to use this. Now move away from the radio, slowly."

Eric shook his head sadly. "I've never thought you were either foolish or frightened." He took another step toward her. "But I don't think you can blow a man's head off either."

"Eric! Stay back!"

"I'm coming, Nicky. Either use the rifle or give it back."

As he took another step, she dropped the muzzle, aimed just wide of his feet, and squeezed the trigger again. As the bullet plowed into the dirt and forest debris, Eric jerked backwards and fell to the ground, writhing violently. "My eyes! My eyes!" he screamed, digging at his face with his clenched fists.

Nicole gaped at him in stunned surprise. She had missed him by almost two feet—unless the bullet had ricocheted or kicked dirt into his eyes. Cautiously she moved around the fire toward him, rifle ready.

Eric rolled wildly, moaning in agony, but suddenly as she neared him, his feet shot out, smashing into her leg just below the knee. With a startled cry she went down, the rifle flying from her grasp. She rolled frantically, but Eric was already to the rifle, and he spun around to face her. For several moments, he didn't move, just stood there, half hunched over, breathing heavily. Then he straightened. "Well," he said softly. "I can see I've been taking you for granted."

Nicole stared at him. Then she felt the tears of rage and frustration well up. Without a word she got up, limped past him, crawled back into her shelter, and buried her face into her sleeping bag, biting back the tears. A moment later she heard his footsteps. She yanked off her shoes and burrowed into the sleeping bag.

"Nicole?"

She pulled the bag over her head. "Please go away."

He sighed wearily. "I'm sorry. I really am."

"Please! Just leave me alone!"

For a moment he was silent, then she felt a sudden weight lifted off the sleeping bag. She jerked up into a sitting position. "What are you doing? Why are you taking my shoes?"

"You've proven yourself to be a very resourceful young woman," he said softly. "I can't take you for granted anymore."

"But why my shoes?" Then suddenly she understood. Barefooted people don't go very far in the mountains.

He moved away, not answering.

"You must be real proud of yourself, Mr. Lloyd," she said. "Real proud."

CHAPTER

21

The full moon had cleared the trees and bathed the tiny clearing and campsite in softly diffused light. The fire had nearly died, leaving only a few glowing embers. Even with the bright moon, the clarity of the star-filled sky was breathtaking. Eric sat and stared across the embers into the night, hunched in his jacket against the chill. The soft hoot of an owl mingled with the sighing of the wind in the trees, giving the night a quiet sense of peace and tranquillity—a feeling totally lacking in Eric Lloyd. By noon tomorrow he would join up with Cliff and the others. At five-thirty he would walk onto the top of the dam, very likely into a trap.

Irritated at the tightness in his stomach, he glanced at the lean-to where Nicole was asleep. As he peered into the darkness of her shelter, he acknowledged another conflict churning inside him. Since her attempted escape, they had settled into a sullen truce that left him filled with a nagging sense of guilt. She spoke only when it was absolutely necessary and steadfastly ignored him whenever he tried to be even minimally sociable. And yet, over the past three days he had developed a grudging admiration for her stubborn courage. Only today had his own body begun toughening up, the chafed skin callousing over and the crippling stiffness leaving him. And he had spent his life on a horse! Yet never once had Nicole complained or asked for an early stop. Part of that was the result of her anger at him, but part was sheer courage.

He picked up a log and set it carefully on the fire so as not to awaken her, but Cricket suddenly stood up and trotted to his side. Eric reached over and scratched behind her ears as she lay down next to him contentedly. A moment later Nicole emerged out of the shelter. She walked over to the fire, picking her way carefully in her stockinged feet, and sat down across from him.

"I'm sorry," he said. "I didn't mean to wake you."

"You didn't wake me. I was already awake."

"You too?"

"Yes."

"Tomorrow's a big day. For both of us."

She didn't reply, and for several minutes they both stared at the flames licking hungrily at the log Eric had added to the fire.

"Nicole?"

"Yes?"

He hesitated, trying to sort out his thoughts. "Are you sure you want to go back?"

Her head came up slowly, and in the moonlight he could see a look of disbelief on her face.

"I mean, well, I know you want to go back home, but do you think you really can go back to Central Control and be a Guardian again?"

"Again? I didn't realize I had stopped."

"I heard what you said to Travis that night in your living room. You don't want to be a Monitor anymore, right?"

"That was before you came back," she snapped. "That changed a lot of things."

He ignored that. "It's open war now, Nicole. I wish we could stop the Major without an open confrontation, but we can't. Are you ready to face another Cliff Cameron choice? Because that's what it's coming to."

She brushed that away. "You're free. Tomorrow your family will be free too. Why can't you just go away?"

"What about the rest of my village—do I just write them off? And what about the other villages and towns dragged into this mess—do I have any obligation to them?"

"Is it your obligation to save the whole world?"

"Look," he said, suddenly weary of the verbal fencing, realizing she had steered him away from what he wanted to say. "I've said some things about you during the past two months, about your lack of concern, about your commitments, and about your insensitivities. I want to apologize for them."

"What? Do I hear something that sounds faintly like a conscience?"

"You have a lot of reason to be bitter, but then so do I. So for once why don't we stop talking to each other as if it's an artillery duel. I want to say something and your blistering replies don't help."

She looked at him steadily and then finally said, "Okay, I'm listening."

"In the past three days you—well, frankly, you've really surprised me. I thought I was going to have to drag you every step of the way."

"And you haven't!" she snapped.

He stopped and sighed, shaking his head in frustration.

Her eyes softened slightly, and the tightness around her mouth gradually relaxed. "I'm sorry. I'll just listen."

"I knew it was going to be a rough few days. I expected you to be—" He shrugged. "I don't know. I thought you were going to be a pampered, whining female and that by the time these four days were up, I'd be a screaming wreck."

"I have been all you say. It's just that I've kept it all inside."

"Maybe so, but even that says a lot. I was wrong about you. You are courageous, determined, and, I've got to admit, you've earned my respect."

That took her by surprise, and for once she had no reply.

"You lack only one thing for making an outstanding Guardian."

Instantly she was defensive again, the coolness back in her voice. "Oh?"

"You've got the courage and the ingenuity and the determination—"

"But?"

"What you lack is conviction. You don't have the emotional nature, or perhaps a better word would be *spiritual* nature, to be a Guardian."

"And maybe," she said quickly, "the problem is that you don't really know my nature."

"I meant that as a compliment, but you may be right. I don't know Nicole the person, only Nicole the Monitor. But I do feel I know *her*. If the Major or Travis had had the rifle the other night, they wouldn't have shot at my feet."

"I wish I hadn't either."

His head came up slowly, and his eyes challenged hers. "Do you really mean that?"

"Yes."

He laughed softly. "I think you do."

"I do!"

"I don't believe you."

"I'd be free now."

"Free of what?"

"Free of you!"

"If you'd killed me the other night," he said, "you'd never be free of me again, and you know it. That would haunt you for the rest of your life."

Nicole stared at him, the anger draining slowly out of her. He was right. "Were you the resident psychiatrist in your village?" she muttered, not willing to openly acknowledge what he had said.

He smiled. "I don't have a diploma on the wall, but my references are impeccable." When she didn't answer, he went on more soberly. "Should I be really honest with you? Give you the full diagnosis?"

"Can I stop you?"

"You could always go for the rifle again."

She shook her head. "Is turnabout fair play?"

"Of course."

"Okay, you first. I'm braced."

"You said the Major pushed the buttons to terminate Cliff. Right?"

In a flash, and against her will, he had thrust her mind back to that horrifying moment. She stared down at her hands, unaware that she was twisting the ring on her left hand around and around.

"Why? Why could he do it and you couldn't? He may pontificate about his great love for mankind and his desire to protect us from everything from first-degree murder to dirt under our fingernails, but however benevolent his dictatorship may appear on the surface, when the crisis hit, his real nature surfaced. He's willing to kill to maintain his little empire."

"You killed three Guardians when you dynamited the truck that was headed for your village. That was a crisis too. What does that mean?"

He shook his head slowly. "A man is justified in resorting to violence as a solution to his problems only under a very limited set of circumstances—when he is defending his life, his liberty, or his family, and when he has no recourse to normal law-enforcement procedures. We approached your men in peace, and they shot Cliff down without warning. Come on, Nicky. Are you telling me that what I did trying to protect the village and what the Major did to Cliff are equivalent acts?"

After a long silence, she finally shook her head. "No."

"But let's get back to that night in the monitoring room. The Major pushed the buttons, but you were caught in exactly the same crisis situation as the Major. You were faced with the same choice, but you refused to terminate Cliff. Why?"

When she looked up, he could see in the firelight that her eyes were shining. "I just couldn't."

"Exactly, which makes you a very different person indeed."

But Nicole went on as though she hadn't heard him. "The Major didn't know which buttons to push. When I wouldn't push them, he demanded that I show him so he could. I couldn't do that either."

"Who did show him?" he asked gently.

She looked up, startled as his question broke into her thoughts. "What?"

"Who did show him which buttons to push?"

She turned her head away, shaking it quickly.

"It was Travis, wasn't it."

A long silence stretched out between them before he spoke. "I rest my case."

When her head came around slowly to meet his gaze, he added, "You make a lousy Guardian, but a remarkable woman."

Suddenly she was angry—at him, at his perceptiveness, at his accurate guess about Travis, at the tears abruptly threatening to spill over. "Okay, Dr. Lloyd," she said. "Now it's my turn."

Startled by her sudden bitterness, he nodded. "Have at it."

"Who are you to sit in pious judgment on others?"

"I—"

"You puff yourself up with pride, telling yourself that your crusade is for the good of man, that you're the great deliverer, the gallant rescuer of a society plunged into the dark ages of slavery. Hogwash! Your motives are as self-serving and self-centered as the Major's."

He rocked back slightly. "There's no need to coddle me, doctor. Give it to me straight."

She leaped up, her eyes blazing. "Don't be cute, Eric! I listened to your little speech. I'm not as clever as you, but now it's my turn."

"I'm sorry. That was uncalled for. Go ahead, I'm listening. Why do you feel that I'm self-serving and self-centered?"

"Because you cloak your true motives in noble and altruistic clothing every bit as much as the Major does. A desire to save mankind is not what's really driving you."

"What is?"

"Revenge. The Major killed your father, destroyed your village, and carried your family here and implanted them."

He broke in dryly. "How could I have gotten so angry over nothing."

"I know that!" she cried. "I know you have reason to be bitter, but then admit it. Admit that that is what's making you do all this. You want to get even. With the Major. With Travis. That's why you kidnapped me and not just any Guardian, isn't it.

180

He shook his head, but there was no stopping the torrent of her words. "You're the destroyer, not a builder. You say the Major's system is grossly evil. But what do you offer in place of it?"

"Freedom."

"No! That's not sufficient. In Shalev we have freedom. The implantation seems so drastic and terrible to you because it's new and painful. But most people never even know it's there or think about it. They live normal, productive lives. In a way, you could even say that implantation enhances their freedom."

"Come on, Nicole," Eric said, angry now too. "Get your head out of the Major's propaganda booklet. Shalev is a festering sore. We've already got a dozen people who are willing to risk their lives to join us. That's how much they prefer our brand of freedom over yours. Okay, I'll grant you that the Major's desires, though misguided, are sparked by noble sentiments. But what happens when he's gone?"

"What do you mean?"

"The system he has devised has an incredible potential for evil. Suppose you get a man who sees other possibilities in the wrist computers and the implantations? Suppose he threatens a woman with the Punishment Mode if she doesn't grant him sexual favors?"

"I—I never thought of that."

"A really inventive mind could bring about the most effective tyranny in the history of the world."

Nicole's anger gave way abruptly to an earnest pleading. "Eric, I was born an orphan because six animals, with long hair and beards, were running around 'free.' So you've got to offer us something better than simply freedom, Eric. Much better."

"No one can fault the Major for his dream of a society where men have learned to control themselves, but he overlooked the most important element of that dream. Even infinite power cannot make men *be* good. You can make them *act* in good ways, but to really *be* good, an individual must choose good things freely. It's man's most basic and sacred stewardship—to serve as the guardian of his own behavior."

His eyes were in deep pools of shadow, but Nicole could almost feel them burning into her flesh as he stared at her and continued. "And it's man's blackest and most fundamental evil to try and overthrow that stewardship. You cannot—no matter how highminded your motives—you can *never* make a man good. Not with guns, not with the rack, and not with a silicon chip planted in the back of his neck."

Shaken by his intensity, Nicole met his gaze for almost a full minute. Then finally, her voice barely a murmur, she asked, "Is implantation so horrible?"

His chin came up sharply, but he saw that she was not challenging him, but was accepting what he had said. It was her way of saying she understood. His hand came up slowly to rub at the back of his neck. "Before coming here, I might have asked that question myself," he said. "But never again, Nicole. Never again."

CHAPTER

22

For unknown millennia, the south fork of the Flathead River had been relentlessly chewing its way deeper and deeper into the floor of the canyon. Rushing and turbulent in spring, subdued and depleted in late summer, ice-encrusted in winter, the river had for countless generations sent its waters into the massive Columbia River system and eventually on into the Pacific Ocean. Then one day, the newest—and puniest—intruder into the forest had dropped a massive concrete plug into the ravine, wedged it tightly against the shoulders of both hillsides, and cut the water's relentless flow. Now the river had to pay toll for passage by turning the huge generators buried deep in the concrete bowels of the dam.

It was a massive cork for such a narrow river. As high as a fifty-story building and nearly half a mile across the top of the curving arch, the Hungry Horse Dam had finally let the river pass, but not before it had stolen three and a half million acre-feet of water and formed a ten-mile-long lake of incredibly deep blue waters.

Normally the sight brought a quick intake of breath from all who saw it, but today Eric Lloyd had no eyes for the view. He, Cliff, and Nicole were hidden in the trees a few yards from the west end of the dam, and Eric stared out across the concrete roadway where, in a moment, he would step out to meet Travis. He turned and gave Nicole and Cliff one last look. "I guess I'm ready."

Cliff sighed. "You know what we're up against as well as I do, so watch yourself."

Eric nodded. The Major had been pouring men into the area steadily for the past thirty-six hours. In addition to the fifteen or twenty he was openly displaying around the Visitors Center across the dam, he had sent two truckloads a couple of miles up the reservoir to wait for his signal. An equal number had been left down canyon below the dam. A dozen more had been seen going into the powerhouse at the base of the dam. The last group worried Eric the most. The powerhouse was six hundred feet below the area where the exchange would take place, but an elevator connected it with a small concrete blockhouse at the center of the dam. Though it supposedly hadn't been used for years, there was no question but what it would be used today.

Eric patted the heavy padlock in his back pocket. He and his companions had a surprise or two of their own for the group in the elevator shaft. Eric took a deep breath. In terms of manpower, the odds were about twenty to one, but surprise and high explosives would be the equalizing factors.

Cliff lifted his walkie-talkie. "Chet? Are you two all set up there?"

Rod Loopes and Chet Abernathy sat across the dam on the east mountainside, hidden in the trees about a hundred and fifty yards above the Visitors Center. They had rifles, a stun gun, binoculars, and a walkie-talkie. That was surprise number two for the Major. Chet Abernathy answered almost instantly. "Affirmative. We're standing by."

"Dick?" Cliff asked into the radio.

"Roger, I'm ready too. Good luck, Eric." Andreason was on the ridge directly behind them, also with binoculars and a rifle and a clear view of the top of the dam. Surprise number three. In addition, a small radio transmitting device was linked to a detonator planted in thirty pounds of high explosives hidden in an outcropping of rock above the road. Surprise number four. No truckloads of men would be coming up from below the dam.

As soon as Eric called for Nicole to be sent out to join him, Cliff would head south along the lake to where he had planted explosive charges at the base of a huge pine tree. Surprise number five. It wouldn't be as effective as the rock outcropping, but it was the best they could find, and it would slow the Guardians down enough for Eric and his family to get back off the dam and to the horses.

The only question was, how many surprises did the Major and Travis have planned? Eric shook off that thought and squared his shoulders. "Okay, then, I guess this is it."

Cliff touched his arm. "I don't think the Major will call for his dogs until he's sure Nicole is safe, so that should give us a few minutes to get in place, but watch yourself. And bring them home."

He gave Cliff a thumbs-up sign and moved out onto the dam.

He had gone only twenty yards toward the center of the dam when a burst of static at his waist broke his stride. He unclipped the walkie-talkie and pressed the button. "Yes?"

It was Chet Abernathy's voice. "Someone is just starting out onto the dam—tall, dark-haired, wearing a Guardian uniform. He's not armed, as far as we can tell."

"Is he alone?"

"Yes."

"Okay, that's Travis. Have they brought my family out yet?"

"No, not yet. They're still inside the Visitors Center."

"Okay, cover him. I'll leave the transmit button switched on so all of you can hear what is going on."

The engineers who designed Hungry Horse Dam had shaped it into a sweeping concave curve so it could better withstand the almost unbelievable weight pushing at its back. The roadway that spanned the half-mile long crest had been lined with concrete retaining walls chest high, and so, for a minute or two, as Eric walked steadily toward the center of the dam, all he could see of Travis was his head and shoulders. Only as they got to within the last hundred yards of each other did he come fully into view.

Eric slowed his pace slightly and then halted next to the concrete blockhouse that housed the central elevator shaft. He took the padlock out of his back pocket, keeping it behind him, and tested to make sure it was open.

"Hello, Eric." Travis stopped about twenty feet away.

Eric nodded. "Travis." Then he turned and stared at the door of the blockhouse. It was just as Cliff had said. "Well, well," he drawled, "would you look at that carelessness." Moving quickly enough to make Travis jump, he reached the door in three steps, slammed shut the metal hasp on the doorway, and clicked the heavy-duty padlock over it. "Someone could get hurt, leaving a doorway unlocked like that."

He grinned at the sudden flash of anger that swept across Travis's face. But as quickly as the anger had come, it fled, and Travis's face became a carefully controlled mask of composure. "Where's Nicole?"

"Safe. Where's my family?"

"Here. Shall we begin?"

"I'd say it's time."

"You start Nicole out here, and I'll send for your family."

Eric shook his head. "Uh uh. For some reason, we have this nagging suspicion that you and the Major are not playing this completely straight, so you get my family out here first, where I can make sure everything is all right; then I'll bring out Nicole."

Travis shrugged, then turned around, lifted his arm, and waved it back and forth slowly.

From the center of the dam to the Visitors Center measured nearly four hundred yards, so it was difficult to tell for sure, but Eric thought he could see the heads and shoulders of two women. He unclipped the walkie-talkie from his belt. "Dick, can you see them?"

Eric knew the radioman behind him was studying the figures through the binoculars. Then the radio crackled. "Roger. It's a long way from this side of the dam, but I see six people—two women, two children, and two Guardians."

"My, aren't we organized," Travis mocked. "Radios, men on the hillside, guns. This is better than TV."

"Travis, tell your men to stay where they are. My family is to come out alone."

"They will."

Almost immediately Andreason's voice spoke again. "They're starting out onto the dam. The guards have stopped."

Travis and Eric fell silent as they watched the steady progress of the small party coming toward them, but Eric was aware of a prickling sense of uneasiness. Travis was still too confident. Eric's locking of the elevator shaft had set him back, but only temporarily. The battle was not over yet by any means.

When Eric's family came around the gentle curve of the roadway and into full sight, Becky exploded into a run, her short legs pumping like pistons, her ponytail bouncing wildly. "Ricky! Ricky!" she screamed with delight.

Travis turned quickly and intercepted her in midstride, swinging her up off the ground. "Hey, Tiger!" he said, "just hang on a minute."

"Put me down!" she wailed, pummeling Travis with her fists. He swung her back down and gave her a gentle shove into the arms of her mother. "Mrs. Lloyd, stop right there until I say."

"Mother," Eric called. "Are you all right?"

She nodded. "We are now. Are you okay?"

"Never been better. Have they removed your implantations?"

"Yes." It was almost a sob, and Stephanie put her arm around her mother's waist.

"For all of you?" Eric persisted. "You're sure?"

"Yes, Eric," Stephanie answered. "They let Mother and me watch them do it." She held up her left arm. "And they took off our wrist computers too. We're all free."

"*Now* are you satisfied?" Travis sneered.

"Not quite. Mom, Steph, come over here behind me."

"Oh, no, you don't!" Travis snapped, raising his arm to block their progress. "They stay right here until I see that Nicole is okay."

Eric shrugged and lifted the walkie-talkie. "Okay, Cliff. Send Nicole."

As Travis had done with Becky, Eric had to intercept Nicole as she almost broke into a run when she saw Travis. "Just stay behind me, Nicole," he said, not taking his eyes from Travis.

187

"Nicole, are you all right?"

She started to answer but the words caught in her throat, and she finally nodded. Before Travis could answer, a loud thump rattled the steel doorway of the blockhouse, and Eric heard a muffled cry of surprise.

Eric smiled briefly. "Sorry to spoil their little welcoming party."

"Sergeant Decker," Travis shouted, "the door's locked. Just stand easy for a while."

Eric half turned around to face Nicole. "I'm sorry for the last few days. I really mean that."

She stared at him for a moment, her eyes as green as the depths of the sea. "I appreciate your treating me with respect."

"I hope you can find peace within yourself." He turned back to Travis. "Okay, start my family over, and Nicole is all yours."

Becky lurched forward, but Travis's arm was like a steel bar holding her back. "Just like that, huh?" he said softly. "Then we all walk away and everyone is happy?"

Nicole too had started around Eric, but he yanked her back against him, suddenly wary. "Yes. Just like that." His eyes were riveted on Travis's face, and he felt his muscles tensing rapidly.

"Sorry, Eric," Travis said, "but it can't go down that way. If it was simply your family for Nicole, the Major might have bought it. But when you started removing the implantations on other people, that set it in concrete. No way can the Major let it go now. We've got a hundred men closing in on you right now. There's no way to get out of here."

Eric jerked Nicole around to shield him as his hand whipped down to his boot and pulled out the hunting knife hidden there. "Did you hear that, Dick?" he shouted, ignoring Nicole's sharp gasp of surprise.

"I sure did," came the answer from the walkie-talkie. Almost instantly the blast of the explosive rocked the air, spinning everyone on the top of the dam around to look northward. A huge cloud of dust and smoke billowed upward about a quarter mile away.

"So much for those truckloads," Eric said. He looked past

Travis to his family. "Mother, you and the girls start walking slowly toward me."

Travis didn't turn around, but the menace in his voice was like the quiet rustle of a cobra lifting its head to strike. "Mrs. Lloyd, for your sake and that of your children, don't move. A dozen rifles are trained on your backs at this moment." His eyes narrowed as he glanced at the knife. "You're a fool, Eric. We know you won't hurt Nicole. Now that you've brought her back to us, she's home free. You know that and so do we. You can't get away from here."

In an instant, the point of the knife was touching Nicole's throat, and she gave a sharp cry of fear. "I think," Eric said, so softly that his voice was almost lost in the gentle breeze blowing across the top of the dam, "I think you're about ninety-five percent sure of that. But what if you are five percent wrong?"

Travis hesitated a moment then said patiently, as though to an errant child, "Oh, Eric, Eric, what will you do? Cut her throat? Come on."

"Let my family come over here, Travis, or you'll see exactly what I'm willing to do."

Again for one split second, Eric saw the hesitation in Travis's eyes; then it was gone. "Give it up, Eric. You've lost the game."

In an instant, it was clear why Travis hadn't given up. Behind him, a low, throbbing noise was rising rapidly, and then suddenly it exploded into a deafening roar as a helicopter swept over the ridge behind Eric and swooped down toward them. As Eric's head swung around to look up, Travis quickly stepped behind the corner of the elevator tower. His hand darted out, and when he straightened up, he held a deer rifle pointed at Eric and Nicole. "You're playing against the Major now, Eric. Amateur night is over. Give it up. Let her go."

"Mother!" Eric shouted. "Come now. Quick!"

Travis spun around, pointing the rifle directly at Madeline Lloyd's stomach. "You'll start back for the Visitors Center, Mrs. Lloyd," he hissed. When she hesitated, his voice exploded. "Now! Move it!"

She reached out for Becky and Lori, who had both started to

cry, and the little group started back in a dazed, stumbling run. For a moment Eric nearly threw himself at Travis, the rage in him boiling like molten lava, but the helicopter was coming fast now, skimming across the top of the water toward them. As quickly as it had come, the rage was gone, and his mind raced over his alternatives. He yanked Nicole hard against him and backed up. "So much for your loving fiancé," he hissed into her ear. "Stay with me, Nicole. If I have to fight you, you'll get hurt."

"Let her go, Eric. I'm warning you."

"Please, Eric," Nicole gasped. "Let me go. Don't hurt me."

But Eric was too busy swinging her back and forth to answer. He kept her moving, keeping her between the muzzle of Travis's rifle and the muzzle of the stun gun held by a Guardian hanging out the doorway of the helicopter. Dick opened fire from behind them. The clattering roar of the engine drowned out any noise from the shot, but suddenly the window of the chopper exploded in a shattering spray of glass. Eric had a fleeting impression of a terror-stricken face, and then the helicopter peeled off sharply, seeking escape from the attack.

Travis stopped dead, his eyes wide with shock. "Hey!" he screamed.

At that moment a second shock wave rippled through the canyon. Cliff had just dropped the tree across the road from above.

Eric dragged Nicole backwards again. "Sorry, Travis. There goes your second source of help."

Like a raging bull, his face contorted with fury, Travis whirled around and ran to the door of the elevator shaft. At point-blank range, he fired at the lock Eric had clipped into place, then kicked the door in. Instantly, orange-clad bodies came pouring out like popcorn spitting from a popper.

"Hold your fire! Hold your fire!" Travis screamed at them. "He's got Nicole. Form a line. Take your positions." He grabbed a man by the shoulder. "You! Get the Lloyd family back to the Visitors Center."

By now Eric was in a half run, pulling Nicole back with him, and was nearly thirty yards from Travis.

"Stop, Eric, or we'll shoot!" Travis had formed a skirmish line with his men and was moving swiftly toward him. The Guardians held no stun guns now, only deer rifles.

Eric knew that Travis's threat was a bluff. They wouldn't dare shoot with Nicole in the way, but why hadn't Dick opened fire on the Guardians pouring out onto the dam? Then in a flash he understood. His family was just starting to disappear around the curve of the dam, out of the line of fire.

"Form a line! Stay behind me!" Travis waved his men into position behind him. "Don't shoot. The others are coming. They'll cut him off."

Eric watched his family go around the curve of the retaining wall. *Now!* It was an inward shout, but as though Dick Andreason had heard it, the flat crack of a rifle, followed swiftly by another, burst out from behind him. The man next to Travis gave a sharp cry as the bullet slammed into him, cutting him down like a scythe.

"Under fire! Under fire!" Travis's warning was totally unnecessary, for the orange-suited Guardians were already scrambling wildly for cover. But the top of the dam offered no cover, not from the vantage point of the hillside where Dick sat. The third shot sent another Guardian thudding off the retaining wall.

"Let's go!" Eric shouted, grabbing Nicole by the arm and breaking into a pounding run for the west end of the dam.

Travis fired at them twice, but the shots were wide and high, and Eric knew he was still afraid of hitting Nicole. He risked a quick glance back as they ran, and saw the earlier scene reversing itself. The only cover on the top of the dam was the elevator tower, and the open doorway was sucking men back into it like a concrete vacuum cleaner. Off to his left, up the lake, the clatter of rifle fire split the mountain stillness. One seventy-year-old man had locked battle with two squads of Guardians.

By the time Eric got off the dam and dragged Nicole up to the ridge where Dick Andreason was methodically firing at flashes of orange, both he and Nicole were gasping for breath. As he released her arm, she dropped to the ground and rolled into a ball, holding her stomach.

"We've got them pinned down for now," Andreason said. "But Cliff won't be able to delay those others for too long. We've got to get out of here."

"I've got to go help Cliff," Eric blurted between breaths. "Watch Nicole."

But as he got back up to his feet, their radios blared simultaneously. "Eric, this is Rod. Can you hear me?"

He jerked up his radio. "Yes, this is Eric. Go ahead."

"They've brought your family back into the Visitors Center. If you could draw off the troops to your side of the dam, we think we can get to them."

The surge of exultation that flashed through him was like a jolt of electricity. "Understood. We'll do our best."

"We have a stun gun, but right now the men are afraid to go out on the dam when you command the heights. Get them to come to you—it looks like the Major will leave only a man or two with your family. We've held our fire so far, and they have no idea we're here."

"Good work!" Eric exclaimed. "We'll draw them to us." He turned to Dick Andreason. "All right, Cliff's on his own for now. We've got to make it look like we're falling back so they'll come after us. Shoot once or twice more, then hold your fire. Let them come clear to the edge of the dam, if necessary, before you open fire. Then we'll engage them long enough for Rod and Chet to get clear."

Dick stood up. "Eric, you've got to get Nicole out of here. Take two of the horses. I'll cover the dam."

"No!"

"Eric, don't be bullheaded."

Stubbornly he stood his ground. "Not until I know about my family."

Andreason held up the walkie-talkie. "Eric, by the time you reach the spot where you left your horses, you'll still be in radio range. If Rod and Chet can get them out, you'll know it. If they don't . . ." He shook his head. "Cliff and I will stand a better chance of getting away if we don't have you two."

He was right, and Eric knew it. "Okay. Good luck." Eric

turned and reached for Nicole's elbow. She was still lying on the ground, her chest rising and falling rapidly as she tried to get her breath from the hard run. "Come on, Nicole. One shout and I'll gag you, out of breath or not."

"No, Eric. Please. I can't. I can't go any further."

"You can and you will," he said firmly, pulling her up and putting his arm around her to support her. "It's only a hundred feet, then the horses will do the work. Come on!"

Eric had just released their lathered mounts and was untying their own horses when the radio at his belt burst out again. "Eric, this is Rod."

He swung up the walkie-talkie. "This is Eric. Have you got them?"

"That's affirmative, Eric," came the jubilant cry in his ear. "We're away and clear. We're headed up now and hope to get another half an hour or more head start before they even know we've gone."

Eric's head dropped momentarily, and the breath went out of him in a great whoosh of relief. "Thank you."

"You are most welcome! See you at Home Base. Over and out."

His arm slowly lowered until the radio hung limply by his side. When he finally looked up, he saw Nicole watching him. "They got my family out," he said.

She nodded. "Believe it or not, Eric, I'm glad." Then she turned and walked quickly to her horse and untied the reins. As she put her foot in the stirrups and started to swing up, the horse shied a little, and she lost her balance, nearly falling. She moved to try again, and Eric strode over and took her elbow. "Here, let me help you."

She spun around as if he had laid a hot iron on her arm. "Don't you touch me!"

Eric jerked his hand away in stunned surprise. Tears had spilled over and left wet streaks down her cheeks, but her eyes were twin sparks of emerald fire behind the glossy shininess.

"I was just going to help you up," he apologized.

"Don't you understand?" she shouted at him through the tears. "I hate you. I hate what you're doing. To me, to my city, to everyone you touch. Now leave me alone!"

She gave the reins a vicious yank, tried to mount again, this time successfully, and sank her heels into the mare's flanks.

"All right, Miss Lambert," he snapped, swinging up onto his horse and yanking on the lead rope of the packhorse. "Have it your way. But I don't think I'm the only one you're angry with right now."

CHAPTER

23

Eric watched Nicole climbing out of her sleeping bag and gave her a tentative smile. "Good morning."

She nodded curtly, still bitter from the day before. "May I have my shoes, please? It's very cold."

He scrambled to his sleeping bag, retrieved her shoes, and tossed them to her, then sat down on a stone next to the creek. "Sorry," he murmured. "I wish I dared make a fire, but the mountains will be crawling with company today." When she didn't answer, he looked up at the sky. "The sun will be high enough soon to take off the chill."

Nicole slipped into her shoes without looking up, then tied them with an angry yank. She stood up and ran her hands through her tousled hair, her back turned on him.

"Nicole," he ventured, "look, I'm sorry about yesterday. I—"

She spun around. "Are you?"

"Yes." He took a deep breath. "Yes, I am."

"Then let me go!"

He shook his head slowly. "I can't, Nicole."

"Your family is free!" she cried, clenching her fists. "You can let me go now!"

Eric stood up. "Cliff hasn't come back to the camp yet. They think he was caught."

Her head shot up in surprise; then her eyes narrowed into angry slits.

"And so it goes, huh? Everytime your little revolution loses somebody, Nicole is dragged back up the mountain."

Her fury was suddenly so intense that she no longer trusted her voice. She grabbed her tote bag and, without so much as a second glance, stalked off toward the creek.

"Nicole," Eric called as she disappeared into the trees. "Don't forget to shout every minute or two."

He gave her a full five minutes before he called the first time. By then she had washed and was pulling a brush through her hair with short, angry strokes. His voice floated through the trees, almost lost in the gurgle of the stream.

"Nicole," he added after his third call, "I know you're angry. But if you don't answer now, I'll have to come down there."

"Go ahead," she muttered, stuffing her brush back into her bag.

"Nicole!" His calls were coming more rapidly and sounded louder now. "I'm not playing. Either you answer or I'm coming down."

"Don't bother," she said to herself as she stood up and picked up her bag. Suddenly her eyes widened. *What if you do come down!* The thought nearly took her breath away. Quickly she scanned the ground and found what she was looking for: a stout tree limb with a thick protrusion on one end. Her heart pounding, she dropped her bag and snatched up the limb. It was heavy, and she clutched it tightly to steady the trembling in her hands. She looked around quickly, then darted up the trail a few feet and ducked behind the thick trunk of a towering spruce. As she raised the club high in the air, her eyes widened in terror. Cricket! What if the dog came around the tree first and started wagging her tail? Nicole felt her knees go weak as the crunch of Eric's feet could be heard coming through the trees. Cricket gave a sudden yelp, and Nicole heard her crash off through the forest, barking wildly.

"Be quiet, Cricket!" Eric hissed, now only a few yards above

Nicole. "You'll have every man on the mountain after us over a stupid rabbit. Nicole, don't you be stupid either." He was muttering to himself now as he came down the trail. "If you're trying to run away, I'll—" Both his words and footsteps stopped simultaneously, and Nicole knew he had spied her bag on the trail.

With an exclamation of surprise, he leaped past her hiding place and crouched down to look at the bag. She took two steps forward and swung the club down, putting four days of frustration, pain, and bitterness into the blow. The knobby end of the limb caught Eric above his right ear. With a sharp grunt, he sprawled forward, crashing onto his face.

Nicole flung the club away, turned, and ran blindly up the path. Not until she had gone fifty or more feet did she get a hold on her panic and pull herself to a halt, leaning against a tree to catch her breath. As she stared back down the path, she straightened slowly, exultation shooting through her. Eric hadn't moved. She had done it! She was free!

For a moment Nicole nearly turned back to see how badly she had hurt him and to get his pistol, but then panic hit her again, and she broke into a run back toward the camp.

Eric had left the horses saddled in case they were discovered by Guardian patrols and needed to move swiftly. Now she murmured a quick thanks for that. She undid the halter rope of the packhorse, slapped its rump sharply, and yelled. The horse leaped forward in fright and bolted off through the trees.

In an instant she grabbed the rifle from Eric's sleeping bag, untied the other two horses, swung up on the mare, and, yanking on the reins of Eric's mount, dug her heels into the mare's flanks.

By the time she had dragged Eric's horse through the heavy timber for over an hour, Nicole decided he wouldn't be able to find it again. She emptied the food and extra ammunition out of his saddlebag and shooed the horse away to fend for itself.

Two hours later she heard the helicopter. At first she felt it as much as heard it. When the pulsating waves became the distinct roar of an aircraft, she gave a cry of joy. Swinging down quickly, she wrapped the reins of her horse around a tree limb and ran toward a large area where the trees were widely scattered and the brush was low. But before she reached the clearing, the helicopter came in at about five hundred feet, almost directly overhead. She screamed and yelled and waved her arms wildly, but she was still in a fairly thick stand of trees, and the helicopter swept over her and was gone.

With disappointment so sharply bitter it almost made her choke, Nicole slowly lowered her hands and turned back. "Hey!" Her mouth dropped open as she saw her horse, frightened by the pounding noise, disappearing through the trees, taking her bag, the rifle, her food, and her transportation with it. She leaped forward, dodging branches and jumping over logs in a wild attempt to catch it. "Come back here!" she screamed.

For a maddening half an hour she tried to recapture the horse, but every time she got within thirty or forty feet of it, the wild-eyed animal bolted headlong into forest. Exhausted, on the verge of tears, afraid that Eric was conscious now and looking for her, she finally gave up and let it go.

With a moan that was half pain and half pleasure, Nicole peeled off her socks and thrust her throbbing feet into the icy water of the stream. Wearily she lay back on the grassy bank and closed her eyes, letting the sun, now full of afternoon heat, beat on her face. The warmth soothed and relaxed her, and for the five-hundredth time she cursed her stupidity in tying the horse so carelessly.

In the three hours since she'd lost the horse, her feet had felt every rock, every twisted root, every uneven stump and log she'd stumbled over. Soon after the horse bolted, Nicole had found a small creek and followed it downward. It joined another creek and then another until it formed a small, turbulent river, now a good fifteen or twenty feet across. Three times she had had to ford streams, and her wet socks and tennis shoes only added to the misery of her feet.

She thought about Eric. She had no doubt he would try to find her. She was certain he could track the horses, but she'd been on foot for the past three hours. That would make it far more difficult, if not impossible. And even if he could do it, it would certainly slow him down considerably. He'd be at least two hours behind, perhaps three or four.

Nicole sighed, telling herself to get up and race the night and the man coming after her, but her body rebelled, and she decided that she had a right to pamper it for once. She closed her eyes again and thought only of how good the sunshine and the cool water felt.

Nicole awoke with a start and lifted her head, looking around wildly until her eyes focused on the river and she remembered where she was. She sat up with a jerk, and her hands flew to her cheeks, feeling the hot, sunburned skin. She squinted up at the sun and gave a cry of dismay. It was noticeably lower. Perhaps an hour, maybe an hour and a half, had passed since she had lain down.

Berating herself for her stupidity, she reached for her shoes and socks, but her hand froze in midair. A loud crash in the under-brush off to her right was clear and distinct, and with a start she realized that that was the sound that had awakened her. She scurried the few feet to the nearest clump of brush and dove into the foliage, her heart pounding furiously.

For a moment she heard only a curious shuffling sound, then the distinct noise of something heavy moving through the brush. Suddenly she went deathly still. It was not Eric. From around a thick clump of mountain-currant bushes, a massive brown shape lumbered into view, sniffing at the ground. Though it was still nearly forty or fifty yards upstream, the golden-tipped fur, the jutting front shoulders, and the square snout were clearly visible. It was not just a bear—it was a grizzly!

Not daring to move, Nicole watched in horror as the animal stopped and stripped several branches of their berries, then pried up a rock as big as a bread box with ease, looking for grubs. If it smelled her—she shuddered. For the moment the wind was blow-

199

ing downriver, carrying her scent away from the grizzly, but in a few more yards the animal would be close enough to catch her scent no matter how the wind blew. It splashed into the river, looking for fish, and turned its back on Nicole's hiding place. Gently and with infinite care she backed out the other side of the bush, giving her shoes and socks one last longing glance.

In a sudden flash of inspiration, Nicole decided to circle wide and head back up the hill. The bear was moving downriver, and she wanted to be where it had already been, not where it was going.

By the time she had moved in a wide circle around the bear, her hopes were soaring and she moved a little more quickly. She was concentrating so hard on watching the brown mass in the river that she didn't see the cubs until she nearly stumbled onto them behind a mountain birch tree. They had their backs to her and were trying earnestly to pull open a rotting log half buried in the forest soil. They gave one startled bawl, leaped straight up in the air, raced across the ground, and shot up the nearest pine tree like two simultaneously ignited brown rockets.

With a roar that split the mountain stillness, the mother grizzly swung around and exploded into a lumbering run of incredible swiftness. Bare feet forgotten, Nicole leaped into motion, her legs a blur. She covered the tiny clearing in three great leaps, then darted back to her right when the thick trees cut her off. The mother bear didn't even slow down to check on her cubs—she had the threat to her offspring in sight and was bearing down on it like a missile.

Nicole screamed and changed directions, cutting back down the hill toward the river to get greater speed. But the brown mass of fury instantly corrected her own charge to head her off, closing now at three times Nicole's speed. Intent only on escape, Nicole did not see the sharp stone protruding out of the soil, and her bare foot slammed down on it with full force. She gave a sharp cry of pain and sprawled headlong, like a baseball player in a desperate slide toward home base. Too close to brake its lumbering attack, the bear overshot her and hit the river in a great spray of water. The momentum carried it completely across the stream, and chunks of turf flew as the animal clawed at the ground, trying to halt her charge and change direction.

Comprehending only that she had been given another few seconds of life, Nicole scrambled to her hands and knees just as a white streak flashed past her, snapping and snarling as it hit the river to meet the onrushing bear head on. Nicole stared for a moment, then cried out with a sob of relief, "Cricket!"

The German shepherd, though outweighed by nearly a thousand pounds, was a flashing fury of its own, darting in to nip at the grizzly's flanks, then barely jumping clear of a swipe that would have taken her head off had it connected.

"Nicole! Run!"

She jerked around. Eric was running pell-mell down the river bank toward her, pistol in his hand. She leaped up, only to collapse instantly as her foot hit the ground, leaving a smear of blood.

Eric reached her and jammed the pistol back in its holster. "Come on," he said urgently, jerking her to her feet and putting his arm around her waist to support her. "Let's get out of here!"

The mother grizzly saw the movement and, with a blood-curdling roar, caught Cricket with one massive paw and sent her tumbling tail over nose and yelping in pain. The bear crossed the river again in two splashing leaps.

"Run, Nicole!" Eric shouted, giving her a hard shove as he spun around, yanking at the pistol. As it came out of the holster, the bear was on him. He had time only to hurl it into her face as he dove to the side. The gun caught the bear just above the eye, causing her to jerk away, but her paw flashed out as she hurtled past him, catching Eric's leg in a sweeping blow that turned his diving fall into a head-over-heels crash into the brush.

"Eric!" Nicole's scream was lost as the bear wheeled around. But once again Cricket smashed into the fight, slashing at the bear's hind flank and heading off the attack. With an astonished cry of rage, the grizzly swung around to meet her attacker, forgetting Eric. But Cricket had learned a painful lesson. A snarling, snapping fury, she circled the bear again and again, driving her slowly down the hill but always staying clear of those massive, flashing paws.

Nicole reached Eric in a hobbling run. He rolled over, writhing in pain, and she gasped as she saw his upper thigh. A two-foot-long patch of his pant leg had been sheared away as cleanly as if cut with scissors, and even as she stared in horror, four bright red streaks blended into one great smear of blood.

"Eric, help me!" She put her hands under his arms, trying to drag him up the hill. "Help me! We've got to get away!"

"Get out of here!" he cried hoarsely, trying to pull himself up. Then suddenly his eyes rolled back and he collapsed, dragging out of her grip.

"No, Eric! No!" Nicole sobbed. She tried to drag him but his dead weight was too much to move more than an inch or two.

The battle between Cricket and the grizzly was still raging only twenty or thirty yards from where Nicole and Eric lay defenseless. Another lucky swipe of the paw and Cricket would be—

With a cry of surprise, Nicole spied the pistol lying on the ground a few feet away. She scrambled for it, then hobbled to her feet. Fearful of hitting Cricket, she pointed the gun above the bear's head and pulled the trigger.

The grizzly jumped five feet sideways with a startled roar, and as Nicole fired again, it broke into a lumbering run into the trees and out of sight with Cricket at her heels. Nicole continued firing blindly, compulsively, until the hammer clicked on already spent shells; then, trembling violently, she let the pistol drop, put her hands to her face for a long moment, then hobbled back toward Eric's still form.

CHAPTER

24

Eric's eyes fluttered open. For almost a full minute he stared up into the trees without blinking, as if in a trance; then his eyes closed again slowly. Five minutes later they opened again, revealing wide, gray pools of pain. Suddenly they widened, and Nicole knew he was remembering. His head turned slightly until his eyes met hers.

"Hello," she said softly.

He started to lift himself up, but the pain contorted his face, and he sank back again. His hand came up and touched the bare skin of his chest, then ran across his stomach.

"I had to use your shirt for bandages," Nicole said. "I didn't have anything else."

Gritting his teeth, Eric tried again and got up on his elbows high enough to see the crude bandage around his leg.

"There are four deep gashes," she explained. "There was a lot of blood, but no arteries were cut. I don't think your leg's broken."

He nodded, his head dropping back to the ground. Then he caught sight of another strip of the red plaid material from his shirt wrapped around her foot, over which she had slipped her tennis shoe. His eyebrows shot up.

"I stepped on a sharp rock," she said with a shrug.

"*That's* why you fell. Be grateful. The bear went right over the top of you. It saved your life."

"*You* saved my life," she whispered, tears welling up again.

He sank back to the ground. "And you saved mine. What happened? I must've passed out."

"Cricket held the bear off long enough for me to get the pistol. That scared it away."

Again a sharp stab of pain twisted his features, causing him to draw in his breath quickly. "Where *is* Cricket?" he said finally, turning his head to look. "Is she—?"

"She's limping badly, but I think she'll be fine. She's out exploring again now, so she can't be hurt too badly."

"Good." He forced a wan smile. "That's a ridiculous name, you know."

Nicole laughed. "I know. When she was a small puppy, it seemed to fit."

"The Cricket and the Grizzly. It sounds like a fable or something."

"Is the pain terrible?" she asked, watching the lines etch deeper into his face.

His hand raised slowly to touch the lump behind his ear. "First time I've ever been attacked by two she-bears in the same day."

Nicole dropped her head. "I'm sorry! But—"

His hand reached out and touched her arm. "No, please don't. I—" He closed his eyes again, breathing deeply to combat the pain.

"So what do we do now?" Nicole asked.

"Make camp here. I don't think either of us will make it very far for a while."

"Make camp! With what? Night's coming on, you don't even have a shirt, we have no food, no ammunition, no tools—and an angry grizzly is prowling in the neighborhood."

"Let's not lose hope," Eric said. His voice was strained but his eyes were teasing beneath the pain. "I have a knife in the sheath underneath me."

"A knife?" she said bitterly. "Good. I'll go hunting."

204

"That's a good idea. We could use some of Cliff's pain pills and that antibiotic he gave us. A couple of sleeping bags would also be appreciated."

"Please. I know you're trying to cheer me up, but don't. Okay?"

"If I were to provide all that, would you let me call you Nicky without getting angry?"

"Eric!"

"Is it a deal?"

"Yes. Now what are you saying?"

"I left the packhorse tied up in the trees above us."

Nicole's mouth dropped open. "But I drove it away when I left you."

"True. But it only went a few hundred yards and started grazing. I didn't take time to pack everything, but I got the essentials."

"Really?"

"Yes. I spotted you lying down by the river from up on the ridge. I was trying to sneak up on you. Then I saw the bears heading downstream. I didn't dare yell to warn you. I was afraid you'd jump and run. So anyway . . ." He let the words trail off, and she could tell he was tiring quickly. "Do you think you can hobble up there and find it?"

"I can't believe it. I've been sitting here for an hour worrying about how we're going to survive a night in the mountains in the open."

"Now haven't I taken better care of you than that?" Then he went on quickly. "Sorry. Don't answer that."

"How did you catch me so quickly?"

"Cricket. Once she caught on that we were trailing you, I just followed her, and we made good time."

"I am so glad," she said, the relief flooding through her again.

"So am I, Nicky," he said gently. "So am I." Again a spasm of pain caused his jaw to clench.

"Hang on," she said, limping to her feet. "I'll go get the horse."

. . . .

Nicole pulled her jacket around her more tightly and held her hands out to the fire. Cricket's head lifted and she yawned widely, revealing her teeth, then dropped her head again. Nicole reached over and pulled Cricket's body against her own. Though it was not yet nine o'clock, the chill was deepening rapidly. She turned to look at the dark shape in the sleeping bag next to her and listened to his deep breathing.

The pain pill had put him under quickly, almost before he could direct her on securing the camp. Wrap the food in plastic bags—carefully so as to not attract shuffling brown visitors—build a fire, get enough wood to keep it going all night, hobble the horse and turn it loose. No wonder she was exhausted, hopping around, chopping wood, drawing water from the river.

She had finished fifteen minutes ago, but instead of crawling inside her bag, she had sat and stared at the fire, trying to sort through her thoughts. In a way it would have been easier if Eric hadn't come. Her feelings had been clear enough up to that point: bitterness, resentment, determination to get free of him. Now? As much as she longed for home and a bath and clean sheets over a mattress, she knew she couldn't leave him. The image of the mother grizzly bearing down on her, and Eric standing between her and the hurtling fury with nothing but a pistol in his hand, was etched so deeply in her memory that she would never be able to put it fully from her mind. Once he could cope on his own, the debt would be paid, but for now, she had to stay.

But it was more than that. Eric's words about freedom and individual rights kept battering at her as they had done for the past two days. Today she had come within a fraction of losing her life, and never had it seemed so sweetly precious. Why was it that life meant so little to Eric and his friends that they would risk it so easily? Or was freedom of greater worth than life itself? Had she taken the loss of others' freedom so lightly because she herself had never lost it? Until this week.

She shook her head, and suddenly her thoughts flashed to the events at the dam—and to Travis. She frowned as she thought of the expression in his eyes when Eric had put the knife to her throat and challenged Travis's willingness to sacrifice her. At that moment Travis's eyes had flicked to hers, then to the knife at her throat, and then away, and she knew the answer. He *was* only ninety-five percent sure Eric wouldn't hurt her. And yes, five percent was acceptable.

Nicole ran her fingers through her hair, hating how dirty it was, hating the hard ground and the chill air, hating the turmoil churning inside her. She sighed and stood up, wearily tossed four more logs on the fire, and turned to her sleeping bag. As she knelt down to unzip it, she stopped short. Eric was watching her.

"Oh!" she said, startled. "I didn't know you were awake."

"How come *you're* still awake?" he mumbled, obviously struggling to sound alert.

She shrugged and sat down to take off her shoes.

"How's your foot?"

"It's okay."

"Did you take a pain pill?"

"Yes, just a few minutes ago. How's *your* leg?"

He pulled a face.

"Are you ready for another pill?"

He started to shake his head, then caught his breath as the pain hit him. When it passed, he let it out in a long sigh. "Yes, maybe I am."

Nicole found him a pill and poured him a cup of water from the canteen. She helped him sit up enough to get it down. When she was finished, she crawled into her bag, grateful even for the hardness of the ground as long as she was lying on it rather than standing.

They fell silent for several minutes, both looking up at the brilliant stars spread out like a protective net overhead, until Nicole felt the drug starting to work on her. Or maybe it was just sheer exhaustion.

"Nicky?"

Her eyes came open with a tremendous effort. "What?"

"I . . ." She heard him sigh.

She half turned in her bag so she could see him. He had his hands under his head, staring up at the stars. "What?" she asked again.

"You are really something else. Did you know that?"

His earnestness caught her by surprise. "Something else? What's that supposed to mean?"

"I mean today. After all I've done to you these past few days. After yesterday at the dam. Why didn't you leave me?"

She looked down. "You forget, I'm not in very good shape to travel either."

"And?"

"You saved my life!" she whispered fiercely, shuddering at the vivid memory of the grizzly hurtling down on her. "If you hadn't come when you did—" She took a deep breath, then turned to look at him.

"If I hadn't come when I did, that night in your house, you wouldn't have been in the mountains trying to get away from me," he said.

"Well, I certainly can't disagree with that logic."

"I know, and I'm very sorry."

She leaned on her elbow and stared at him. "How sorry?"

"We'll have to stay here for a day or two at least. I don't think either of us is in any shape to go very far. But then, if you'll help me get to base camp, I'll have one of the men take you down."

"Do you really mean that?"

"Yes, Nicole, I really mean it. I'll see that you get home again."

CHAPTER
25

They'd been there for two long, lazy days. Nicole hobbled around with a makeshift cane, keeping the fire going, getting water, and fixing simple meals. Other than that, they rested on their bags, letting the sunlight warm them as they talked, or lay silent, or dozed off and on. Even Cricket seemed content to take a day off from her wide-ranging explorations to let her body mend.

By unspoken agreement, Nicole and Eric never approached the topics of conversation that laid bare so much emotion and conflict. The Major, Travis, implantation—all were tacitly avoided. Instead they talked of life in the valley, of life before Termination, of what life was like for a girl growing up in Shalev.

This was a side of Eric that Nicole had not seen before—relaxed, pleasant, often showing a wry humor. She sensed the warm affection he had for his family and the steady but pleasant life of the village. And she realized more and more why this eagle had so hated the chains of bondage.

Now, as dusk settled in, she almost wished they didn't have to leave it all tomorrow, go back to face the pain, the choices, the conflict.

Suddenly Eric rolled over and pulled up into a sitting position with a grunt of pain. He gritted his teeth and tried to stand up.

"Eric? What is it? What do you need?"

"I've got to get up."

"Why?"

"It's sundown. I've got to call the others. They should have a new base camp set up by now. Where's the radio?"

"It's with the other stuff. Can't it wait until morning? You'll be stronger then."

He was up now, grimacing with the pain. "No, we set sundown as the time for calling. They won't be listening any other time. I should have called the night before last, before they moved, but neither of us was functioning very well then. I couldn't get them last night, so I've got to try again. They'll be worried sick about us."

She sighed. "Sit down, I'll get it for you."

Nicole's foot still hurt, but she managed to drag the heavy radio to him, then sat down and stared into the fire.

He flicked the switch, waited a few moments for it to warm up, and pressed the mike to his mouth. "Home Base. Home Base. This is Eagle One. Do you read me?"

The radio crackled in response almost instantly, as the rich, deep voice of a woman came through. "Eric, is that you?"

"Mother? Yes, this is Eric. How is everything?"

The relief in Madeline Lloyd's voice was evident even through the tinniness of the speaker. "Thank heavens. Where have you been?"

"Nicole and I had a slight run-in with a bear. We were kind of out of it, but—"

"A bear! Are you all right?"

"Yes," he soothed. "It autographed my leg, but I'll be fine. We think we can come to you tomorrow. What about Cliff? Did he finally show up?"

There was silence for a moment, then, "No, I— Wait a minute. Here is Dr. Abernathy."

"Eric, this is Chet. What's this about a bear?"

"Nothing serious. What about Cliff? Have you heard from him?"

210

"Yes."

"What?" Eric demanded.

"They captured him at the dam."

The air went out of Eric's lungs in a sudden burst of pain. "Oh, no."

"Yes. We've been monitoring the radio broadcasts from Shalev."

"Was he hurt?"

"No. But—"

"But what?"

"An announcement came over the air about four this afternoon. All citizens of Shalev are to report to the soccer stadium tomorrow afternoon at one o'clock. All stores and businesses, except for critical services, will close at noon. Attendance is compulsory."

"Attendance at what? What's going on? And what has that got to do with Cliff?"

Again there was a pause. Then, "They're putting Cliff on trial."

Nicole watched Eric tear her long-sleeved, cotton blouse into long strips and bind them tightly around his bandaged leg. He finished and looked up. "Will you hand me my boots, please?"

"Eric, this is insane. You can't use that leg." Her voice was pleading, tight with worry.

His chin jerked up, and in the flickering light of the fire, his eyes were glittering, hard, bright. She flinched and finally crawled over to where his hiking boots lay next to his sleeping bag.

"Will you help me put on the left one?"

"No. I won't help you lose your leg. I understand how you feel about Cliff, but you can't—"

He leaned over, gritting his teeth against the pain, fumbling with his boot. Finally Nicole shook her head and knelt down in front of him. "I know why you feel this way, but there's no way you can ride or walk. You can't help Cliff this way."

"I've taken another pain pill, and I'll take more if necessary."

"You can't even be off the mountain by noon," she pleaded, "let alone into Shalev."

"Chet's going to meet me at the bottom."

"You won't make it to the bottom! And if you do, then what? Don't you think the Major is doing this to lure you down? Don't you know he'll be expecting you?"

"I hope so."

She tied the boot with a vicious yank and looked up at him. "Spoken with the courage of a lion and the brains of a bean."

His eyes surveyed her for a long moment. "I appreciate your concern, but Nicole, I've got to try. You know as well as I, this is no trial. It's a public hanging, an execution. I've got to try!"

"Yes, I suppose you do." She stood up and moved to her own bag, picked up her tennis shoes, and sat down to put them on.

In one lurching motion Eric was at her side and snatched her shoes away. "No, Nicole. Not you."

She stared up at him, too stunned to speak.

"We have only one horse, remember? With the pack on it to carry the essentials I need, there isn't room for two people. One of us would have to walk, and neither of us can do that."

Suddenly she was frightened. "You can't just leave me here."

"As soon as I get down, we'll call the Guardians and send them for you."

She glanced quickly at the darkness of the surrounding forest. "Eric, no, please, not alone. I can walk with my cane. My foot is feeling better. I'll keep up."

He shook his head.

She jerked away angrily. "I'm going. Give me back my shoes."

He moved away to the packhorse and stuffed her shoes into a small bag tied onto the pack. "No, you know you can't walk very far." He dragged the radio over and hoisted it up and tied it on the pack.

"Then at least call the Guardians now. Tell them where I am. Have them come for me."

He shook his head.

"Why?" And then she knew the answer. "Eric, I won't tell them about you. I won't let them know what you're doing."

He finished tying the radio down and turned to face her. "Come on, Nicky, be realistic. That won't work, and you know it."

"It will. I promise I won't give you away."

He bent over the pile of gear, then straightened. "Here's the hatchet. The flashlight is under my pillow. I wish I could leave you the pistol, but I may need it tomorrow."

"Please, Eric. Please don't leave me alone. I give you my solemn word I won't tell them anything. Perhaps I can persuade the Major not to hurt Cliff. I can tell him that you let me go. Why won't you believe me?"

"I do believe you," he said as he hauled himself up on the horse. "But I know Travis and the Major too well. They'd have it out of you in two minutes."

"But why are you taking my shoes?"

"I'm afraid you'll try and follow me and get lost. Then they'll never find you."

"So much for promises," she cried bitterly.

"Please sit down until I'm gone, Nicole. And tie Cricket up so she doesn't follow me. She'll keep animals away from the camp."

"Please sit down until I'm gone, Nicole," she mimicked. *"Here are some things for your safety, Nicole."* Her voice sparked like the edge of a knife striking a whirling stone. "My, aren't we just full of manners this evening, Mr. Lloyd? *I'm sorry to have to abandon you, Nicole. I'll leave you with a hatchet and a flashlight and my good wishes, Nicole. Of course, I must take your shoes with me, Nicole. Please forgive me, Nicole.*"

The urge to cry or scream or hurl herself at him was so overpowering that for a moment she just stood there trembling. Finally she ducked her head and dropped to her knees. "Come here, Cricket," she said, fighting to maintain control of her voice.

Eric reined the horse around. "I'll have someone here shortly after we get down."

She didn't look up as she slipped a rope through Cricket's collar. "Whatever you have to do to ease your conscience."

"I don't want Cliff Cameron on my conscience," he snapped.

"Oh no!" she cried, her throat tight. "I can't stop you from

213

going, but don't leave here with righteous piety swelling your breast. I told you I'd help you help him. Taking me with you now won't make that much difference to Cliff Cameron. Cliff is just your excuse. The Major has won another round, and you can't stand the thought of that. It's the Major you're really after, isn't it?"

She had stung him, for when he answered, his voice was heavy with anger. "It's the Major who has Cliff Cameron and two hundred thousand others under his electronic thumb."

"Oh? Tell me, Eric, other than in numbers, how do you differ from him?"

In the dim and dancing firelight she could not read the expression on his face. For a long moment he just looked at her across the fire, and then he spoke softly. "Good-bye, Nicky."

She leaped to her feet. "You brought me an eagle chained to a limb," she shouted as the horse started away from her. "Did you do that to make me feel sorry for you? Well, it worked. So go, Eric. Go down and save the world. But while you're going, just ask yourself one question. You have my shoes in your bag. How is that any different from putting a black box in the back of my neck?"

Nicole woke up with a start and groped for the hatchet before she realized it was just Cricket. The dog had stood up and crossed over Nicole's feet to reach the end of her tether. With a sigh she slid the hatchet back under the sleeping bag near her head and lay down again. Eric had been gone for an hour and a half, perhaps two, and she still had five or six hours until light. It seemed an eternity.

Suddenly Cricket gave a low growl, and Nicole heard a crash in the brush across the river. In an instant the adrenalin pumped through her system, causing her heart to pound violently. Groping for the hatchet once more, she leaned forward, straining to read the night. Cricket exploded into a frenzy of barking as the noise sounded again.

Nicole leaped up, forgetting her foot, and gave a cry of pain as it nearly crumpled beneath her. She sank to her knees, the terror leaving her as suddenly as it had come. Gripping the hatchet firmly, she reached out and put her hand on Cricket's back. "Be quiet, Cricket. Shhhh!"

And then she heard it, the voice floating softly on the night air, and the relief was as hot and as swift as the terror had been. "Nicky! It's Eric. It's all right. I'm coming in."

"Eric?" Nicole whispered, unable to believe her ears. The hatchet slipped out of her fingers and hot tears of relief burned at her cheeks as she fumbled to untie the rope from Cricket's collar. Like a shot Cricket leaped free and was gone into the night.

Finally Eric stopped across the fire from her and slid off the horse, his face drawn with pain and weariness. "Hello, Nicole," he said softly.

"Hello." Her voice surprised her. She had not shouted it nor had she thrown herself at him. He had come back and, at least for the moment, had ended the terrifying aloneness of the night, and she had merely said hello. She felt a quick burst of pride that she could demonstrate such control. "Did you forget something?"

"Yes, as a matter of fact I did." Moving almost in slow motion, he untied the sack from off the pack animal, set it on the ground, and fumbled inside it. When he stood, he had her tennis shoes in his hand. "I forgot these."

"Oh?"

He hobbled slowly around the fire until he came within two feet of her. She stood straight and unmoving, watching him closely. "I also seem to have forgotten a lifetime of teaching as well," he said. "I would consider it an honor if you'd let me help you put these on."

Though her eyes had suddenly misted up, she didn't look away from him. "That isn't necessary. I can do it."

"Yes, I know, but I can't think of any other way to say I'm sorry."

"You came back. That says enough."

"I should never have left. But if you'd like to put these on, I'll go find the radio."

"The radio? But you took it."

"I know, but I dropped it off in the trees a short distance down

215

river to lighten my load. Perhaps once you have your shoes on, you could throw whatever wood you have left on the fire."

She stared at him, unbelieving.

He smiled briefly. "The bigger it is, the more quickly the helicopter will spot it."

"What about Cliff?"

"I'll start down again as soon as I'm sure they've picked you up. I know I have no right to ask anything of you, but would it be too presumptuous to suggest that when they arrive, you might tell them you escaped from me and don't know exactly where I am?"

She nodded, blinking at the sudden burning behind her eyelids.

"You could tell them you hit me over the head with a club."

Nicole laughed and brushed at the corner of her eyes with the back of her hand. "Yes, I guess I could say that."

"Good." He started to turn away, then swung back. "You wouldn't need to tell them that you did it twice."

"Twice?"

"Yes, once with a length of spruce—once with some very blunt words."

CHAPTER

26

Nicole checked the time on her wrist computer, trying to ignore the quick flash of irritation. She had barely left the helicopter and been ushered into Central Control before the Major had slapped a new wrist computer on her arm. It was all done very cordially, but the Major's underlying nervousness at her bare arm was evident.

They had not finished at Central Control until nearly 6:00 A.M. Then Travis had brought her home, and she had collapsed into an exhausted sleep for five hours. Now the dread of what was coming lay heavy on her mind.

Frowning, she limped to her closet, reached in, and had her dress uniform half off the hanger when she stopped. For a long moment she stood there indecisively; then, with a quick shake of her head, she put it back and took out a tailored, navy-blue blazer and gray skirt and dressed quickly. As she buttoned the last button and peered at herself in the mirror, the doorbell chimed.

"Come in," she called loudly.

"Hi, honey," Travis called through the shattered door to her bedroom. "Are you ready?"

"Almost. I just need to put on my shoes."

"Would you like me to help you?"

The memory of Eric standing before her with her tennis shoes flashed into her mind. "No," she called out quickly. Then more slowly, "No, I'm all right. I'll be just a moment."

Travis, in full dress uniform, looked trim and fresh, as though he had not been up half the night rescuing girls from mountain campsites. He stood up and started toward her as she came into the living room. "You look lovely, Nicole . . ." His eyes dropped to note her clothes, and his voice trailed off.

"But?" she supplied for him.

"But the Major said we were to wear our uniforms. He said so this morning, just before we left. Don't you remember?"

"Yes, I remember." Her eyes met his calmly.

"Then . . ." He was obviously flustered, but he quickly recovered. "Whatever. You really do look lovely." He swept her into his arms, crutches and all, and bent down to kiss her. She stood motionless, accepting it dutifully.

"I *am* glad you're back home."

"Me too." She pulled away. "My purse is there on the desk. If you'd carry it for me, I'll see if I can't get the hang of these crutches."

"Of course." He retrieved her purse and moved to hold the door for her. As she came alongside him she stopped and looked up, searching the depths of his face. "Travis?"

"Yes?"

"Is this really a trial, or is it to be a public execution?"

"An execution?" He gave a short laugh. "Of course not. The Major just wants the citizens of Shalev to see what happens to those who try to overthrow our society. Dr. Cameron will be punished but not executed."

"Can you promise that?"

"I guarantee it. Now let's get going, or we'll be late."

As they entered the dressing room under the grandstand of the stadium, Nicole stopped short. The Major stood nearly hidden in a cluster of blue and orange uniforms, but as she and Travis entered, a sudden hush fell over the room; then the group broke into a babble of welcome and congratulations. Clayne Robertson was the first to reach her. "Welcome back, Nicole."

She pulled her eyes away from the Major, who was staring at her. "Hello, Clayne."

"When I told Adrienne you'd been found, she cried. She's been worried sick about you. The kids too. They remember you in their prayers every night."

Her eyes softened and she smiled. "They're sweet."

"You up to a good dinner tonight, or do you want to recuperate for a couple of days first?"

"I'd like that. I'm going to Mount Pleasant tomorrow, to stay with my aunt and rest up. But after almost a week of camp food, Adrienne's cooking sounds wonderful."

His eyes dropped to her foot. "Eric do that?" he rumbled, his mouth tightening.

"No, I—" Suddenly she didn't want to try to explain with everyone listening. "I had my shoes off and stepped on a sharp rock."

"Good. I kept telling Adrienne that Eric wouldn't harm you. I—"

"Nicole?"

Clayne stepped back as the Major approached.

"Yes, sir?" Unconsciously she hitched the crutches back a little to make herself stand up straighter.

"Again, welcome back." His eyes flicked down to her clothes and then back to lock into hers. One eyebrow raised slightly. "We're so glad everything has worked out to bring you back safely."

"Thank you, sir."

He glanced at his wrist computer and turned around briskly. "It's 12:55. Bring out the prisoner."

Every head swung to face the corridor leading to the equipment room, where Cliff Cameron had been kept under guard.

Cliff emerged first, walking easily, his head erect. He was dressed in a navy blue suit, long sleeved white shirt with gold cuff links, and maroon tie. With his wavy gray hair and craggy fea-

219

tures, he looked every inch the distinguished brain surgeon he had once been. A step behind him came another man, also in a suit and carrying a briefcase, and Nicole assumed this was his attorney. As they came out into the dressing room area and Cliff turned to face the Major, Nicole saw the fresh bandage at the back of his neck.

Suddenly he turned and saw her. A smile broke out across the somber face, and he stepped quickly to her. "Ah, Nicole. I heard you had gotten away from Eric. I'm glad. I haven't felt good about that whole thing from the very beginning."

Before she could respond, the Major cut in curtly. "Dr. Cameron, it's time to go. If you would follow me, please."

"Yes," he said, his eyes still on Nicole. "As we used to say in the old days, 'On with the show.'"

As the group walked out into the bright sunshine, the silence of the crowd was almost stifling in its intensity. For one quick moment Nicole wondered about Eric. Had he made it down? Was he here? But then she saw the numerous orange uniforms scattered throughout the crowd and posted at nearly every exit, and she knew he could not have made it in, even if he had made it down from the mountain.

The procession of prisoner, lawyer, and Guardians proceeded to the center of the field, where some risers provided a platform about thirty feet by thirty feet. Several rows of chairs had been placed in front of it. On the platform were three tables, one large and imposing, two smaller ones side by side in front of the big one. To the left of the large table was a single row of chairs. A television camera crew was perched on the one corner of the platform, filming as the procession approached.

Nicole saw a second group of people, men and women, coming from the visiting-team tunnel. As she sat next to Clayne, they filed past and sat on the back row of chairs on the platform.

"Who are they?" she whispered.

"That's the jury. The first jury to hear a criminal case in the history of Shalev."

"Ladies and gentlemen, would you please rise?"

The Major spoke into a microphone in front of the risers as Travis escorted Clifford Cameron and his attorney to the first small table on the platform, then joined another man at the second table. Nicole assumed the man next to Travis was the prosecuting attorney. Behind them, the jury sat quiet and sober-faced.

Slowly, reluctantly, almost rebelliously, twenty thousand people came to their feet in response to the Major's command. If he noticed their reticence, he gave no sign. "Ladies and gentlemen, the Honorable Judge Lorenzo R. Bradford, who will be presiding at these proceedings."

From the row in front of Nicole a man stood, clothed in long black robes, and moved to take his seat at the center table on the platform.

"You may be seated."

The sound of the crowd settling back onto their seats was a soft rustle, but no other noise could be heard—no talking, no laughter, no cheering, no cries of disappointment—none of the sounds that were so typical of this stadium. As Nicole peered upward at the people, then dropped her eyes to study the Major and those on the stand, she felt a sudden bitterness. *This isn't a trial. Cliff was right. Before it had ever begun, he had known. It was a show. A well-staged, manipulated event.*

And then as she scanned the sullen faces of the crowd, she understood, and knew the Major understood as well. It *was* a show, and the show was for them—for every one of them who had asked himself the question, "What will I do if Eric Lloyd and his men ask me to join them?" Television coverage alone was not sufficient to answer that question. Only a live demonstration, where the shock and reality would be undiluted, would suffice. And then the Major spoke and pulled her thoughts away from the crowd.

"Citizens of Shalev." His voice gave the impression of one caught in sudden mourning. "For the first time in our eighteen-year history, we begin a trial—not the first civil trial, for we are still human and have had to work out our differences with the aid of the courts and counselors and legal processes—no, for the first

221

time, we convene to conduct a *criminal* trial. And I cannot fully express the inner feelings that tear at me now. How many times in all of history has mankind gone eighteen years without a single criminal action? How many times have they gone two decades without crime, violence, or unrestrained passion?"

He half turned so that he could see Dr. Clifford Cameron. "Now, for the first time we have had violence, we have had killing, we have had treason. One of the men responsible for that breach of history is here now. He must answer for robbing us of our chance to extend that remarkable, unequalled record of peace and security and harmony to three decades, or four. Or even a century. That was my dream."

The two men locked gazes, the Major's expression a mixture of sadness and anger, Dr. Cameron's one of curious amusement.

The Major turned back. "Ladies and gentlemen, we will now proceed with the case of the Alliance of Four Cities versus Dr. Clifford C. Cameron."

Judge Lorenzo R. Bradford smacked his gavel against the table and leaned forward into the microphone in front of him. "Will the defendant and his counsel rise and approach the bench?"

Cliff and his attorney stood and came around to stand before him. Travis also stood, unhooked the microphone on his table, and handed it to Cliff's attorney.

"None of us have a lot of precedence for conducting a trial of this nature," the judge continued, "so we shall proceed as best we know how."

He picked up a long sheet of paper before him. "Dr. Clifford C. Cameron, you stand here today accused of the following charges: eight counts of high treason through the illegal removal of the implantations of citizens of the Alliance of Four Cities; six counts of aggravated assault; six counts of illegal manufacture, possession, and use of high explosives; three counts of illegal possession and use of dangerous weapons; four counts of conspiracy to commit treason; and one count of being an accessory to forcible abduction and kidnapping."

He leaned back in his chair, his face grave. "Those are the charges. Do you understand them?"

Nicole saw Cliff nod, but heard no answer. "I'm sorry, Dr. Cameron, but would you speak into the microphone. Would you repeat your answer, please?"

As his attorney held the microphone up to him, Cliff's voice boomed out over the speakers in the stadium. "Yes, your Honor, I understand the charges."

"And how do you plead?"

"To these particular charges?"

"Of course."

"Guilty."

Nicole's head jerked up as a gasp of surprise swept the stadium. "No," she whispered.

"What was that again?" the judge said, leaning forward in his chair.

"I said guilty. I plead guilty to the charges read."

Cliff's attorney stepped forward and took the microphone. "Your Honor, may I speak?"

"Yes."

"Your Honor—" He paused, evidently as stunned as everyone else. "I don't think my client fully understands the implications of what he's saying. He doesn't—"

Cliff gently took the microphone back. "Your Honor, I appreciate Mr. Wingate's concern, but I do fully understand what I am doing. The Major, in his opening address, charged me with trying to overthrow peace, introduce violence, foster crime. Now if those were the charges, I would plead not guilty and defend myself vigorously. But you said I am charged with operating on people and taking out their implantations, with using weapons and explosives," he shot Nicole a quick glance, "in aiding and abetting in a kidnapping. To those charges I must plead guilty."

"Well . . ." The judge gave the Major a searching look, pleading for help.

Cliff continued, his voice amiable and friendly. "Does there have to be a trial now? I mean, do we still need to call witnesses, argue the case, all of that?"

"Well, I—no, I mean, I guess not. If you refuse to deny your guilt, I guess we just—sentence you."

Again the judge glanced at the Major, who nodded curtly.

"Good." Cliff turned and surveyed the crowd, then looked up at the sky. "Well then, your Honor, Major Denison was kind enough to give all these good people half a day off from work. It's a hot day. Instead of sitting here sweltering in the sun, why don't you hurry and pronounce sentence and leave them some time to catch a swim or take a picnic to the lake or something."

As a startled wave of laughter swept through the crowd, punctuated with shouts of approval and a smattering of applause, Nicole stared at Cliff Cameron, and suddenly her eyes were swimming.

"What do you say, your Honor?"

Totally bewildered, the judge again turned to the Major for support, and again Nicole saw the almost imperceptible nod of the head.

He cleared his throat quickly. "Well, then. Since the defendant pleads guilty to all charges—uh—I guess we're ready to pass sentence. Would the defendant please—oh, yes, you're already standing." He cleared his throat nervously. "Dr. Clifford C. Cameron, as the judge over these proceedings, I hereby sentence you to be remanded into the custody of the Guardians. Stage Three implantation is hereby declared permanent."

Clayne whispered into Nicole's ear, "They knew what the sentence would be before this ever happened." The disgust in his voice was evident.

"And also," the judge intoned, "you are to be placed in a confinement cell for the rest of your natural life."

Once again the sudden intake of twenty thousand pairs of lungs caused a rippling of sound across the stadium. Nicole felt the tears well over and trickle down her cheeks as Cliff Cameron nodded.

"That concludes this trial," the judge said, banging his gavel. "Court is adjourned." Cliff nodded again, then turned and walked back to his seat, leaving his attorney staring at him.

In an instant the Major was up and to the microphone in front of the platform. "Ladies and gentlemen, may I have your attention, please." The babble of noise quickly died, and the people

224

sank back into their seats. "We want to express our thanks to Judge Lorenzo R. Bradford and to the jury members, who, fortunately, were not needed today." His voice was tinged with a hardness Nicole had heard only once or twice before.

"The accused now becomes the convicted, by his own confession." He turned to look at Dr. Cameron. His hand came up and covered the microphone, and Nicole heard his savage whisper. "Travis!"

Even as Travis came off the platform to join him, the Major was back at the microphone. "Dr. Cameron has graciously suggested that we cut these proceedings short. We shall do that, only delaying you a moment or so longer."

Again his hand came over the mike, and Nicole leaned forward, straining to hear what he said as a low murmur of disappointment rippled through the crowd. "Travis, get on your radio and patch us in to Central Control. I want a direct radio link with the Monitoring Room."

The Monitoring Room! Nicole stared, the first glimmer of horror pushing against her stomach.

"Ladies and gentlemen," the Major said smoothly, even as Travis, obviously caught off guard, unhooked his radio and began speaking into it. "It appears that while Dr. Cameron has confessed his guilt, he has exhibited no real remorse. And it may even be that some of you are thinking that his punishment is not all that bad. Confinement for life is a depressing thought, but considering that he tried to overthrow our entire society, the magnitude of the crime seems to demand a more severe punishment."

He glanced over at Travis, who nodded. Up came the hand, and once again the microphone was covered so the crowd did not hear the exchange. But Nicole and those around her heard it clearly. "Tell them to stand by on Dr. Cameron's frequency. I want them prepared to give me ten percent increments of his Punishment Mode on my signal."

Several members of the press corps and the television crew audibly gasped, and next to her, Clayne Robertson started in his chair. Nicole stared numbly, knowing better than any of them what the Major was up to.

"Travis! That's an order!" The Major's voice snapped out like a rifle shot, and Travis flinched. Then slowly, he lifted the radio to his mouth.

"Under no circumstances are they to exceed eighty percent of the maximum. I don't want him killed. Tell them that!"

"Yes, sir!"

The Major swung back to the microphone, and his eyes scanned the rows of faces staring down at him. "Some of you may think that Dr. Cameron has gotten off easily, but that is only because you do not fully understand what Stage Three implantation entails. Few people in Shalev have it, and so relatively few of you have seen its effects. Perhaps a demonstration is in order. Travis, if you'd hand me the radio, please."

The walkie-talkie changed hands slowly. "Now, will you go up and stand by Dr. Cameron. Hold the microphone for him. I wish the people to hear whatever he has to say."

As Travis moved back onto the platform, Cliff stood up slowly. He licked his lips once, then straightened and squared his shoulders. His right hand came up slowly until it touched his forehead, and with dignity he saluted the crowd.

"Ten percent!" the Major said quickly into the radio.

Cliff gave an involuntary gasp, and his arm jerked away from his forehead, but he forced it back, biting his lip to stop the violent trembling of his upper body.

"Twenty!"

A sharp cry was torn from Cliff's lips as he dropped to his knees and grabbed his head with both hands.

"Ladies and gentlemen, what you are now witnessing is only twenty percent of the Punishment Mode under Stage Three implantation." He turned and looked at the trembling figure. "Dr. Cameron, are you ready to express regret for your crimes?"

"No." The word was barely audible, but Travis had lowered the microphone to the kneeling figure so that it was touching Cliff's lips, and his answer went booming out over the speakers.

"Thirty percent!" the Major commanded.

Cliff screamed in agony as Nicole clamped her eyes shut, her fingernails biting into the flesh of her palms.

226

"Fifty!" The Major's voice was an angry bellow. "Now, Dr. Cameron, now are you ready to speak to us?"

"Yes! Yes, oh help me! Yes! Please, yes!"

"Cut the power," the Major said quickly, nodding in satisfaction.

A great sob of relief echoed out of the body that suddenly collapsed and went limp.

"Travis," the Major said, now fully composed again, "will you help Dr. Cameron up? I believe he is ready to make a statement now."

Travis's arm went around Cliff's waist. He was trembling so violently that he could not stand alone. Travis helped him to his feet, heavily supporting him. Cliff's eyes were bulging and he was gasping for breath as Travis held the microphone to his lips.

For a long moment the only sound in the air was the tortured rasping of his breath. Then suddenly his head came up. "*Eric!*"

It was a cry of such anguish that it tore through Nicole and went bouncing off the grandstands in echoes that would haunt her forever. "Eric, don't give up! Help free this people!"

For a split second the Major stared, his mouth open in stunned surprise. Then his hand flew up, jamming the radio to his mouth. "Eighty percent!" he screamed hoarsely. "Eighty percent capacity! Now!"

Cliff's body jerked so violently that he was torn out of Travis's grip, as though hit at point-blank range with a high-powered rifle. One long scream rent the summer air before Cliff collapsed into a crumpled heap at Travis Oakes's feet.

For a full ten seconds there was not a sound in the stadium. Every eye was riveted on the still form on the platform in the center of the field. Then suddenly, high up in the center bleachers, a man leaped to his feet. In the stillness his voice echoed like a pistol shot, the sarcasm twisting it into a mocking cry. "Let's hear it for Major Denison and the Guardians," he shouted, "keepers of the peace, protectors of our freedom."

And then he began to clap his hands. Almost instantly someone else leaped up, and then another. Like gasoline vapors ignited by sparks from a torch, twenty thousand people exploded, leaping to their feet. There was no open anger, for years of instantaneous punishment had long ago flattened such responses. But they were up, pounding their hands, many of the women with tears streaming down their cheeks, paying tribute to the crumpled figure on the stand, and, as openly as they dared, rejecting the man who had put him there. The sound rolled down out of the stands in a smashing wave, engulfing the small group of people standing in the center of the soccer field. Nicole stared straight ahead, seeing nothing because of the burning in her eyes.

CHAPTER

27

Nicole set down her book and unfolded her legs as the soft chime of the door bell echoed through the house. She stopped briefly to look at herself in the small entryway mirror, then pulled the door open.

"Hi."

"Hello, Travis." He gave her a quick kiss, which she accepted absently. Then she stepped aside so he could enter the living room.

"Did you get unpacked?"

"Yes, I was nearly done when you called."

"And how was Mount Pleasant?"

"Beautiful. It's such a lovely place there."

"Yes, it is. And how's your aunt?"

Nicole smiled. Outwardly Travis seemed his usual confident self, but these were exactly the same questions he had asked her on the phone. "She's fine. Lonely since Uncle Arthur died, but doing quite well. Please, sit down."

Though she sat on the couch, he chose the easy chair opposite her. *He really is unsure of himself tonight,* she thought. For a moment there was an uncomfortable silence. Then he turned and looked down the hallway where the shattered door frame to her bedroom could be seen. "Now that you're back, we'll have to get that fixed."

"Yes, I'll have to do that." *Before I sell the house,* she nearly added, but caught herself. Finally she asked, "How's Dr. Cameron?"

He shrugged, not meeting her eyes. "About the same. The doctor says that it's as if he had a massive stroke. At this point they can't tell whether the paralysis is permanent or whether it's just a temporary shock to his nervous system."

"And still no sign of Eric?"

"None. We expected a real blow-up after the trial, but there's been nothing. I can't believe he's given up or been scared off."

Nicole nodded. Except for the ticking of the mantel clock, the living room was filled with silence. Finally Travis drew a deep breath. "Nicole?"

"Yes?"

"I've been thinking about us, and . . ."

His inward nervousness had finally surfaced. His hands were up, fingertips to fingertips, and he was tapping them.

"Yes?"

"And . . . well, I've decided I've been a fool about our marriage, saying we ought to wait until next summer. If you want a Christmas wedding, that's fine with me. Or we can even do it sooner than that if you want."

Do it? What a peculiar choice of words. As though it were a task to be gotten out of the way. But she showed no response. She had known this was coming sooner or later, had even told herself she welcomed it so she could stop agonizing over what she would say. But now that it had come, her courage wavered. Just two weeks ago—*was it only that long ago?*— what she would have given to hear those words.

Travis was watching her closely, the drumming of his fingers increasing in tempo. "I mean," he added, "it's clear to me now just how flimsy my excuses were. Since you've been gone, first with Eric, now with your aunt, I realize just how much you mean to me. And I—"

230

She took a deep breath and plunged in. "Travis?"

He stopped.

Once started, her words came out in a rush. "Travis, when I report to work Monday morning, I'm turning in my resignation from the Guardians."

"What?" The stunned look on his face was almost comical. He had played his best hand, and she had just trumped it.

"Yes. Effective immediately. Then I'm moving to Mount Pleasant to stay with my aunt for a while."

"But why?"

"I've talked with a computer manufacturer there. They have an excellent opportunity in their testing department." She reached down and slipped off the engagement ring. "I think it's better if you take this back for now. Maybe later, if we can get the whole thing sorted out, then . . ." She trailed off, not sure how to finish.

"But why, Nicole? Why?"

"I can't be a Monitor anymore. I think you're right. I don't think Eric has run away. I don't think the battle is over. If I stay, there will be more commands to push the red buttons, more Dr. Camerons in the hot summer sunshine. And—and I don't have any more of those battles in me. I can't face those options. Maybe they have to be done, but not by me."

She moved over in front of him and held out the ring. "So I think it's best if you take this back now."

He just stared at her, so she dropped the ring in his hand and moved back to the couch.

"It has something to do with what happened at the dam, doesn't it."

Nicole considered for a moment, then finally nodded. "Yes, in a way it does. Not as much as you think, but some."

"Nicole, I didn't have any choice. The Major wouldn't let Eric's family go."

"I know. And I guess I understand, but have you ever considered what the game of soccer must be like from the ball's point of view?"

He didn't answer.

"Well, I was the ball that day—to you, to the Major, to Eric—and that isn't a very uplifting feeling. But it's much more than that, Travis. Much more."

"What?"

Showing the Major which buttons to push, holding microphones to a seventy-two-year-old man's lips as he screams in agony. But she merely shook her head. "Maybe after it all dies down, things will return to normal, and we can start building something again."

Travis stood up quickly and came over to sit next to her. He took her hand. "Nicole, do you still love me?"

"I—" Her head dropped, and she stared at their hands. "I don't know. I need time to sort this all out in my mind."

He sighed deeply, then finally nodded. "Okay. I guess I can understand how you feel." He stood up abruptly. "Well, then, I guess I'd better go."

The hurt in his voice was obvious, and for a moment she almost relented. Then something inside her stiffened, and she stood up too. Suddenly he put his hands on her shoulders and pulled her to him. His kiss was gentle, longing, imploring. One part of her ached to return it, but she couldn't.

"Good-bye, Nicole."

"Good-bye, Travis."

At the door he abruptly stopped. "Have you considered what leaving the Guardians means for you?"

A thousand questions from friends, loss of one of the best-paying jobs in the city, giving up this home, which was furnished by the Guardians—her mind flicked quickly over the things she had already considered. "Yes, I think I have."

"Implantation?"

Nicole faltered, the color draining from her face.

"I didn't think so," he said. "But you know that's true."

"I—"

"With your uncle dead, you're not immediate family anymore. The Major won't make an exception, especially not now."

Nicole's mouth was a pale, tight line across the chalky hue of her face. How stupid. That above all should have occurred to her, and it had never crossed her mind.

"Look," Travis said, moving to her and taking her by the shoulders, "you've still got until Monday to think about your decision. That gives you another thirty-six hours. If being in Central Monitoring is what concerns you, just ask for a transfer. You could go in—"

They both spun around at the sound of scratching at the door. "What's that?" Nicole said. Then, as she opened the door, she cried out in surprise and delight. "Cricket!"

The German shepherd was sitting down, her nose pressed to the screen, her tail beating furiously against the porch.

Nicole threw open the screen and dropped to her knees. "Cricket, where did you come from?" She laughed with delight as the dog tried to lick her face.

Travis stepped out onto the porch and peered into the night. "That's what I want to know too. Where did she come from? You said Eric had her when you escaped from him. Do you have a flashlight?"

"Do you think Eric is *here?*" she asked incredulously.

"I don't know, but I'm going to find out. Do you have a light?"

"No. Surely, Travis, he wouldn't be here. He had no reason to try and keep Cricket with him. She probably just came down on her own. I've been gone—she could have been back for days."

"Maybe, maybe not. But he did come here for you once, so let's be sure he hasn't come again." He stepped off the porch and began a methodical search of the yard.

For a moment or two Nicole watched, a little angry at the sudden clutch of anxiety for Eric's safety. She had spent the last week telling herself she was through with Eric Lloyd and his futile little rebellion. Then she shook it off as Travis moved around the back. "Come on, Cricket, let's get you something to eat."

She had just opened a can of dog food when Travis knocked at the back door. "It's open, come in."

"Nothing," he said, shaking his head. "But I'd better get back to Central Control and alert them just in case. Lock your doors and shut all the windows. If you see or hear anything, call me." He gave her a quick kiss on the cheek and was gone.

Nicole moved out onto the front porch and watched him

233

drive away, amused, half sad. "Well, so much for all those regrets over broken engagements," she murmured. "Half time is over, the ball game resumes. Only this time, they'll have to find another ball to play with."

She sighed and went back inside, shutting the door. As she turned back into the living room, she gave a startled cry. Eric was kneeling behind the couch, elbows on the back of it, his head resting in cupped hands.

"Hi," he said with a smile.

"Eric! What are you doing here?"

"If I promise to stay across the room, would you mind if we talked with the lights out?"

Nicole's eyes flicked to the front window, but Travis had gone. Curiously, she was glad. "I—why are you here?"

He held up his hands quickly. "No abductions, no shattered doors this time. I promise."

"Good. I couldn't help but wonder." She walked over and clicked off the lights, leaving only the light from the kitchen doorway.

Limping noticeably, Eric stepped over to Cricket and reached down to rub her neck. "You rascal. How did you get out of the garage? I locked you in there."

"That was your first mistake," Nicole said. "I used to lock her in the garage when I wanted to go for a walk without her. Then she learned to climb up on the workbench and push the little sliding window open with her nose."

"Well, she about did me in. That was a little too close."

"How did you get in here?" And then her face colored slightly. "And how long have you been behind the couch?"

"About two minutes is all," he answered quickly. "I had just started up the front porch when I saw the headlights coming." He grinned. "Believe it or not, I was going to call on you in a normal fashion for once. When I saw it was Travis, I dove into the bushes around the side of the house. I was going to wait until he left. Then Cricket started scratching on the front door. When you two came out the front, I scurried around the back and came in here."

When she nodded, obviously relieved, he grew serious.

234

"However, I must tell you, I was hiding directly under these windows." His thumb jerked over his shoulder.

"So you did hear?"

"Yes. I didn't want to eavesdrop, but I was afraid to move for fear Travis would hear me. I'm sorry."

She shrugged. "I appreciate your telling me."

"I felt I owed you that."

"How's your leg?"

"Coming. How about your foot?"

"Fine. The doctors in Central Control opened it up again the morning I got back and cleaned it all out. I had the stitches out yesterday. If I'm careful, I hardly know it's there."

"Good. I saw you on crutches at the stadium."

"Were you there?"

"No, we didn't get down until almost dusk. But I watched the news broadcast that night."

"I see."

"That's why I'm here."

"I'm not surprised."

"Where is he, Nicky?"

"What?" she blurted. "No 'didn't I tell you so, Nicky'? You told me that if I returned, I'd be forced to face unpleasant alternatives. It took less than eight hours to prove your seeric gift. Why don't you call that to my attention before you ask me to betray my employer?"

"Nicky, I—"

"Don't call me Nicky!" she cried. "Please, don't call me Nicky."

He was watching her steadily. "It was Nicky who dragged me away from the claws of the bear. You'll always be Nicky to me."

"And *Nicole* works for the Major, right?"

"Nicole," he corrected slowly, "is a woman of remarkable grace, courage, and integrity. She has more of my respect and admiration than any woman I've ever known. And to call her Nicky in no way lessens what I think of Nicole."

For a long moment she stared at him. Then finally she murmured, "Please don't."

Eric looked surprised. "Please don't what?"

"Don't be nice. Not now. I don't want to like you. I want to get away from you and Travis and the Major and Shalev and Cliff Cameron and—" She had a sudden thought. "Were you going to ask me to join you?"

"I have no right to ask that. If you remember, I was one of those who played soccer, using you as the ball. I have no right to toss you back into the game now. Except for Cliff. If you'll tell me where Cliff is, I'll leave you alone."

"So you can get him out?"

"Yes. Your people abandoned you on the dam. We can't do that."

Her voice was barely a whisper. "Even if he won't know that you've gotten him out?"

Eric's eyes were stricken. "I heard what Travis said." She saw him swallow hard. "It doesn't matter. We'll get him out."

"He's heavily guarded."

"It doesn't matter!" he shot back angrily. "Will you tell me where he is?"

Nicole stood up, walked to the fireplace, and leaned on the mantel, looking away from him. "If I did that, it would mean treason," she said. "I don't have to go with you into the mountains, or operate on somebody. Even the simple act of telling you where they're holding Cliff Cameron becomes treason against the Guardians, against my people, and against everything I've always believed in. With one word I become as guilty as if I held the knife."

"I understand."

She whirled to face him. "Do you?" she cried. "You're asking me to risk everything—my career, my freedom, Travis—"

"You've already—" He bit back the angry retort.

"I've already what?" she demanded.

"Nothing. I have no right to say that either. I'm sorry I bothered you, Nicole. You're correct, I have no right to ask such a thing of you."

"I've already lost Travis. That's what you were going to say, isn't it?"

236

Eric knelt down by Cricket. "Good-bye, old girl. Take good care of her, will you?"

"Say it!" Nicole cried, taking a step toward him. "You're thinking it. Why won't you say it?"

He straightened slowly, his eyes gentle. "If I ever ask a woman if she loves me and her answer is, 'I don't know' . . ." He shrugged.

Surprisingly enough, she did not flash back at him.

"Up in the hills you accused me of being the village's resident psychiatrist," he went on. "At the risk of supporting that accusation, let me say something. My father used to tell us that love and goodness are interwoven and interdependent. The more goodness a person exhibits in his life, the easier it is to love that person. Selfishness, cruelty, exploitation—any evil act makes it harder and harder to feel love for a person. And you and Travis—" He stopped and then shrugged. "I think your head is still struggling with what your heart has already decided."

"I know," she said, almost in a whisper. "Every time I think about him, I can't blot out the image of him showing the Major the terminal voltage buttons on the computer."

"Or last week in the stadium?" Eric asked softly.

"Yes, that too." Her shoulders straightened, as if the saying of it had relieved her of pain.

"I'm sorry. Travis is a good man in many ways."

"I know." She took a deep breath. "So what now?"

He smiled, the slightest touch of teasing in his eyes. "I could always drag you back to the mountains again."

"Against my will, of course."

"Of course." He laughed gently, then instantly sobered. "What about implantation, Nicky? Travis is right—the Major won't make an exception."

"I know."

"Nicole, I—" Then he stopped and his shoulders dropped.

"What?"

He took a breath, hesitated as though ready to speak, then finally shook his head.

"Ask me, Eric," she said.

"I lost my right to ask you anything."

"I know. But you earned it back when you brought me my shoes. So ask me."

His hands came up, as though he was about to take her by the shoulders, then they dropped again. But his eyes were steady and his face determined. "Nicole, come with us. Help us free this people."

He used almost exactly the same words Clifford Cameron had screamed out as his final answer to the Major, and they hit Nicole hard. When she looked up at him, tears were streaming down her cheeks. "Why did you come back? I don't want to be part of this. I want to get away and not think about it anymore."

"Yes," he said, thinking of the valley and irrigating in the warm summer sunshine. "That does have its attractions."

Suddenly Nicole walked into the bedroom. When she returned, she held the carved redwood figure of a tortured eagle straining upwards. "Why did you give me this?"

"He sighed. "I carved that because it was me, then. It represented everything I was feeling."

"And why did you choose to give it to me?"

Eric took the statue, turning it over in his hands as he looked at it carefully. Finally his eyes lifted to meet hers. "I told myself it was to throw you off, to confuse you, but I really think it was because I wanted you to understand me. I wanted you to know why I had to do what I did."

Once again her eyes were glistening. "Is freedom so precious?" Before he could answer, she went on quickly, talking to herself as much as to him. "I guess having always had it, I've never thought about it much. Implantation never appeared that horrible in others. They seemed happy. I kept telling myself it was really for their good. But as I've watched you and the others—" Her voice caught for a moment. "Cliff saluting the crowd—I . . . How can I go on supporting the very thing that denies that freedom to tens of thousands of people? How could I ever have been part of that?"

"Nicole," Eric said, his own voice husky with emotion. "Come with us."

"And if I say yes, then what happens?"

238

"I'll take you with me right now. We'll cut your wrist computer, and as soon as we get Cliff free, we'll go back to base camp. You can meet Mother and my sisters."

"I'd like that very much."

"And—"

"But that's not the answer, is it?"

He looked startled.

"You don't need me in the mountains. Not really. What you need is someone in Central Control."

"No. That would be too dangerous."

"Eric," she pleaded, "for the past week I've been agonizing with myself, wondering what to do, not wanting to face what I feel has to be done. Now you've given me another option. I don't like it. I don't want it. But if I'm going to join with you, then put me where you need me."

"After what you've told Travis, it'd be very dangerous."

"I know, and I'm frightened to death. I'll have to tell him the threat of implantation changed my mind. But Eric, do you really need me?"

He stared at her for several moments, then slowly handed her the eagle, putting his hand over hers as she took it from him. "Yes, Nicole, we really need you. Will you join us?"

She smiled, a strange mixture of relief and sadness. "I joined you up there in the mountains. I just needed you to come and let me know that I had."

CHAPTER

28

Nicole was in the cafeteria on her afternoon break when it began. She had forced herself to go with Shirley Ferguson, though her stomach was tied in knots. With tremendous effort she managed to smile and respond at the proper places and tried to avoid looking at the clock a dozen times a minute.

"Nicole?" Shirley's voice penetrated her thoughts. "Are you all right?"

"Oh, yes. Yes, I'm fine."

"You look pale. Are you sure you should have come back to work this soon? You haven't been yourself all day."

A wave of panic went flooding through Nicole. Shirley was a whiz on the computers and a steady and reliable Monitor, but definitely not one of Central Control's more perceptive lights when it came to interpersonal relations and interactions. If Shirley had noticed her distracted state, she was flirting with disaster with the Major and Travis. The Major had interviewed her relentlessly when she came on shift. "Why did you come to the stadium out of uniform?" "Why were you going to resign?" "Why did you break off your engagement with Travis?" "What changed your mind about resigning?" "What if you falter in the Monitoring

240

Room in the next crisis?" She had answered him honestly wherever possible, telling him everything except the decision to join Eric. She had satisfied him, and he agreed to allow her to continue as a monitor, but she knew she was on probation and would be watched closely.

Suddenly the public-address system blared out through the cafeteria, the feminine voice high-pitched and clearly excited. "Attention, all personnel. Attention, all personnel. We have a Stage One Alert. All personnel report to your duty stations immediately."

"Stage One!" Shirley exclaimed as they both raced for the door. "That's a full-scale emergency. What's happening?"

It's Eric! Nicole nearly shouted out loud, her heart soaring with relief. But she just shook her head quickly and broke into a trot toward the Central Monitoring room.

When they reached the room, Travis was already there, a phone in one hand, staring at the monitoring board above the blue-and-orange computer consoles. Three lighted panels were blinking brightly.

Three! Nicole stared. If they had removed three implantations at the same time, they'd be slowed down considerably and highly vulnerable to capture.

And then, even as she slid into her chair, the big board clanged sharply and a fourth set of flashing letters began to wink on and off.

WARNING! WARNING! WRIST COMPUTER #116543, DONALD LEON BROWNLEY, HAS BEEN SEVERED. TERMINATION VOLTAGE SEQUENCE NOW INITIATED. DONALD LEON BROWNLEY IS NO LONGER READABLE VIA WRIST COMPUTER.

"Four now!" Travis shouted into the phone, then spun around to Shirley and Nicole. "Eric's back. They've removed four implantations. Nicole, I need a tracking on where they were when the wrist computers were severed."

"Right." Her fingers began to fly across the terminal keyboard.

"Shirley," Travis barked, "pull up personal data files on each of these people and stand by."

"Yes, sir."

At Nicole's command the computer searched its massive brain with breathtaking swiftness and fed the data to the screen. For one split second, she thought about delaying the data for Travis in order to give Eric even a small margin of time, but then she rejected the idea. Eric had specifically warned her against doing anything that would give her away. Even as the letters began flowing across her screen, she called out to Travis. "Richard Dawson was at the Kooska Mill and Lumber Company, 345 Green Street. That's in the northwest sector."

"Kooska!" Travis shouted, stabbing his finger at the flashing lights on the board. Nicole looked to where his finger pointed and saw the next two names, Stanley R. Kooska and Darla B. Kooska.

"Check the last one, check Brownley." Without waiting for her response, Travis picked up the phone again. "Units Two and Four, Code Three to 345 Green Street. Watch for any vehicles or personnel fleeing the vicinity."

He turned back to stare at Nicole's monitoring screen, where the impersonal brain was spewing out the information on Brownley's location at the time of severance. But before it had finished, another sharp clanging shattered the silence.

WARNING! WARNING! WRIST COMPUTERS #124667, #124668, #137125, AND #138976, CHARLES KEITH METCALF, DAWN JOANN METCALF, LISA RAE METCALF, AND JAMES CHARLES METCALF, HAVE BEEN SEVERED. TERMINATION VOLTAGE SEQUENCES NOW INITIATED.

Travis swore softly, the first profanity Nicole had heard since she was a small child. But it wasn't Travis that had her shocked attention. She too stared at the screen. *A whole family. Four at the same time.* And that was in addition to the other four. But before she could comprehend what that meant, the flashing lights on her screen reverted to the message on Brownley's tracking.

Travis, looking over her shoulder, burst out with another expletive. "Brownley's somewhere else!"

"Yes," Nicole answered with a cool precision that in no way revealed the exultation sweeping through her at that moment. "This time it's in south central sector, 1461 Page Lane. That's the home of—"

"The Metcalfs!" Travis exclaimed. "That means they have two operating teams." Again he began to bark orders into the phone, sending additional teams racing to the second site.

"Captain Oakes," Shirley broke in, "I have the data files on the first four."

"Good. Read them out to me."

Before she could speak, the door to Central Monitoring flew open and the Major strode in, his face red. He stopped and stared at the flashing board. "What?" he shouted. "Eight!"

"Yes," Travis said quickly, "done in two different locations. I've got teams on the way to both places right now."

"I can't believe this!" the Major shouted.

"Shirley is giving us a run-down on who's been operated on."

"Proceed," he snapped, not turning away from the screen.

"Richard Dawson," Shirley began to read in a timid voice, "age twenty-five, male, Caucasian, single, born in Toledo, Ohio, came to Shalev—"

"Yes, yes," Travis prodded. "Just give us his name, age, and occupation for now."

"He's a medical student, presently in his internship at Shalev General Hospital."

"A doctor!" Travis cried out. "Who's he doing his residency under?"

"I don't have that here. Just a moment." She punched some keys. "Dr. Chester Abernathy, sir."

"Abernathy!" the Major exploded. "I should have known."

"What about the others?"

"Stanley R. Kooska is forty-seven and owns his own lumber mill. His wife does their bookkeeping. Brownley is a chemistry professor at the Technical College and is also a partner in the Flathead Chemical and Fertilizer Company."

"I have the Metcalfs," Nicole said. "Care to guess who the other partner in Flathead Chemical and Fertilizer is?"

"So," the Major said, stepping back to glare at the monitoring board, which was now nearly covered with flashing lights, "they're tapping their close associates. That's how they choose their next victims."

"But why take the whole family?" Travis said, staring at Nicole's screen. "The girl is sixteen, the son eighteen. Why take them?"

"I can answer that," Nicole replied. "I heard them one night on the radio. They said they'd take only single men or whole families, in case you tried to apply pressure through their relatives."

"Thus providing a very close and tight-knit group," the Major added.

"The teams should be arriving at the two locations any moment now," Travis said. "Maybe we'll catch them."

"Don't count on it," the Major snapped back at him. "Eric's no dummy. He knows how swiftly we can pinpoint the locations. He's got some kind of transportation away from the site, and he'll fix them up someplace else."

"They must have found additional heavy-duty bolt cutters," Nicole volunteered. "All four of the Metcalfs were cut so close to the same moment that the computer registered them all at the same time."

"Yes," the Major said. "But now they're going to have to fix their people up. They have eight bleeding people; they're not going to be easy to hide." He glanced up at the clock. "Nicole, how long ago was it when the first person was severed?"

She punched a button again, recalling Dawson's profile. "Dawson was cut at 3:13, nearly eight or nine minutes ago."

"Okay," the Major said. "They can't have gone far. Travis, tell your men to start cordoning off both sectors. Once they are secure, begin a house-to-house search. I want every garage, every basement, every possible hiding place covered."

"Yes, sir."

The phone rang sharply, and Travis snatched it up. "This will be the first team reporting in now, sir." He jammed the phone to his ear and barked, "Captain Oakes speaking . . . Yes, put him on." He covered the mouthpiece. "It's Captain Burton from Serenity. I—yes, this is Captain Oakes. Hello, Cal, what is it?"

And then his face blanched. "What?" he shouted. He listened for a moment longer, then stared at the Major. "Burton is in Serenity's Central Monitoring Center, Major. They've just had five wrist computers severed there. All of them are people from Eric's village."

By 6:30 that evening, Central Control looked like a castle under siege. Orange-uniformed men and women rushed here and there, their faces drawn, stopping to share the latest shock of news in hurried whispers. The call from Serenity had come in at 3:22 P.M. At 3:29, Travis's first group commander called to report that the Kooska Lumber Mill and surrounding areas were deserted. At 3:31, his second commander reported that the house on Page Lane was likewise empty except for some bloodstained sheets and four wrist computers and implantation chips on the floor. Neighbors reported that a brown van had driven off swiftly a few minutes before the Guardians arrived.

At 3:44, Captain Burton called again from Serenity to report six additional removals, all family members of the previous five.

At 4:17, Shalev General Hospital sent in a fire alarm. A small blaze had started in the basement laundry. It was quickly contained, but ten minutes later a shamefaced corporal rushed into Central Control to report that while he and his men were downstairs fighting the blaze, two men in orderlies' uniforms entered Cliff Cameron's room, stunned two Guardians into unconsciousness, and disappeared with Dr. Cameron.

At 5:11, the monitoring board clanged again. WARNING! WARNING! WRIST COMPUTER #G2632, JOSEPH PAUL JENSEN, HAS BEEN SEVERED. TERMINATION VOLTAGE SEQUENCE NOW INITIATED. JOSEPH PAUL JENSEN IS NO LONGER READABLE VIA WRIST COMPUTER. TERMINATED SUBJECT WAS A MEMBER OF THE GUARDIAN STAFF. Shirley Ferguson went white. Joe was a corporal on the city patrol, and he and Shirley had been dating steadily long enough that the office had been buzzing about a potential marriage. With a long face but soaring heart, Nicole called that bombshell to the Major, who had gone to his office with Travis to try to get ahead of the escalating crisis.

At 5:15, even as Nicole was still trying to find out where Joe

Jensen's duty station had been, a call, almost incoherent, came from the sergeant in charge of a road checkpoint leading north out of Shalev. A large truck covered with a tarp had pulled up to the checkpoint. Just as the sergeant and one of his men yanked back the tarp to reveal a mass of people huddled in a hollowed-out pile of lumber, a man with a stun gun had sprung from the thick underbrush on the side of the road. That was surprise enough for the sergeant, but worse still, one of his own men had joined the stranger in attacking the other Guardians. When the sergeant came to, his tires were flattened, his radio shattered, two of his men were still unconscious, and the third had fled with the truck and the people. The traitorous Guardian? Corporal Joseph P. Jensen.

And finally at 5:57, a patrol near Hungry Horse Dam called in to report they had found the abandoned lumber truck hidden in a stand of pines. Numerous horse tracks were found around the truck and disappeared into the forest.

Even Nicole was reeling by the time the Major burst back into the Monitoring Room at 6:30, Travis at his heels. The Major seemed under perfect control again now, but Travis was looking hounded, his face strained and lined with weariness. The Major came straight to Nicole and thrust a paper into her hand. "I want this to go out on all wrist computers immediately."

"Yes, sir." She cleared her terminal and pushed the keys that would set her up for a general broadcast to all citizens of Shalev. Only then did she look at the paper. Her eyes widened, and she looked at the Major.

"Send it."

"Yes, sir." Her fingers punched away even as her mind pictured the effect this was going to have throughout the city.

ATTENTION, ALL CITIZENS. EFFECTIVE IMMEDIATELY, SHALEV IS UNDER A STATE OF EMERGENCY. RETURN TO YOUR HOMES AT ONCE. ALL WORK AND RECREATIONAL ACTIVITIES ARE HEREBY TERMINATED FOR THE EVENING. SERVICES AND ACTIVITIES OF A CRITICAL NATURE THAT ARE EXEMPT WILL BE NOTIFIED IMMEDIATELY. ALL OTHERS MUST BE IN THEIR HOMES BY EIGHT P.M. FAILURE TO COMPLY WITH THIS ORDER

WILL TRIGGER THE PUNISHMENT MODE IN YOUR WRIST COM-
PUTERS. REPEAT, AUTOMATIC PUNISHMENT MODE WILL RE-
SULT FOR ALL CITIZENS FOUND OUTSIDE THEIR HOMES AFTER
EIGHT P.M. UNLESS ON EXEMPT STATUS. A GENERAL AN-
NOUNCEMENT AND FURTHER DETAILS WILL BE GIVEN ON THE
TEN O'CLOCK NEWS THIS EVENING.

When she was finished, the Major nodded. "Nicole, there will
be a special meeting for all section heads at 9:00 P.M. in the general conference room. I'd like you to be there. Also, I want you to
contact the president of the AFC, the mayor of Shalev, all city
council members, the editors of both papers, and the directors or
presidents of both the radio and television stations in Shalev.
They are all to be in attendance. This is *not* optional." He spun on
his heel and strode out, Travis right behind him.

"Wow!" Shirley said softly, leaning back in her chair.

"Yes," Nicole answered. "Wow indeed!"

CHAPTER

29

"Ladies and gentlemen, may I have your attention?"

The Major's request was totally superfluous and about five seconds too late. The moment he entered the conference room, the excited babble of hushed voices came to an immediate halt. Now every eye was on the somber face.

"I have a brief statement to read," the Major said, letting his eyes sweep across the faces in the room. "After that, you may ask questions."

Roy Hartford, editor of the *Shalev Daily Herald*, lifted his pencil to his small notepad. The movement caught the Major's eye.

"Roy, I'll have copies of the statement for each of you when you leave."

"Good. Thank you."

The Major lifted a paper and adjusted his glasses slightly, looked up once more, then began to read in a clear voice, enunciating each word carefully.

"'A state of grave crisis exists in the city of Shalev and throughout the Alliance of Four Cities tonight. The security and peace of our society face a challenge potentially more deadly and destructive than at any time in our eighteen-year history. Therefore, as authorized in section nine, article four of the Laws of Incorporation of the Alliance of Four Cities, we hereby declare a formal state of national emergency and put the entire Alliance under martial law.'"

He paused to let the ripple of shock flutter through the assembled group, then went on firmly. "'Beginning at 8:00 P.M. this evening, a state of emergency went into effect. It will remain in effect until further notice. Under martial law the following rules will be in effect: One. All civil government in the AFC, including the senate, the courts, and elected officials, will be temporarily suspended, and the Guardians will assume all governing powers until further notice.'"

Nicole saw the stunned look Peter Dobson, president of the AFC, gave Estelle Hardy, Shalev's mayor, and heard the exclamations of dismay even as her own mind reeled.

"'The Commander-in-Chief of the Guardian forces will be the chief executive officer and director of government. He is directly responsible for all law, all policies, and all enforcement of the same for the duration of the state of emergency.

"'Two. For as long as martial law is in effect, all citizens of the AFC are on restricted movement status. All travel outside the city of residence is forbidden without a written permit from the Guardians. A strict curfew will be in effect from 8:00 P.M. until 6:00 A.M. each day. Only those with evening or night employment or those carrying special permits will be allowed outside their homes during those hours. All noncritical activities and services will cease until further notice. Violation of the curfew or travel restrictions will be subject to the Punishment Mode response via the wrist computer.

"'Three.'" If the Major was aware of the battering effect his words were having on the group, he gave no sign. "'Beginning at 8:00 A.M. tomorrow morning, all citizens of the Alliance not now implanted will report to their nearest hospital for Stage Two implantation.'" He went on swiftly, overriding the startled cries from the senior Guardian officers. "'This will include all family members of the Guardian staff, heretofore exempt, and all Guardian personnel in noncritical positions. Lists of exempt personnel

249

will be given to Guardian commanders immediately after this meeting. Failure to report for implantation will warrant maximum Punishment Modes.'"

Maximum! Maybe the others in the room didn't understand what that meant, but every Guardian did. Maximum meant termination voltage. Nicole looked up at Travis and flushed. It was an effort to keep her face expressionless, for her mind was hurtling through white-water rapids of thought. Monitors were classed as critical personnel, so she was under no threat personally. But her aunt would be implanted, and that made her stomach drop. Then she saw Clayne Robertson sitting in front of her, and she felt ill as her mind leaped to Adrienne and Sarah and Timmy.

Eric's final sardonic comment as he slipped out the back door Saturday night had been, "I think it's time to see if we can bloody the Major's nose a little, goad him into action." He had gotten his reaction all right, and Nicole felt a burst of despair. Eric was underestimating the Major. Shalev had just been clamped down so tightly that Eric's rebellion would be crushed like a bug under the wheels of a juggernaut.

"The fourth rule," the Major continued, cutting into her thoughts, "will be in effect, but is not included in the official statement. It will not be announced to the people, but will affect some of you in this room directly. The fourth order of action is that during the state of emergency all media reports—broadcasts, press reports, any announcements—must first be approved by a special public communications committee in Central Control."

"No!" Roy Hartford of the *Herald* had leaped to his feet. "You can't do that!"

The Major sighed. "Roy, of all the requirements of this sordid mess, that one causes me the greatest sorrow. We have never had censorship of the media in Shalev." His voice grew suddenly hard and cold. "But Eric Lloyd is depending on the media to make him into some kind of twisted folk hero, to turn the hearts of this people so they support him. To some degree, that has already been happening. The media are partially responsible for generating a base of action for Lloyd and the other criminals who have joined him."

250

His fist crashed down on the table. "And that is going to stop!" he thundered. "You will not in any way help this man. Is that clear?"

The editor rocked back, stunned by the savagery in the Major's face, but he was not totally cowed. "May I ask what events have justified this? All we know is that everyone has been put under curfew."

The Major's anger disappeared with the same swiftness with which it had flared up. "Yes. That finishes the formal statement. I'll now answer your questions. The rebels have begun a major offensive. Nine people in Shalev have had their implantations illegally removed since three o'clock this afternoon. Arsonists set a fire in Shalev General Hospital today to cover an attack on the team guarding Dr. Clifford Cameron."

"Cameron?" Charles Cowles, the president of KSHV-TV, asked. "Was he rescued?"

"Rescued? I think kidnapped would be a better term."

"Nine people?" The voice was that of Karl Francis of KAFC radio. "Have any of them been found?"

"Not yet. A Guardian checkpoint north of Shalev was attacked this evening and a truckload of people broke free to the mountains. We assume all nine were in that truck along with some of the other rebels."

The editor of the *Morning Tribune*, whom Nicole did not know, stood up. "If they've escaped, why the martial law now? Isn't that a kind of shutting-the-barn-door approach?"

Nicole expected the question to trigger another flash, but the Major was now in complete control, and he responded evenly. "Bob, I'm partially responsible for what has happened today. I've been dealing with Eric Lloyd as if he were simply a minor skirmish, an irritation on our rear flank. Obviously that's my mistake. This is an all-out war, and I won't make the mistake of underestimating him again."

The editor started to speak, but the Major went on quickly. "We were not able to get a count of how many were in the truck. But as you know, Eric Lloyd and Dr. Cameron removed the implantations from several others prior to the battle at Hungry

Horse Dam. It's possible that some of those—perhaps Lloyd himself—remained in the city. My secretary will furnish you with pictures of all the people who have joined the rebellion thus far. You will begin to publish and circulate the pictures immediately with a warning to all citizens to report any information they have on the whereabouts of these people." A hand came up, and the Major acknowledged the president of the AFC. "Yes, President Dobson?"

"You said the state of emergency was being declared for all the AFC. Not just Shalev?"

The Major nodded. "Unfortunately, yes. Eleven implantations were also removed in Serenity this afternoon. Thus far, it has not spread beyond that. But we must assume nothing. This is war now. And we are acting accordingly."

Clayne Robertson rose slowly, bringing a sharp frown to the Major's face, but he finally nodded toward him. "Yes, Clayne."

"Sir, why are you implanting our families?"

The Major took a deep breath. "I said the restriction on the media was the saddest decision I had to make. The recommendation for implantation of Guardian personnel and their families was the hardest. But as you know, Clayne, two members of the Guardian staff have defected—Rod Loopes from Central Monitoring, and Joe Jensen this afternoon. When there is no implantation, all a person has to do to beat the system is to cut his wrist computer. This makes it very simple for Guardian members to defect. Since we cannot implant certain key personnel without inhibiting their ability to function as needed, the implantation of family members will discourage any of them from considering foolish alternatives."

"I see," Clayne said, not trying very hard to hide the bitterness in his voice.

"Once martial law is lifted, those implantations will be removed."

"Major Denison?" Estelle Hardy, the mayor, spoke.

"Yes?"

"You said that the Punishment Mode will be applied to people breaking curfew. Surely that is not the same as treason. Is such drastic action really necessary?"

"Mayor Hardy," the Major said patiently, "these rebels can only function effectively with the help of the citizens—either deliberate help or unsuspecting help. We must isolate them, cut off their ability to move freely about the city."

He smiled, and Nicole supposed it was meant to be a kindly smile, but in the context of what he was saying, it became grim, almost macabre.

"Actually, for tonight, the first night, we will use only small increments of the voltage, just give them a sharp jolt or two. But—" his voice rose sharply, "thereafter, it will be a very painful experience. And for anyone found helping or abetting the rebels in any way, the Punishment Mode will be the maximum. And that means a very painful death. Please make that very clear to the people. Treason threatens our very society and, therefore, will bring the maximum penalty."

"Major?" It was Roy Hartford again. He spoke quietly into the hushed silence that followed the statement. "You said all media reports on the crisis had to be cleared by committee. How is this to be done, and how long will it take?"

"Good question. Our intent is to expedite the clearance as much as possible. Captain Travis Oakes will chair the public communications committee. He has personnel already standing by to clear your reports of this meeting immediately after we close."

Charles Cowles, president of KSHV-TV raised his hand.

"Yes, Chuck."

"And violation of this media blackout on our parts would also constitute treason. Is that correct?"

The Major's eyes narrowed into icy blue slits. "Yes, that's correct. I don't like to—"

A sudden sharp buzzing filled the room, causing Nicole and everyone else to jump and stare at their wrist computers. They were all buzzing in synchronized rhythm. Nicole stared at the face as a message flowed across it in bright yellow letters.

ATTENTION ALL CITIZENS OF SHALEV. AN IMPORTANT ANNOUNCEMENT WILL BE SHOWN ON KSHV-TV BEGINNING EXACTLY THREE MINUTES FROM NOW. PLEASE TURN ON YOUR TELEVISIONS AND STAND BY.

Then it began again. ATTENTION ALL CITIZENS—but the
Major's angry roar jerked Nicole's attention away from her wrist.

"What's going on?" he shouted. "Chuck! What's the meaning
of this?"

But the president of KSHV-TV was as stunned as anyone in
the room. "I don't know," he stammered, his face white. "I told
them to stand by with normal programming until they heard from
me."

"Who's sending out unauthorized messages on the wrist computers?" Travis said. "That's what I want to know."

Once again the Major demonstrated his ability to take a shock
and recover quickly as he began barking orders. "Chuck, there's a
phone there in the corner. Call your station immediately and find
out what's going on. I want whatever announcement they are
making stopped until it's cleared. Travis, get down to Central
Monitoring and find out who's sending out messages to the wrist
computers. Clayne, there's a TV in the training room. Get it up
here on the double."

The buzzing of the wrist computers stopped, leaving the room
in hushed silence as Travis and Clayne hurried out the door.

Clayne was the first one back, pushing a television on a cart.
He was still in the process of getting it plugged in when Travis
burst back into the room. He ran to the Major and whispered urgently into his ear. And for the first time in her life, Nicole heard
the Major swear.

"The line is dead," Cowles called from the corner. "I don't understand it. I know someone's there."

"I understand it," the Major hissed. "It's Lloyd again. Shirley
Ferguson, one of our monitors in the computer center, is missing.
She programmed the announcement into the wrist computers and
then fled. We're looking for her now."

Shirley! Nicole nearly fell off her chair. Plain, plodding Shirley Ferguson? That was the same as being told that your donkey
had just won the AFC Race of Champions. And then Nicole remembered Joe Jensen. He and Shirley—of course. She shook her
head, stunned.

"We've dispatched a team of Guardians to the station," the

Major said, "but I'm not sure they can get there in time to stop the broadcast. But if they *are* there—"

"Here it is!" Clayne called as the insipid comedy on the screen went blank. He turned up the sound, and for a moment the soft hiss of static filled the room. Then the face of Mark Van Dam, KSHV-TV news anchorman, appeared on the screen.

"Van Dam!" Cowles shouted. "What's he doing?"

"Good evening, ladies and gentlemen of Shalev. We interrupt our regular programming to bring you a very special announcement."

The announcer was easily one of the most widely recognized men in Shalev and immensely popular. But now his face was as somber as Nicole had ever seen it, and tinged with pain. And Nicole understood. His implantation had not been removed, and he was suffering the consequences.

"At eight o'clock this evening, the city of Shalev was put under strict curfew," Van Dam said, speaking softly. "We have all been wondering what is happening and why. At this very moment, Mr. Charles Cowles, president of KSHV-TV, is in a meeting at Central Control with other media representatives and Curtis Major Denison, commander-in-chief of the Guardians. At this time we can only speculate what is being announced in that meeting, but we feel certain it bodes evil for the citizens of the AFC."

"I want him stopped," the Major commanded Travis. "Tell that team to hurry."

"Listen!" Clayne exclaimed, bringing every eye back to the screen and the face of Mark Van Dam.

"—felt that you, the citizens of Shalev, should fully understand what is going on, we have arranged an exclusive interview with the man who began this whole movement for freedom and who now leads the rebellion against the Guardian forces." His face twisted, and Nicole could see his lower lip trembling slightly. "Ladies and gentlemen, I am proud to introduce Mr. Eric Lloyd."

The camera moved back slowly to reveal Eric sitting next to Van Dam. He was dressed in a light blue sports shirt, and his expression was as serious as the anchorman's. He reached out and gripped Van Dam's arm, giving him an encouraging nod.

255

Nicole felt her heart drop. Guardians were speeding to the studio and would be there momentarily.

"Good evening," Eric said, looking as though he realized he was staring directly into the Major's eyes. "I bring you greetings from the free people of the AFC."

"Nicole!"

"Yes, sir." She jumped, startled by the Major's sharp call.

"Get on the phone to Central Monitoring. I want a location trace put on Mark Van Dam as quickly as possible."

"Yes, sir."

"Major." It was the president of KSHV-TV. "This isn't live. It's a videotape." Nicole looked down quickly, afraid the relief sweeping through her would be evident for anyone to see.

"Are you sure?"

"Yes. Look at the window behind them. It's still light outside, probably a little before dusk. I'd say it was shot about two hours ago. They probably started the videotape and then fled."

"Do it anyway, Nicole. Van Dam's in on this, and I want him."

"Yes, sir." She strode to the phone and dialed quickly. A minute later, as she hung up, she forced a frown. "Mark Van Dam's been cut loose," she said. "He and Shirley were cut together near Alliance Square a few minutes ago. They've both disappeared. The Monitoring Room was trying to call us, but the line's been busy."

The Major swore again and slammed his fist down against the table.

"So he's done it again," Travis raged, his fists clenched as he stared at the screen.

Eric went on evenly. "We must talk swiftly, since the Major has undoubtedly already sent his troops out for us. Citizens of Shalev, our intent is not to simply be free, but to free all of you, to overthrow this twisted, sick attempt at paradise that Major Denison and Dr. Gould and the others who stand with them have forced upon you. We hereby declare our implacable opposition to the Major and all he has done here. We do not expect you to come out openly to join us. You saw the Major's reaction to opposition last week at the soccer stadium. We do not expect you to put your lives or those of your families in jeopardy. But you can help us. Let us move freely among you without betrayal. Let us strike at the Major from within the confines of Shalev and slip away undetected. We can hide from the eyes of the Guardians, but we cannot hide from you and still succeed. We ask only that you become blind for the next few days. For that we shall free you all. That is our pledge."

"And I pledge to you it shall not be!" the Major shouted.

As though Eric heard the cry, his head suddenly lifted and he stared into the camera. "Major Denison, I know you're listening, so let me close with a word to you. Hear me well. We feel it only fair that you should do more than simply sit on your orange and blue throne and pronounce lofty judgments upon us and the people who willingly help us. You are the cause of the war; therefore you should not be immune from its effects."

The room had grown deathly quiet except for Eric's voice, and every eye stared at his face on the screen.

"At first we toyed with the idea of sending a Punishment Mode to your wrist computer. That would be poetic justice, I suppose."

The Major visibly started, and the eyes of the group swung to him.

"But strangely enough, what you deem necessary for your subjects, you yourself decline to share. You have no Punishment Mode in your wrist computer, do you, Major. And yet," Eric went on, "you can't be left untouched when it's your claws that tear at the vitals of this people." Eric brought his hand up in a mock salute. "So, Major, we bring the battle to you."

Suddenly Eric disappeared, and for several moments the screen went dark. No one in the room spoke, but several glanced furtively in the Major's direction. Then the screen flashed on again. It was obviously nighttime, and a huge, well-lit house, surrounded by what appeared to be acres of lawn and gardens, could be seen dimly. The camera was badly out of focus, and the details were heavily blurred.

"Ladies and gentlemen." It was Eric's voice again. "Mr. Van

257

Dam has gone downtown to have his implantation removed and has not yet joined us. He asked that I continue without him. We are now broadcasting live. I am here at the outskirts of the city, standing at the edge of the thick lawn that marks the beginning of the palatial estate of one of Shalev's foremost citizens.

"Most people in Shalev have never seen this view, since the estate is walled off and hidden in a thick stand of trees." Eric spoke slowly and clearly, as though doing a documentary for a group of school children. And then the cameraman began to bring the house slowly into focus.

Before it reached full clarity, the Major gave a sharp cry. "That's my home!" For one long moment he stared, his eyes wide; then he spun around and darted out the door, Travis hard on his heels.

"Perhaps Major Denison has recognized where we are by now," Eric said, as the stately French Provincial home finally came into sharp focus. "We're at the edge of the estate of Dr. Curtis Major Denison, commander-in-chief of the Guardian Forces in the Alliance of Four Cities."

"Major," Eric said, stepping into view in front of the camera, "your wife is here with me. She has not been nor will she be harmed. I suppose it would be to our advantage to take her hostage, hold her for some concessions, but she's an innocent bystander in this affair and therefore should be exempt from the war. Your maid and cook have likewise been escorted out."

The camera swung around to reveal three women. One was dressed in a long, white, silk pantsuit with her hair swept back off her face, and Nicole recognized Mrs. Denison immediately. The other two cowered close to her, dressed in robes and slippers.

"Oh, yes," Eric said as the camera revealed three still figures stretched out on the ground, each clad in an orange and blue uniform, "and the three Guardians you left here to watch things are likewise safe, though sleeping peacefully at the present.

"Major, we have checked the house carefully to make sure no one is there. Even your poodle is safe here with us." The camera swung once more to verify his word, revealing briefly a gray poodle on a leash held by Mrs. Denison. Then it swung back to Eric.

258

"We have no desire to hurt innocent people, only to let you know of our intent to bring you down." He turned his back to the camera to face the home and lifted his hand. For one moment it was poised there, like an ax over a chopping block; then it dropped.

With a shattering roar, the front of Major Denison's beautiful French Provincial mansion bulged outward and then exploded into a thousand thousand pieces as an orange-yellow ball of flame burst out of its puny confinement. The roof lifted up, then settled down on the billowing blast of flames, flattening them as they swept outward.

Even as she stared, Nicole felt Central Control shudder, and the windows of the conference room rattled softly. She and the others ran to the windows and threw back the drapes. High up, near the base of the mountain that formed Shalev's western flank, a tiny ball of orange light flickered upward, pushing back the darkness around it.

Behind her, Nicole heard the television speaker. It was Eric's voice, and he spoke only two words. "Goodnight, Major."

CHAPTER

30

It was nearly two-thirty in the morning when Travis came down the deserted halls of the fourth floor suite of offices and knocked softly on the Major's door, then slipped inside when he heard the muffled command to enter.

The Major sat behind his desk, looking as fresh and tireless as if he had just risen from a long night's sleep. His suit and tie were still immaculate. Sometime since the shattering loss of his home, he had taken time to shave. Travis shook his head wearily as he sat down, rubbing at the stubble on his own jaw. He felt rumpled, strung out, and ready for a shower and bed.

"No sign of them, I presume," the Major said.

"None."

"That's no great surprise." He leaned back, his reflection clearly mirrored in the polished expanse of the empty desk top, and his hands came up to form a fingertip steeple.

"Major, I haven't had much chance before now to say this, but I'm sorry about your home."

The older man shrugged. "Houses can be rebuilt." Then in a musing tone he continued slowly. "In a way, it has value, for it's revealed a flaw in Eric Lloyd that could prove very helpful to us.

Eric is a man of principle and has a rather highly charged sense of fairness."

"Your wife, you mean?"

"Yes. He could have taken her hostage or even killed her and done me great harm. But he didn't. If he won't go for the jugular when he has the chance, that gives us a decided advantage."

Travis shook his head dubiously. "Maybe."

To Travis's surprise, the Major smiled. "Actually, in addition to Eric's high principles, we have another strong advantage."

"What?"

"Joe Jensen."

"Joe Jensen?"

"Yes."

"Do you mean—"

"Yes. Joe came to me a couple of days ago. He and Rod Loopes are old friends. Rod had called him and offered him a chance to join Eric. Joe played along with them. Said he wanted time to consider it. Then he came directly to me."

"Well, well, well," Travis breathed in admiration as he leaned back in his seat.

"I told him to go along with anything up to serious injury of our people. If it comes to that, he's to get out."

"And Shirley?"

"Yes. Her too. We figured that having Joe ask her to join him was a natural for Eric to swallow." He groaned. "I didn't expect her to send that message over the wrist computers. But on the other hand, I gave her the same instructions as Joe. I suppose it's worth it. I think Eric has bought their authenticity."

"Have you heard anything from them?"

"Not yet. It's still too early. I told them to watch for a chance to use the radio, call in to us when they can. If we could find that base camp . . . But they are to risk calling only if they can bring us to Eric or if something critical is going to happen. I don't want the others without him."

"Well, well, well," Travis said again, his spirits suddenly soaring.

"I thought you'd be pleased. I think you can understand why I didn't tell you earlier. I wanted your reaction to be completely natural."

"Of course." Travis sat back, unable to believe that the tide had just turned in their favor. "So the Trojan horse is inside the enemy camp."

"Yes, but the battle isn't won yet. I—" At that moment, a soft knock came at the door. "Oh good, that's Dr. Gould now. Come in."

The short, balding man entered, still clad in the brown suit he had worn at the conference the night before, his face lined with weariness. They exchanged greetings, and, as Dr. Gould sank into the chair with a groan, the Major sat back down. "What did you and Max decide?"

"Yes, he says he can do it. In fact, he brought a unit that will fit inside her wrist computer nicely. We're ready any time you are."

Travis started. *Her wrist computer?* But the Major broke into his thoughts.

"Do you remember Max Grant from our Research and Development Department in Mount Pleasant?" the Major asked.

"Yes."

"I sent the chopper for him last night. He and Wayne have been working on an idea."

"Good."

The Major rubbed his chin thoughtfully. "Well, you may not think so when you hear it."

"Oh? Why not?"

"It has to do with Nicole."

"Nicole?"

"Yes. First of all, let me say that my hope is that with the help of Joe and Shirley, we can find Eric and put an end to the whole matter. But if not . . ." He took a deep breath. "Travis, I think Nicole has gone over with them too."

For a long moment Travis stared back at the Major. "Why do you think so?" he finally said softly.

The Major held up the fingers on one hand and began to tick them off with the index finger of his other. "First her 'miraculous' escape. She says she hit Eric over the head and fled, yet she had the presence of mind to take the packhorse, the radio, matches, and so on, so she could signal us for the rescue."

"Don't underestimate Nicole's resourcefulness."

"I don't. But the whole thing looks a bit too pat."

"Then why did she come to the stadium without a uniform? Why did she insist on running to Mount Pleasant to see her aunt? If she was with Eric, she would have come right back to us. Why did she tell me she was going to resign from the Guardians?"

"All excellent questions, and I must admit they threw me too. But number two, why did she suddenly change her mind when she felt so strongly about it? And third, why all of a sudden is she so cooperative, almost eager to please?"

"I—"

But the Major went on, swiftly overriding his answer. "When I called her in after the meeting last night, why did she agree to continue in Central Monitoring during the period of martial law? If she's so squeamish about what happened to Dr. Cameron, why is she willing to stay on now when we are threatening maximum Punishment Modes all over the place?"

"So she won't be implanted."

"Maybe," the Major agreed. "Yes, that's a possibility. But I still wonder. I think Eric let her go in the mountains. She wasn't completely convinced then, but she was wavering. She wanted time to think. After talking to you Saturday night, she finally decided. Or maybe Eric or one of his men finally got to her and convinced her to join them."

"What do you want to do?" Travis asked.

"Put another Trojan horse inside the gates. Only this time even the horse won't know it."

"How?"

"Two things. First, we want an electronic bug on Nicole's person. If she is teamed up with the rebels, that will be the quickest way to know it."

Travis took a deep breath and let it out slowly. "And second?"

Dr. Gould leaned forward and turned to look at Travis. "In the early stages of our research, even before Termination, Dr.

Denison and I experimented with different kinds of implantations, and—"

"No!" Travis shouted. "No implantation! It will destroy her!"

"Hear him out, Travis," the Major said gently.

"It was crude by our standards today. We took a tiny radio receiver with two stubby little electrodes and inserted it under the skin at the base of the spinal column. A patient would be put under observation. If he misbehaved, we triggered a signal that pumped an electrical charge into the spinal cord. Intense pain resulted as long as the signal was maintained. But it was very unwieldy and impractical because the person had to be kept under twenty-four-hour observation, and only outward behavioral symptoms could be punished. That's when we started developing an internal, automatic control system implanted in the brain."

"There is no automatic punishment response in this system, Travis." The Major waved his hand. "She won't even know it's there. Unless we push the button, she'll never have any pain."

"You insert a radio receiver in her back, and she doesn't even know it?"

"Yes. I'll explain how in a moment."

"Why the implantation?" Travis demanded, obviously wavering. "Bugging her wrist computer will lead us to Eric, if—" he paused, his eyes bitter, "—if she's really with them. So what's the purpose of implanting her?"

The Major looked away, unable to meet Travis's demanding stare. "We think something may be developing between Eric and Nicole, Travis. I'm sorry, and I sincerely hope we're wrong. But if we're right and somehow he cuts her wrist computer and she slips away to him, the implantation will give us leverage. We'll have a hold on Eric. We can trigger intense pain from virtually any distance."

Travis was silent for almost a full minute, his face drawn. Finally he nodded. "How can you implant her without her knowing it?"

The Major smiled. "We have arranged for a minor accident to happen tomorrow in the Monitoring Room."

CHAPTER

31

Clayne Robertson stared at the patches of white on Sarah's neck as she bent over the stack of blocks to help her younger brother. He looked away angrily.

Adrienne leaned across the table, pushing aside the dishes from the quick dinner she had fixed for him, and put her hand over his. He looked up, his own eyes softening when he saw the moistness in hers. He swung around to face her, covering her slim fingers with his massive palms. "Hi."

"Hello, big man."

"I love you."

The tears welled up and spilled onto her cheeks. "And I love you," she whispered fiercely.

He started to rise, but she reached out with her other hand to hold his on the table. "Clayne, do you really want them to catch Eric?"

His eyes narrowed. "What's that supposed to mean?"

"You liked him, didn't you?"

"Once," he snapped. "Once I thought he liked *me* until he blasted me with my own stun gun."

Adrienne nodded, "He was hardly himself that night."

Clayne shook his head stubbornly. "Be that as it may, my feelings have nothing to do with it. He'll be caught, and the Major won't be as lenient with him as with Clifford Cameron. Eric will be executed."

"I know," she whispered, " and yet what he's doing is right."

"Adrienne!"

"Well it is, and you know it."

"That's treason talk, and I won't hear any more of it. The Major is not playing. He'll stop Eric and anybody who tries to help him. Now that's enough."

"What if Eric asked you to join him?"

"Adrienne!" Though he had meant to whisper, his voice was so sharp that both Sarah and Timothy looked up, their eyes wide. Clayne leaned closer to his wife. "Adrienne, I mean it," he said in a fierce whisper. "No more!"

"I have a right to ask that question, because whether the answer is yes or no, it profoundly affects me and the children. So I want to know, Clayne. What would you do if Eric said, 'Clayne, come with us'?"

"I'd whip his fool tail into custody so fast he wouldn't know what hit him."

"Would you?"

"You'd better believe it. The man's insane to try this."

"Is he?"

Clayne leaped to his feet. "Woman, what's the matter with you tonight? You're acting as crazy as he is."

Once more her eyes swam with tears. "You know as well as I do that even if you were to catch Eric tonight, the Major will never remove our implantations. He's losing his grip on the city, and even killing Eric won't change that. Not ever. He can't risk decontrolling us again."

"That's not . . ." His voice trailed off, and he looked away.

"Your children and your wife are very soon going to be just like everyone else in Shalev. Is that what you want?"

He put his hands on the table and leaned forward, his eyes stricken. "Adrienne, the Major implanted you and every other family member of a Guardian officer precisely for this reason. One

266

misstep and he will terminate you or one of the children. There will be no more mercy."

"I know that."

"I waited ten years to find you and start a family. I would rather have you and the kids implanted and alive than—" He broke off and shook his head angrily. "No, Adrienne. The risk is too great."

"Eric has freed almost two dozen people now. Not one has been either punished or caught."

"Except for Dr. Clifford Cameron."

"All right. One. And that was only because he stayed behind to cover Eric's escape. Whole families have been freed, Clayne. *Whole families.*"

"Not since martial law was imposed," he countered angrily. "It's a whole new ball game now, Adrienne. They've rigged up the computers so that the moment someone's wrist computer is cut, it begins an automatic trace on them. Nicole says they can pinpoint the location of removal in under thirty seconds. And Travis has blanketed the city with roving teams of Guardians so they can respond quickly. No, Adrienne," he finished firmly. "I can't risk losing either you or one of the kids."

A figure suddenly stepped out of the hallway that led to the bedrooms, and Clayne shot up out of his chair, sending it crashing to the ground.

"Is that the only thing stopping you?" Eric asked. "The risk?"

"Come in, Eric," Adrienne said calmly. "As I told you, he isn't very easy to convince."

"Eric!" Sarah and Timothy leaped up and threw their arms around his legs.

"Hi, kids." Eric bent down and swooped them into his arms and swung them around. When he came full circle, he came face to face with the muzzle of Clayne's stun gun.

"Put them down, Eric."

Eric smiled. "Hey, big fella, you don't need that. I came unarmed, and I sure don't want to tangle with a moose like you."

"Put them down!"

Eric let them slide down his arms to the floor. "Okay, kids, away you go. Your dad and I need to have a little talk now."

267

Adrienne motioned toward the family room. "Okay, you two. It's time for television. Off you go."

"But, Mama," Sarah wailed plaintively.

"Now!" thundered Clayne, causing both children to jump and scamper into the next room. Timothy stopped long enough to peek around the door and give Eric one last wave.

Adrienne stepped directly in front of Eric and stared at her husband. "Clayne, I let him in."

"You what?"

"About ten minutes before you got home. At least listen to him."

"Clayne," Eric said, stepping out from behind Adrienne, "you're in it now, like it or not. Your wife has committed a treasonable offense by even letting me in the door. So what have you got to lose by listening to me? If I can't convince you, you can still take me in. Tell the Major you set me up in a trap."

The muzzle of the weapon lowered slowly, and Eric plunged in. "I find it interesting that in countering Adrienne's arguments, you only talked about the risk."

"So?"

"I heard no cries of betrayal, no speeches supporting the Major's cause, no affirmations of loyalty. Suppose I told you we have eliminated the risks. Then what?"

"Garbage!"

"Not all the risks, of course. You'd be in with us, and until this is over, that means danger. But what if I could guarantee that the Major cannot terminate your family via implantation?"

"Stop the snow job, Eric. You heard what I said about the computers."

"Clayne," Eric said softly, "Adrienne and the kids are not implanted."

Both husband and wife stared at him in stunned surprise.

"They're not," Eric continued calmly. "They were operated on, but nothing was inserted. We have a doctor and a nurse sympathetic to our cause who operated on Adrienne and the kids. An incision was made and the implantation was palmed. Then they were simply stitched back up again."

268

"I don't believe you."

"Adrienne, have you felt even one pain response since your operation?"

"No. But I've been careful."

"Have the children?"

"No," Clayne said. "But there again, we've been making a special effort to prepare them."

"If I can prove to you that they are not implanted, will you join us?"

Clayne shook his head slowly, but Eric eagerly pressed in. "You're right about the increased risk now. We don't want to jeopardize people's lives, so we've changed our strategy. We're planning one swift and final blow, one stroke designed to end it all and put the Major's little black boxes out of commission for good. Everybody is out of the city now except me and two others. And we're going tonight. If you come with us, your family will be safe."

"You can't get out of the city," Clayne said firmly. "We've doubled the patrols and—"

"We've sent six people out in the past two nights."

"I don't believe it," Clayne retorted, but it was obviously more of a startled reaction than an open challenge.

"We need you, Clayne." Eric's voice was full of earnest pleading. "We need your courage, we need your leadership, we need your knowledge of Shalev."

The older man watched Eric steadily, unblinking.

"And besides that," Eric added softly, "I think a great deal of you and your family. I'd like them to be free and safe from all this. I can't promise you no more snubs at the country club, but I can promise you that when people treat you right, it won't be because they've been electronically blackmailed into it."

Clayne finally turned to Adrienne. "And you knew this all along?"

"No. He only asked me to get you to listen to him."

"You keep forgetting this is the little twerp who blasted me unconscious."

Eric laughed softly. "The Bible says to turn the other cheek, to pray for them that despitefully use you."

Clayne looked first at his wife, then at Eric. Then he nodded. "Okay, how can you prove Adrienne isn't implanted?"

"Hit me, Adrienne."

"What?"

"Hit me. Slap my face. If you're implanted, you'll get an instant response the moment you lift your hand."

"I—I can't do that."

"Let me do it," Clayne broke in with a wicked grin.

"No way, you moose," Eric said. "You're not the one implanted. Come on, Adrienne, do it before he does."

Still she shrank back.

"Adrienne, hit him! It'll serve him right for sneaking in here and making a revolutionary of my wife."

The swiftness of Adrienne's hand caught both men by surprise, and the sharp sound of palm against cheek cracked like a rifle shot. Instantly she grabbed Eric's arm. "Oh, Eric, I'm sorry! Are you all right?"

He nodded as he rubbed his cheek. "Are *you* all right? That's the question."

Her hand shot to the bandage at the base of her skull. "Yes. I'm fine." She whirled around and threw her arms around Clayne's neck. "I'm fine!" she whispered, burying her head against his chest.

"Okay, Eric," Clayne said, his voice husky. "You can add four black folk to your little slave rebellion." He stuck out his hand.

Eric gripped it firmly. "It's a growing company," he said, "and you're getting in on the ground floor." Then he became businesslike. "Okay, Adrienne. Pack a few essentials. Warm clothing primarily. Remember we have to carry everything on horses once we hit the mountains. Clayne, bring your weapon and good hiking boots. Let's take your stun gun and your squad car. Any other vehicles may be stopped in the curfew."

"I've got a deer rifle and a hunting pistol."

"Bring them. Any ammunition too. Hurry, we've got another stop to make."

Clayne's bushy eyebrows raised. "Oh?"

"Yes. We've got one more person to persuade to join us."

270

With a sigh, Nicole set the book down and turned off the light over her bed. Sleep would probably still elude her, but . . .

She sat up suddenly as a soft rap on the screen was followed by an urgent whisper. "Nicole!"

She snatched her robe from the chair where she had thrown it and was at the window in three quick steps. "Eric? Is that you?"

She put her face next to the screen and saw his, split with a wide grin. "Hi, Nicky," he said softly.

"What are you doing here? We thought you'd left the city."

"May I come in?"

"Of course. Come around to the back door. I'll get dressed and be there in a moment."

She dressed swiftly, leaving the lights out, then moved through the house and unlocked the back door. Eric pulled open the screen and entered, a very happy Cricket at his side. As she pushed the door shut again and locked it, Eric clunked a set of heavy bolt cutters on the kitchen table.

"One of these days I'm going to come calling on you properly, ring the doorbell, come in the front door—the whole works."

"Why're you here? It's so dangerous. What if they're watching me?"

"They're not. I've spent the last half hour checking very carefully. Hey, what happened?" He gently touched the small strip of adhesive tape on her forehead.

"Oh, that. I got hit by a falling ladder."

"You what?"

"It was nothing really. Tuesday one of the custodians was changing a fluorescent tube over my monitoring station. He lost his balance, and he and the ladder fell on top of me."

"Are you okay?"

"Yes. It knocked me out for a few minutes, but other than a bad headache, a small cut on my back, and a few bruises, I'm fine." She looked up at him and smiled. "After a mother grizzly bear, a man with a ladder is hardly worth talking about."

"Good."

He picked up the bolt cutters. "Hold out your arm."

"What are you doing?"

"Nicky, we're leaving tonight. You're coming with us. It's getting too dangerous."

"But—you said you needed me in Central Control. Hasn't the information I've been sending you been valuable?"

"Extremely so. But we're pulling out now. The lives of too many people are at stake, yours included."

As he stepped toward her, raising the cutters, she grabbed his arm. "Now more than ever you need someone in Central Control. Isn't that true?"

"No. We need you with—"

"It *is* true. I'm terrified every moment, but if that's where you need me, that's where I'll stay."

Eric stared at her for a long moment, set the cutters on a chair, and took her by the shoulders. "Nicky, I wish there was time to say all this just right, but there's not. So here it is, straight out. I want you to come with me. I don't care how much we need you in Central Control—I can't leave you there any longer. I won't risk losing you. Do you understand that?"

Nicole's lips parted softly as she looked up into his face, wanting so much to believe what she thought she was hearing. "Eric, I—"

He shook his head, then put his arms around her and gently pulled her to him. "I'm saying I want you with me. Okay? I want to sit with you in the mountains again, talk about trivial things, throw pebbles in the river. I don't want to take any chances of that not happening."

She tipped her head back and looked up into his face. "I'd like that too, Eric. Very much."

A sudden urgent knock behind them spun Eric around and brought a sharp bark from Cricket. He unlocked the door and yanked it open, and Clayne Robertson thrust his head in.

"Eric, we've got to get out of here. They're coming!"

"What?"

"The radio's gone wild. They know you're here. Every available unit is on its way here right now. Let's go!"

Nicole stood rooted in place. "Clayne?" she cried in shocked surprise.

272

"Give me your arm," Eric commanded, snatching up the cutters. He inserted the jaws over the band, ignoring the sudden warning buzz, and snapped through the band, then whirled to Clayne. "Give me yours. We'd better cut you loose now too." Again there was a sharp snap, and Eric thrust the cutters at Clayne. "Cut Adrienne and the kids. Hurry!"

"Adrienne?" Nicole asked, still half stupefied by the sight of Clayne.

"Yes." Eric grabbed her elbow and propelled her toward the door. "Clayne and his family are going with us. They're out in the alley."

"But my clothes and things—"

"Go!" he thundered.

By the time they darted out through the garage and into the alley behind Nicole's home, Clayne was leaning through the window of the squad car and cutting Adrienne's band. The crackling of the radio shattered the quiet. As he pulled back out, Adrienne leaned forward, her face twisted with fear. "They're coming Code Three, but with no sirens," she said.

"They want to catch you by surprise." Clayne's expression was grim.

Eric opened the back door of the car. "Nicky, get in and help Adrienne cut the kids loose. Cricket, you get in there with them." Without waiting for compliance, he darted around to the back of the car, where Clayne had left the trunk open. He snatched up the deer rifle and a box of shells, slammed the trunk lid shut, tore the top of the box off with a savage jerk, and began jamming shells into the magazine.

"Listen, Clayne. The people who will get you out are at 536 Fairfax Avenue. They're expecting us. I'll try and keep these guys busy long enough for you to get clear."

Nicole's head popped out of the back window. "Eric, you can't stay!"

He ignored her. "Go to 536 Fairfax and tell them what happened. Now get out of here!"

Clayne hesitated for a fraction of a second, then nodded and moved swiftly to his door. "Good luck," he called softly. The door slammed, and the car shot forward in a spray of gravel. Eric caught a glimpse of Nicole's face, white and torn with fear, and then they were gone.

"All right, Major," he muttered, "one surprise deserves another." He broke into a run toward the front of the house. Less than a minute later, he saw the flash of headlights, and then the first car rocketed around the corner onto Nicole's street, tires squealing in protest. The round plastic top and orange and blue markings were unmistakable.

One quick breath, half out slowly, squeeze the trigger.

The windshield of the car shattered with an explosive spray of glass, and the car careened wildly to the right, hit the curb, bounced upward, then plowed into a chain-link fence with a shriek of metal on metal.

The second car, hard on the tail of the leader, slammed on its brakes when the first car veered off, then skidded broadside, rubber shrieking. Eric dropped the muzzle slightly and sent his second shot slamming into the front tire. It was like kicking one leg out from under a three-legged stool. The car flipped over, bounded hard on its side, then seemed to float momentarily before it slammed down on its bubble top and came to a shuddering halt in the middle of the street.

Eric heard the screech of brakes, car doors slamming, and the excited yells of men. Lights flicked on up and down the streets, and he prayed that none of the people would come out to see what was happening.

He scooped up the box of shells, crossed the sidewalk in two quick leaps, and vaulted the fence around Nicole's house. As he hit the grass, he gave a sharp cry of pain, and his left leg buckled under him. Nearly two weeks had passed since the grizzly's claws had laid him open, and the surface cuts were all but healed, but his leg was still too weak to take that kind of punishment. Biting back the pain, he pulled himself up, blasted off a quick round, then headed for the back alley in a lurching, hobbling run.

The alley that ran down the center of Nicole's block had no lights, and Eric welcomed the darkness. As he cut around her garage, he turned left, hugging the deeper shadows of a high wooden fence. But before he had gone ten steps, the sharp sound of shoes running on gravel spun him around. Two dark, barely discernible figures were running hard down the alley toward him. He swung the rifle up and pulled the trigger even as it cleared his hip. With a startled cry, the two figures split, each diving for a different side of the alley. Before Eric could lever another shell into the chamber, he saw the first dark shape rise, and then a blast of air smashed past his head, sharply enough to feel like a slap against his cheek.

Directly across from Eric's position, a high grapestake fence ran the length of the lot, coming to an end in a gate next to the garage. Taking a deep breath, he raised the rifle and snapped off a shot up the alley, then hobbled across to the gate—but not quickly enough. The stun gun blasted out with its highly concentrated and focused ultrasonic sound waves, catching him shoulder high. Had he been facing his attackers directly, he would have been knocked unconscious, but since he was moving sideways across the alley he took the main force of the shot in his upper arm and shoulder. Even then it slammed him backwards, spinning him into the fence. His head cracked against the wood, and his hands jerked out wildly, grasping for support. He was dimly aware that the rifle had been torn loose from his grip and clattered to the ground. He felt his legs buckle, and with a soft moan he went down. Through the daze he tried to push himself up, groping desperately for his rifle. But the footsteps came pounding up, and with one swift kick, the rifle was sent skidding away from his reach.

"Well, well!" Travis's voice was shrill with triumph. "Look who we have here!"

CHAPTER

32

"It's not like you to leave your back unguarded, Eric," Travis said as he jammed the muzzle of the stun gun into Eric's ribs and searched him quickly. "Where's Nicole?"

Eric got up on all fours, then staggered to his feet, as dazed by the bitterness of defeat as by the stunning blast he had taken. Travis grabbed him by the arm and shook him savagely. "Where's Nicole?" he shouted.

"I don't know. She left."

"I know that. With Clayne. Where are they? Where were they going?"

Again Eric shook his head. Travis slapped him hard across the face, the blow cracking sharply in the narrow alleyway. "Where are they?" he thundered.

Eric looked at Travis as a trickle of blood oozed from a split lip. "They took the dog for a walk."

Travis's eyes narrowed into slits, and he thrust his stun gun at the second man and said, "Hold this." When he turned back, his fist was cocked, pointed at Eric's face.

Eric tried to roll away from the blow, but it slammed him against the fence with stunning force. Travis grabbed him by the hair and yanked his head up roughly, his fist raised again. "Let me ask that question one more time, Eric. Where's Nicole?"

"I'm right here, Travis."

Travis and the sergeant whirled as Nicole stepped into the alley behind them, a stun gun raised and pointing at them. Her first shot took the sergeant squarely in the solar plexus. His hands flew up into the air, and both stun guns went flying. Travis lunged to the left, diving for the corner of the nearest garage, but Nicole had squeezed the trigger even as he jumped. The blow caught him in midair, flinging him clear of the garage. He bounced once on the gravel, then slid to a halt on his back.

"Nicole?" Eric cried, unable to believe his eyes.

She ran past him, kicked the stun guns away, and looked quickly at the two still figures lying in the alley. Satisfied, she whirled back to Eric and put her arm around his waist. "Come on, we've got to hurry. There'll be others."

Half running, half stumbling, she got Eric through the gate and shut it behind her. He stopped, dragging her to a halt. "What are you doing here?" he demanded, still half in shock, swiping at the blood on his mouth. "You're supposed to be with Clayne. Where is he?"

"Gone," she said. "Now let's go!" She grabbed his arm and pulled him forward again. "We've got to get across the next street before they start fanning out to cover our escape." She dragged him along with her, past the dark shape of a house, then along a length of hedge lining a driveway out to the curb.

"Can you run?" she asked, peering up and down the empty street.

Eric's head was clearing fast, and he nodded. "More or less. Let's go."

They leaped up, and Nicole supported him as he half ran, half hobbled across the street and into the deep shadows of a large willow tree. Suddenly the sweep of headlights filled the street as a Guardian squad car swung around the corner and moved toward them.

"Quick," Eric whispered urgently, giving her a shove toward the house, "into the bushes."

Nicole burrowed into a lilac bush while Eric made a leaping dive into a thick tangle of pfitzers, ignoring the fiery clutch of the needles. The squad car went by swiftly, its electric engine a low hum, and Eric breathed a sigh of relief. "We've got to get out of here," he whispered, rolling out from under his cover.

"Wait!" Nicole cried. "He's turning around."

At that instant the front door of the house opened almost directly over where Eric was crouching, and a dark figure stepped out. "Quickly!" a deep voice commanded. "Come inside."

"Come on, Nicky," Eric said, grabbing her by the hand and virtually hurtling through the open doorway, pulling her with him.

The door slammed shut, and a hand touched Eric's shoulder. "Follow me. Hurry!"

All the lights in the house were out, and Eric held Nicole's hand tight as they followed the man through the living room and down a hallway. Then he gave a startled grunt as the man stopped so quickly that he bumped into his back.

"Wait a moment." A small lamp flicked on, causing Eric to blink sharply. A tall, lean man bent over a telephone, his back to them. Nicole stared at Eric for a moment, then raised the stun gun.

"Jeff, this is Don Anderson. I . . . yes, yes. I heard it. It's the rebels. I have two of them in my house. I . . . yes, of course I mean it. I have them right here. Can you take them and send them on? There are Guardians all over the neighborhood."

Nicole dropped the muzzle of her weapon, a great wash of relief flooding over her as she squeezed Eric's hand.

"Good," Anderson said quickly. "We'll come through the garage." He hung up the phone and turned around. "All right, let's go."

"Thank you for what you're doing," Eric said fervently.

The man waved that away and then clicked off the light. "Let's go."

For the next hour, that was the pattern—one neighbor passing them through his house and on to the next. Sometimes they skirted as many as three or four houses, sometimes they crossed

278

the alleys straight across, but steadily they moved farther away from Nicole's neighborhood. Each time there was a quick handshake, a fleeting touch on the arm, and a solemn wish for luck. If any of the people—sometimes a single man, often a couple, once an elderly widow—were thinking of the consequences of their actions, they gave no sign. They were grim-faced and talked little, sometimes moaning in pain as their fear triggered bursts from the implantations, but no one hesitated or seemed regretful.

Eric had lost count of how many homes and yards they had transversed when one of their hosts—a man in his early forties, with two wide-eyed teen-aged boys—stopped them just as they were about to leave his garage. "Wait," he said. "I have an idea." He spun around and went back into the house, leaving his sons posted in the alley to watch.

Eric sank down on the cement and leaned against the car parked in the garage. For a moment Nicole stared at him in the darkness; then she joined him. It was too dark to see her face, but he could hear the anxiety in her voice when she spoke.

"How's your leg?"

"Sore," he admitted, massaging it gently, "but at least it's functioning. I'll be okay. How're you doing?"

"Marvelous, considering. I can't believe these people."

"Neither can I. Aren't they something?"

"That's not what I mean. How can they help us without triggering the implantation more violently than they do? Some seem hardly bothered by it at all. This is treason, a capital crime, and yet it seems to have no effect on them."

Eric nodded. "That's the one flaw in the Major's design. Something inside a man has an inherent sense of right and wrong. It doesn't matter what the Major says—these people know that helping us is not wrong. It's a capital offense only by executive fiat. Therefore, they get little or no pain response. If they were doing more than that, they'd probably have more trouble, but just to help us on our way . . ."

For a moment they were both quiet; then Eric spoke again. "When I see Clayne, I'm going to kick him in the shins for letting you go. However, I'll file a complaint later."

"He didn't *let* me go," she corrected. "When he wouldn't stop, I grabbed his stun gun and threatened to use it if he didn't let me out. I don't think I really scared him, but I did convince him you needed help." She paused. "Are they going to make it?"

"I hope so. If they get to Fairfax, they'll be fine. Clayne has the squad car, and squad cars are running everywhere right now. The way out is all set. I think they stand an excellent chance. In fact, they should be on their way out by now."

"And what about us?"

"Actually, that's an interesting question. I—"

The door behind them opened, and Eric stood up, pulling Nicole up too. "Hold on a minute," the man said, pushing past them. He slowly lifted the garage door and called to his sons. "Watt Thompson should be coming up the alley. Watch for him."

A moment later he grunted in satisfaction and stepped back inside. A short, squat man followed, no more than a darker shape in the thick blackness of the garage. The garage door slid down, and then the owner of the house opened the car door. The dome light inside was dim but provided enough light for them to see each other.

"This is Watt Thompson," the man said, motioning.

Eric stuck out his hand. "I'm Eric Lloyd. This is Nicole Lambert."

"Well," Thompson said in a voice that boomed even though he was whispering, "Lloyd himself. I'm proud to meet you."

Eric turned to the host and his two sons. "We didn't even hear your names and here you are risking your lives for us."

"Bill Johnston. This is Alan and this is Craig." The two boys grinned, half embarrassed, but obviously proud and excited.

"We think we may be able to help you," Johnston went on. "How?"

"I've got a permit to leave the city," Thompson said.

Eric's eyes widened. "A valid one?"

"Yes. I'm the foreman on the graveyard shift at a large lumber mill south of town."

Nicole's heart leaped with sudden hope. "Really?"

"And," he continued, "I happen to drive a camper. There's

some dead space under the benches on both sides of the camper, back where the wheel wells are. It'd be pretty tight for you, but I think you can squeeze in. We'd nail it shut. I don't think they'd ever guess."

"We'll do it!" Eric exclaimed. Then he turned to Nicole. "That is, if you're willing."

She nodded quickly. "It's no more risk than staying in town."

"Good," Thompson said. "I understand your camp is somewhere up toward Glacier Park. Once we clear the checkpoints, I could swing around north and drop you off wherever you say."

"No way," Eric said. "You just get us out of town, and we'll do fine from there."

"Okay," Johnston broke in, "we'll have to hurry. Watt has to leave by 11:30. That's less than half an hour from now."

"How can we ever thank you?" Nicole said, looking first at the father and then his two sons.

Bill Johnston held up his left arm so that the wrist computer gleamed in the dim light. "When it's time, come back and get these things off. That'll be thanks enough."

"Within the week," Eric said. "You have our word on it."

CHAPTER

33

Shirley Ferguson moved away from the campfire, zipping her jacket against the chill night air. She forced herself to walk non-chalantly, as though bored and absently looking for something to do. This took an effort of will, for her mouth was dry and her heart pounding wildly.

It was a beautiful, crystal-clear night, the smell of pine and woodsmoke filling the air, but Shirley had no eyes for the stars, nor was she aware of the scents in the air. She licked her lips nervously as she glanced around the circle of tents. Stephanie Lloyd was at the door of the children's lean-to, and Shirley could hear bursts of childish giggles. Other tents and lean-tos were dark, and only a few women and none of the other children were still awake. Charles Metcalf, the one man left in camp, was fussing around inside his lean-to, and Shirley noticed Madeline Lloyd sitting near the fire alone, staring into the night.

For the hundredth time, Shirley cursed Eric's thoroughness and caution. As soon as he and Nicole had come back to camp, he had insisted that they change locations immediately, moving down closer to the highway. He had also packed the radio in the gear stowed next to his lean-to. Neither she nor Joe had had a chance to get even close to it for a broadcast, so the Major still had no idea where they were or what was happening. Now Joe had gone back to Shalev with Eric and the others, and the final act was unwinding. Shirley had still not been able to get to the radio as Joe had told her she must. They had drawn times for watch turns, and Shirley had tried to maneuver for a night watch, but she had drawn the ten-to-noon shift. With the whole camp up and about and the radio only fifty or so yards away, she hadn't dared even lift the microphone.

At the edge of the clearing, she gave one last look at the camp, then turned and walked quickly toward the creek where Dick Andreason had rigged the aerial up a tall pine tree for better reception.

Dawn Metcalf, a middle-aged, graying woman, looked up in surprise as Shirley approached her through the low underbrush. "Hello, Shirley."

"Hello, Mrs. Metcalf. Any word?"

"None, but it's probably just as well. Charles showed me how to work this thing—" she patted the radio near her feet— "but I'm not sure I could."

Shirley dropped to the grassy creek bank, leaned back on her elbows, and tried to look bored, though once again her heart was pounding inside her chest like a series of tiny, repetitive explosions. *You must give Travis at least three or four hours' warning.* Joe had said it so easily as he had hurriedly kissed her good-bye that morning. He acted as though he was merely suggesting she walk down to the corner phone booth and place a call. *If you can't get to the radio in an inconspicuous way, then wait until after dark and knock out whoever is there. But you must warn Travis and the Major that we're coming.* Joe could do it—or Captain Oakes, if he were here—but Shirley went into cardiac arrest at the sight of a spider. She had never hit a person in anger in her whole life that she could remember.

She thrust her hands under her legs to stop the sudden trembling. Could she hit this kindly woman over the head with a rock? The very thought made her nauseated.

"You ought to be sleeping," Mrs. Metcalf said.

Shirley sat up and hugged her legs. "I tried. I just lay there and worried about Joe and the others."

"I know," the older woman answered. "The waiting is the hardest part." Then she ducked her head. "I suppose in a way that I have the easiest task, what with Charles being left here to supervise the camp. But he wanted to go with them so badly that I—"

"I know. He's still over there banging things around in frustration."

"He's too old. That's what he thinks, no matter what Eric said."

Shirley straightened, holding her breath. "Say, would you like me to take your turn? You could go be with him."

Mrs. Metcalf looked up, startled. "Oh, no, I couldn't do that. You already had your watch today."

Shirley pressed in, trying not to appear too eager. "That's okay. There's no way I'm going to sleep anyway. I may as well sit here as in my tent."

"Well, I don't know if I should."

Shirley felt her heart leap at the hesitation in the woman's voice. "Go on. Your husband needs you. Really, I don't mind."

"Are you sure?"

"Really."

Mrs. Metcalf stood up and brushed off the back of her skirt. "Well, he does need some cheering up. Thank you, Shirley. Thank you for being so thoughtful."

Not until the woman was out of sight did Shirley let out her breath in an explosive burst of relief. "Thank *you*, Mrs. Metcalf," she whispered triumphantly. "Thank you very much."

Madeline Lloyd sat staring into the small campfire, lost in her thoughts, her face lined with worry. As Stephanie came across the clearing and into the firelight, Madeline looked up. "Are they asleep?"

"Yes, finally." Stephanie sank down onto the log next to her mother.

"How many stories did they worm out of you?"

"Well, actually it wasn't stories. They wanted to talk about Eric and Nicole."

"Ah," Madeline said with a smile.

"How come Nicky had to go with the men? Does Ricky like her? Will they get married? Will I get to be a flower girl?"

"Married? Aren't they rushing things a little?"

Just then Adrienne Robertson came out of a small lean-to and walked over to join them. "Who's getting married?"

"Eric and Nicole, if our children have their way," Madeline answered.

"And me too," Adrienne said firmly. "I'm all for it."

"Well, they're hardly to that stage yet," Madeline responded.

"The children saw Eric kiss her last night," Stephanie said. "That's what started all the speculation."

Adrienne nodded. "I saw it too. I don't think Eric realized that half the camp could see them there in the trees."

They all chuckled and then gradually fell silent.

"And so," Madeline said, after a few moments, "here we all sit and worry about our men."

"And one woman," Stephanie shot back. "Why did Eric take Nicole down?"

Madeline's answer was patient. "You know why. She was the one who convinced them that they needed her. Clayne and Joe and Eric all know their way into Central Control, but only Nicole and Rod Loopes know how to run the computers. And Rod will be busy with Eric setting the charges. That leaves Nicole."

Stephanie sighed. "I know, I know. I just can't stop worrying about them."

The lines on Madeline Lloyd's face deepened. "Neither can I."

Adrienne stood up. "It's all this sitting around waiting with nothing to do. Come on, Madeline, let's go for a walk."

"You're right." She stood up. "Steph, do you want to come?"

"No, I think I'll go up and join Shirley at the radio—see if she's heard anything yet."

"Shirley?" Adrienne echoed. "I thought Dawn Metcalf was on the radio tonight."

"She was, but I think Shirley is worrying too, about Joe Jensen. She volunteered to take Dawn's turn."

"Okay," her mother answered. "If you hear anything, call us."

Stephanie, who had already started toward the creek, turned and waved. "I will."

As she approached the clearing through the trees, Stephanie could see Shirley's white sweater in the pale light of a quarter moon. She nearly called out to her; then she heard over the quiet gurgling of the water the murmur of Shirley's voice speaking into the radio. Stephanie felt a sudden clutch of anxiety. Had something gone wrong that they were calling in so early? She quickened her pace, moving through the short grass of the creek bank as swiftly but as quietly as possible, so she could catch Shirley's words. Shirley's first distinguishable sentence froze Stephanie in midstride.

"Yes, Captain Oakes, that's right."

Captain Oakes? That was Travis! Stephanie stared at Shirley's back and dropped into a crouch, inching forward to hear better.

"I will. If they call in, I'll radio immediately. Yes, I'm positive about the target. Eric hasn't given them any of the details, in case someone gets caught going in, but he did tell them what they were going to do. Joe said he'll try to get clear and call you as soon as he gets the details."

Stephanie reached down to the soft earth and pried loose a baseball-sized rock, then straightened slowly as Shirley finished. "Thank you, Captain. I'll call in again if we hear anything."

Shirley took the headset off and ran her fingers through her hair, then jumped and gave a startled cry when Stephanie appeared from nowhere.

"What are you doing?" Stephanie cried. "Charles!" she shouted. "Come up here—quickly!"

Shirley looked around wildly, her eyes large and white in the darkness.

"Move away from that radio," Stephanie said, raising the rock high and starting forward. Then she tipped her head back and screamed again with all the power in her lungs. "*Charles!*"

"No!" Shirley lunged forward, head down, and bulled into

Stephanie, coming up under the swinging arc of the stone. The rock flew out of Stephanie's grip, and the air whooshed out of her with a soft explosion of sound. She flew backward and hit the grass sprawling. With one swift movement, Shirley whirled and snatched up the radio, snapping the aerial with a sharp ping. Raising it high above her head, she hurled it against the rocks in the rushing waters of the creek. Then, like a deer pursued by a pack of wolves, she crossed the water in one splashing leap and disappeared into the trees.

Stephanie was on her hands and knees, gasping for breath, when Charles Metcalf came pounding up. He helped her to her feet. "What's the matter? What happened?"

"Shirley!" Stephanie managed to gasp. Her cry had aroused the camp, and the others were coming quickly through the trees.

Metcalf looked around. "What about Shirley? Is she hurt? Where is she?"

Stephanie shook her head, then blurted out the words between desperate gulps of air. "She ran—she was broadcasting—to Shalev. She told them—about Eric coming. I was too late—couldn't stop her."

Stephanie's mother and Adrienne Robertson had arrived in time to listen to the gasping account, and her mother's hand flew to her mouth. "Oh, no!"

Metcalf ran several yards upstream, his head turning quickly as he searched the night. Then he spotted the canvas bundle in the water. He retrieved the dripping hulk and set it down on the ground to examine it.

"We've got to warn Eric," Stephanie cried. "It's a trap."

"Nobody is going to warn anybody," Metcalf replied. "Not with this."

"That means Joe Jensen is probably one of them too." That was from Darla Kooska, whose husband was with the men.

"Yes," Stephanie said, gradually getting her breath back. "She said Joe will call Travis as soon as they're down there." She turned to her mother, her face stricken. "We've got to warn them!"

Metcalf shook his head and stood up, giving the radio a disgusted kick. "Both Eric and Clayne went down prepared for trouble. We can't do anything for them now. But we've got to get out of here. We have to assume Shirley told them where we are. We don't dare assume otherwise." He turned quickly. "All right, everybody, you know your jobs. We've trained for this very thing. Let's go."

He took Stephanie's arm. "If your mother helps with Dr. Cameron, can you handle the children?"

"Of course."

As one body, the frightened little group turned and ran for camp.

"Shirley called in!" Travis nearly shouted into the phone. "Eric is on his way here now."

"Great!" the Major said. "I'll be right down."

Travis paced back and forth nervously, his mind racing. When the door opened, he spun around. Then, without waiting for the Major to take a chair, he began giving him the report.

When he was finished the Major frowned. "The central computer banks. Then we were right. As much as he hates me, he hates what I have done even more."

"Exactly. That's why he's got Rod Loopes and Nicole with him. He's going for the heart of the system."

"Well," the Major said, "he'll never make it. We'll cut them down like young wheat in a hailstorm."

"Where?" Travis asked slowly.

"*Where?* Anywhere. In the city, at the outskirts. What do you mean where?"

"I have a suggestion."

"What?"

"Suppose we let Eric take Central Control."

The Major shot up out of his chair. "What? Are you crazy?"

Travis went on. "Maybe, but think about it for a minute. We both know that Eric is coming here, but Shirley didn't know exactly when or from which direction. Evidently Joe can't get away or get a radio to tell us what's happening. But we both know that Eric has the sympathy and support of many of the citizens. If

288

we start moving men—the numbers of men it will take to trap him—somebody will see it. Maybe they'll warn him. Eric could slip away from us again."

The Major nodded. "Go on."

"Even if we let him come to Alliance Square and try to take him in the central quad, we still stand a good chance of some of them slipping away. Perhaps even Eric himself. But Central Control is like a fortress. Besides the front entrance, there are only two ways in or out—the fire doors on the north and the south sides. They're heavy metal and locked. He'd have to blow them off to get in that way."

As the Major sat down slowly, Travis went on.

"Eric knows there's a skeleton shift at night, only one man at the front desk. So let's let him take his whole team inside, where we'll have two squads of men set up, one hidden in the cafeteria, the other in the main conference room. Once Eric and his people are inside, we'll have them trapped. And there won't be any citizens around to help him escape."

For a few seconds the Major was silent, considering the proposal. "With explosives, we're taking a tremendous risk. What if something goes wrong?"

"The computer banks are on the lowest level, at the very back of the building. Just to be sure, what if we put a third squad of men in the equipment room, which is just two doors away from the Monitoring Room. If for some reason the other two teams let anyone past them, the third group would still be in their way. For that matter, we could attack too, from the outside, the minute he's inside. We'll cut him off from both directions."

The Major slapped his hand down against the table. "Brilliant. Absolutely brilliant. I agree. How long will it take you to get ready?"

"Less than half an hour. Shirley said the target time was set for roughly two in the morning. That gives us plenty of time." He picked up a pencil and rolled it back and forth in his palms. "We also pinpointed the location of the mountain camp from Shirley's transmission. We'll sweep in there at dawn and get the rest of them. We can end this thing once and for all."

"It's time, Travis," the Major said grimly. Then he gave the younger man a long, appraising look. "And if something does go wrong, we always have our ace in the hole."

Travis's head shot up and then he finally nodded.

"If it becomes necessary, will you be willing to use it?" the Major asked.

"Nicole, you mean?"

The Major nodded, watching him closely. "Shirley confirmed that she will be with them. If it comes to that, can you watch Nicole suffer?"

Travis stared at the table for several moments; then he snapped the pencil in two and let the pieces bounce noisily off the polished surface. "Nicole who?" he said bitterly.

CHAPTER

34

So where is he?

Travis paced back and forth like a caged animal. His head turned each time he changed directions so he could watch out the huge glass windows of the Shalev City Library across the quad toward the dark shape of Central Control. Once again he glanced at his wrist computer. It was seven minutes after two.

The Major watched him check the time and stirred in his chair. "Well," he asked, "where do you suppose he is?"

Travis shook his head, the tension and frustration pulling down at the corners of his mouth. Then suddenly the radio crackled behind him, and the young woman manning it jumped to turn up the volume. "Command Base, Command Base, this is Charlie Four. Someone is coming into the quad from around the president's mansion."

Travis leaped to the microphone. "Charlie Four, how many do you see?" Charlie Four was the four-man team Travis had hidden on the top floor of the building closest to Central Control.

"Just one so far." There was a short pause. "It's a man. Seems to be alone. He has a rifle, but it's slung over his shoulder. He's heading for Central Control. And he's in a hurry. He's running."

"I've got him," the Major said, staring out the window with the field glasses. "But why just one? Surely they'll send more than one to make entry."

"All units stand by," Travis barked into the radio. "Don't anybody move until I give the signal."

Suddenly one of the units, too excited to identify itself, shattered the silence. "It's Corporal Jensen! It's Joe Jensen!"

Travis spun around in time to see 'the lone figure run up the steps of the front entrance and into Central Control. Travis jammed the mike back to his mouth. "Zebra Six, Zebra Six, the man coming in is Corporal Jensen. He thinks we're in Central Control. Send him over to Command Central. Tell him to hurry. I don't want Lloyd's men to see him."

He turned back to the window and nodded in satisfaction as a moment later the dark figure reappeared and broke into a run toward them.

For the past ten years, Donald Brownley had taught graduate chemistry classes at the Shalev Institute for Technical Studies, and for eight years he had been Charles Metcalf's partner in the Flathead Chemical and Fertilizer Company. Neither position had prepared him for tonight, and as he swallowed back the dryness in his mouth, he decided that all the fiction writers who had described the effects of fear on a man had grossly understated the case.

He and Eric were standing in the deep shadows of Central Control's western wall, where it was more than two stories high. Brownley fought back the almost overpowering urge to let his eyes measure exactly how high the wall was. Instead he forced them to watch calmly as Eric extracted a heavy coil of rope and a three-pronged grappling hook from the sack at his waist.

"Did I ever tell you I'm terrified of heights?" Brownley whispered as Eric carefully took the coil in his left hand and the hook in his right.

Eric chuckled softly. "Yeah, me too. Stand back." The hook sang softly in the darkness as he swung it in a cirle, its speed increasing with each revolution. Then he heaved it upward, the rope hissing after the hook. He jumped back as there was a soft clang of metal against brick, and the grappling hook plummeted back to the ground.

Eric again coiled the rope, stepped to the right to get a better angle, and started the hook swinging once more. This time it sailed up and over the top of the wall. He pulled slowly until the hook grabbed, tugged hard two or three times, then tested it with his full weight. Satisfied, he turned back to Brownley. "You want to go first, or me?"

Brownley shrank back from the extended rope. "I'm not kidding, Eric," he whispered. "Heights absolutely petrify me. I can't do it."

"What?" Eric stepped closer to see if he really was serious. What he saw evidently convinced him, because his eyes widened. "Why didn't you say something back in camp?"

Brownley forced a weak smile. "And have all the women think I have no machismo?" Then he added quickly. "I kept telling myself I could do it."

"And you can," Eric said firmly. "I'll go up first and then help pull the rope."

"Look, you don't need me up there. All you do is uncork the bottles and pour them into the air conditioning ducts."

"Oh yeah," Eric retorted. "Heights may frighten you, but that little concoction you put together gives me the jitters. No way am I going to mess with it."

"Really?" Brownley peered more closely at him to see if Eric was putting him on.

"Really! No way am I going up there alone with that stuff. Besides, we don't know what we'll find up there. It may take us both." Without waiting for an answer, he swung the bag so it hung directly behind him and moved up the side of the building hand over hand.

The moment he cleared the small retaining wall around the edge of the roof, he looked around, then leaned over the edge. "Okay, Don," he called softly. "Come on up."

For several anxious moments, Eric didn't think the middle-aged man was going to do it. "Come on, Don!" he urged in a low hiss. "Do it! We've got to hurry!"

For several long seconds Brownley stared up, shaking his head, a mindless, unreasoning panic paralyzing him. Then Eric flipped the rope, and it brushed against his face. With a sudden burst of will, he grabbed at it, bit his lip, and muttered, "Otherwise how will I ever face my fans?" He leaped up, pulling on the rough hemp, his eyes shut tight.

"Climb, Don," Eric urged, the dead weight nearly pulling his arms out of the socket. "Use the building. Help me!" Bracing his feet, Eric started hauling the rope up until Brownley's head appeared, and one hand shot up to grab the edge of the wall. Eric quickly grabbed that hand, then both hands, and hauled him up and over the top.

"Man," Brownley gasped, "that's terrible!"

"You made it! Come on, let's get moving."

"That's easy for you to say, Tarzan," Brownley moaned, gasping for air. "You're only twenty-four. I'm forty-nine—or I was before I started up that wall. Now I'm sixty-nine."

"Let's go, old man," Eric said with a grin. He moved quickly in a low crouch to a dark shape that was emitting a low hum.

Brownley lurched to his feet, muttering to himself, "Which means I'll be eighty-nine when I get down."

"Here's one," Eric said, tapping on the air-conditioning unit. Then he pointed. "There's the other."

Brownley could manage only a nod as he collapsed next to Eric, who was opening the sack and pulling out the two plastic bottles.

"Will the air conditioning send this stuff all the way through the building?"

"Oh, yes," Brownley said. "These will do just fine." He uncorked the first bottle. "Avert your head and cover your face, please," he said, following his own command. "It would be a shame if we took a whiff of this and ended up sleeping peacefully on the roof."

"Are you sure this stuff will work?" Eric put his arm across his face as Brownley poured in the liquid.

294

"Of course. As I told you before, it's colorless, odorless, brings unconsciousness in less than thirty seconds, and the person wakes up in about an hour with no side effects other than a slightly fuzzy head. One of the chemical companies I consulted for before Termination developed it for the CIA and other intelligence agencies."

"And you're sure it'll be gone by the time we're ready to go in?"

Brownley shook his head. "You make me feel a little better about being afraid to climb up that wall."

"Well, this stuff makes me nervous."

"It breeds a healthy respect in me too," Brownley agreed. As they moved across the roof to the second air conditioning unit, he continued. "But, yes, it'll be gone by the time we go in. It gassifies on contact with air and dissipates very quickly." He uncorked the second bottle and, averting his head, poured it slowly into the whirling fans. "All right. That's it."

"Good, let's get out of here."

"Any other way down besides the back elevator?"

"Sure, I'll call you a helicopter."

"Your empathy and understanding are really touching," Brownley sighed. "Why don't you just throw me off?"

They had reached the edge of the roof, and Eric handed him the rope. "That's my second option," he growled, "so get going."

Stanley Kooska, former owner and operator of the Kooska Mill and Lumber Company, liked to tell people he was a big-game hunter. Elk, moose, mountain goat, bear—he'd shot them all, he would say, and watch their eyes widen. Then when they were dutifully impressed, his wife or one of the kids would break in. "Ask him what he shot them with," they would suggest. And then Stan would trot out the finest examples of his photography. Though people invariably oohed and aahed over his work, they were never quite as impressed when they found that his weapon was a camera. This always left Kooska faintly irritated, because his hobby required far greater stalking skills and infinitely more patience than that of a hunter.

That was why Eric had placed him in command of this team, he decided. He stopped in the thick darkness of an aspen tree near the southwest corner of Central Control and let his ears sift the soft sounds of the night.

"No one should be guarding the south fire door," Eric had said. "But it's our way out, and we need to be sure we can use it. If anyone *is* there, you've got to see them without their seeing you. Move as if you were part of the night."

Kooska had taken him at his word, and now it paid off. A soft cough and brief rustle of the foliage were barely audible over the sighing of the wind in the trees, but to Kooska's ears they sounded like a chain saw in the vast silence of a forest. It took him one minute to find the man, sitting in a thick patch of foliage. In ten more minutes he circled slowly and found eight more, all facing the circle of light that illuminated the fire exit, all armed and waiting.

Satisfied that he had located all there were, Kooska backed away slowly, puzzling over what he'd found. Eric's little rebellion had unquestionably put Shalev on alert, and the Major was known to be a careful man, but this was no precautionary guard. It was an ambush, a trap set to slam shut on the first person who stuck his nose out the door. And that was an ominous sign. For the first time since they had left the mountains, Kooska felt the uneasy pricklings of fear rumble in his stomach.

He had left the six other members of his team waiting near the low ridge that protected Central Control's back flank, and it took nearly ten minutes to make his way back there, still moving with the utmost care. As he called out softly, he noted that several of the men jumped, which made him smile. He had moved undetected to within twenty feet of them—and they were watching for him!

"We've got trouble," he said, as he stepped forward to join them. "Get Eric on the radio."

"So do we abort?" Clayne Robertson's voice was angry.

Eric shook his head and drummed his fingers against his leg.

"How long ago do you think Joe left us?"

"We're not sure," Nicole answered. "No one actually saw him go. We thought he had gone with Kooska's team, but Stan said he assumed he had stayed with us. He must have gone not long after we left the van."

"Was he with us when we split into two teams?"

Rod Loopes shook his head. "No, I'm sure of that." The former head of computer services for the Guardians was deeply upset, for he had recommended that Joe Jensen be brought into the movement. "Maybe he just got behind and got lost."

"We have to assume the worst," Clayne broke in, impatient with their unwillingness to grapple with the real question. "Joe's gone, and nine men are waiting at the back door. We've been blown—there's no question about that. So the question is, do we abort or do we go ahead anyway?"

"If Joe *is* the Major's man," Rod Loopes broke in, "then Shirley Ferguson is probably with him."

Dick Andreason, the radioman, nodded. "Which puts the camp in danger."

"These radios," Eric said, touching the walkie-talkie at his belt, "there's no way they can reach the camp?"

Dick shook his head. "No, but we've got the big radio in the van. I can be there in two minutes. We told the camp to keep a watch on the radio all night."

"All right," Eric said. "Go call them. Tell them to pack it up and move out fast. Tell them also to watch Shirley."

"Right." Andreason turned and hurried back up the hill.

"Okay," Eric said, turning back to face the others. "We've got two things in our favor. We didn't tell you any of the details of how we were going to get into Central Control, not because we didn't trust you, but because we didn't dare risk your knowing too much if you got caught. So that means Joe doesn't know the details either. He left before we split into teams. He knows we're going out the side door, but he doesn't know Stan is there and has spotted the ambush. And the Guardians there don't know they've been spotted either. That gives us another advantage. Also, we didn't tell any of you about putting the knock-out liquid in the air conditioning until we arrived here at the building. Only Don and I knew anything about that, so that's another surprise in our favor."

He looked around the circle of anxious faces. "Clayne is right. We have to assume that Joe and Shirley have betrayed us. If so, we also have to assume the Major and Travis have planned a little trap. But why haven't we hit it yet? Why didn't we see any Guardians before this?"

Clayne saw his reasoning almost instantly. "Because the trap is here, at Central Control."

"Inside. They'll be waiting for us inside," Nicole said, also seeing what Eric was getting at. "Which means they too will be knocked out."

"There *are* nine at the south door," Abernathy said, shaking his head. "What if there are others elsewhere out here?"

"A valid possibility," Eric agreed. "But we're committed now. We've put the stuff into the vents. If we do abort, they'll know we were here, and we can never use this tactic again. It'll mean a head-on assault to get to those computers."

The silence hung heavy for a moment. Eric took a deep breath. "If my father or Cliff Cameron were here, they'd say we have yet another advantage."

"What?" Dick Andreason asked. "We need every one we can get."

Eric looked from face to face, finally stopping with Nicole. "Heaven favors the just cause."

"I say we go," Clayne said. "If we don't take them out tonight, then our chance is gone."

"I agree," Loopes said.

"Nicole? Chet?"

Nicole felt her chest tighten and her stomach twist at the thought of what could be waiting for them. "I'm very frightened," she finally answered, "but I think we owe it to Cliff."

Chet Abernathy took a deep breath. "We never thought it would be a piece of cake," he said with a shrug.

Eric turned to his last man. "Don?"

"Will I have to climb any more ropes?"

Eric gave a brief laugh. "No, that I promise you."

"Then I think I can handle anything else."

Eric nodded, feeling a swift surge of pride. These weren't warriors, they were common people, everyday men and women caught suddenly in a web of war. He pulled the radio off his belt. "Stan, are you there?"

"Roger. Standing by."

"We're going in. Can you be ready to neutralize our friends?"

"Roger. How soon?"

"We should be coming out in no more than twenty to thirty minutes. Stay low until you see the door open. No matter what happens, don't let them see you until we come out. Then we'll try to catch them in a crossfire."

"Will do."

"And Stan?"

"Yes."

"If we're not out in forty-five minutes, we're not coming. Pack it up, get back to camp, and get our people clear out of the Alliance."

There was no answer.

"Is that understood?"

For a moment the soft hum of static was the only sound, and then Kooska's voice came soft but clear. "That's a roger, Eric. Good luck."

"Same to you." Eric looked quickly into his team's eyes, then spoke into the radio again. "Mark, have you been getting all of this?"

Mark Van Dam responded instantly. "Yes, Eric. We got it all."

"Are you all set there?"

"Roger. We're inside the studio waiting to broadcast. You buzz the people's wrist computers and wake them up, and we'll talk to them."

"Nicole will program the message the minute we get into Central Monitoring. Tell them we need them, Mark." His voice had lowered, and Nicole could tell he was feeling the strain. "Once we knock out the computers, their implantations will be neutralized. They can help us. Tell them that."

"We will," Van Dam said. "We'll send you the whole blinking city."

"Right. Thanks, Mark."

"Good luck."

When Eric looked up, his face was grim. "That'll be our last little surprise for the Major."

Just then Dick Andreason rejoined them. To Eric's questioning glance he shook his head. "There's no answer. I couldn't raise anyone."

"Oh, no," Nicole whispered, thinking of the children. "We've got to help them."

Eric shook his head, his face unreadable. "If they're in trouble, the best help we can give them is to wipe this building off the face of the earth." He reached out and took her hand. "Let's go."

CHAPTER

35

"You've done a great job, Joe," Travis said. "We'll wait until they're inside, and then we'll close in. There's no way they can get away."

At that moment the radio crackled into life. "Command Base, Command Base. This is Charlie One. We have a group of people coming out of the trees on the north side of Central Control. There are four—no, five—no, seven—seven people in all. One appears to be a woman. They're all carrying rifles, and three have heavy sacks."

"That team watching the north fire door had better stay out of sight," the Major growled. "I don't want Eric to see them and get spooked."

Travis had his binoculars up. "No, they're coming right along the building. Our men are up in the trees, out of sight." He turned to the radioman. "Winters, tell all units to stand by. I don't want anybody moving so much as an eyelash until I give the signal."

Joe shook his head. "There are more than seven. There were fourteen of us altogether."

Travis and the Major both looked startled. "Some of them must be going to wait in back to cover them."

"Or Eric may have sent them around to the south door," the Major said. "Winters, alert the team by the fire exit to watch for them. Tell them to stay out of sight."

Then both he and Travis lifted their binoculars again and peered out the glass front of the Shalev Library.

The men went in quickly, Eric going first, rifle at the ready, the others following. For a moment they stood together in a tight clot inside the main lobby; then one of them (Travis couldn't tell which) moved over and peered behind the desk.

"Where's Hendry?" Travis asked.

"Who's Hendry?" the Major demanded. "And how come they got in so easily?"

"Hendry is the desk sergeant tonight. I told him not to appear too alert and not to fight them coming in. But he's not even at his desk. That could make them suspicious."

"He was there when I went in," Joe Jensen said.

Just then the lights inside the lobby went out, except for a dim light over the desk. Travis half turned. "Winters, tell Zebra Six they're inside and should start moving down the hall any moment now. Tell them to stay alert. I don't know what's going on with that desk sergeant. Tell him to report to us the minute things are secure."

"Yes, sir." The young radio operator began barking out the order into the microphone.

For the next two minutes no sound from the radio broke the growing tension in the room, and Travis grew more and more impatient. Suddenly the Major swore. "What's the delay, Travis? They should have them by now."

Travis stared first out the window and then at the back of the radio operator's head, willing him to make the radio speak. "I don't know. Carlson has probably forgotten us in the excitement." He strode to the radio and snatched up the mike.

"Zebra Six, this is Central Control. Come in, please."

No answer.

"Lieutenant Carlson, this is Captain Oakes. What is your report? Have you made contact?"

Silence.

302

The Major leaped to his feet. "Something's wrong! Why doesn't he answer?"

"Lieutenant Carlson!" Travis shouted. "Anyone in Zebra Six! Come in, please! What's going on over there?"

Suddenly the silence was shattered by the shrill, synchronized buzzing of their wrist computers. As the four men jerked up their hands and stared, the bright yellow letters flowed across the tiny screens.

ATTENTION! ATTENTION! ALL CITIZENS OF SHALEV! STAND BY FOR AN IMPORTANT ANNOUNCEMENT. PLEASE TURN YOUR TELEVISIONS TO CHANNEL FOUR. AN ANNOUNCEMENT CRITICAL TO ALL CITIZENS WILL BEGIN IN EXACTLY TWO MINUTES ON KSHV-TV, CHANNEL FOUR. And then it began again. ATTENTION! ATTENTION! . . .

The Major, his face purple, grabbed Travis's shoulder and spun him around. "What's the meaning of this?" he screamed in fury.

Travis was stunned. "They've gotten into the Monitoring Room. But that's impossible!"

"Van Dam!" Jensen cried. "Mark Van Dam left camp the day before we did. I asked Eric about it, but all he said was that he had to go down and get some things ready for us."

"He's going to announce his victory to the people!" the Major shouted, almost incoherently. "We've got to stop them, Travis!"

Travis broke out of his shock and thrust the microphone up to his mouth. "All units! All units! Something's wrong. The enemy force is inside Central Control. Move in! Move in!" Then, without hope, he screamed into the mike once more. "Carlson! Answer me! Where are you?"

Eric poked his head around the door marked "Authorized Personnel Only" and looked across the Monitoring Room to where Nicole sat at one of the consoles. "Did you get the message off?"

"Yes, it's sent. I repeated it three times. It should wake everyone in the city."

"Good." He pointed to the woman who lay on the carpeting.

"You'd better drag her out of here. Take her far enough away that she won't be hurt when this blows. Then see if you can find the unit locations for the Guardians. If we're in a trap, let's find out."

Without waiting for a response, Eric went to the room where the rows of central processing units lined each wall and took clumps of reddish-gray putty from the sack. He was grateful they had found Don Brownley and Charles Metcalf, both excellent chemists. In the village they had been unable to make anything more complex than dynamite and gunpowder, but this plastic explosive, made by the two partners in Flathead Chemical and Fertilizer Company, was far more sophisticated and better suited for their task.

The plan was very simple. While Nicole stayed in the main room at the console, Eric, Rod, and Dick worked on the CPUs. Moving swiftly from computer to computer, Rod and Eric slapped the putty in large globs at the base of the machines. Then Dick, moving right behind them, inserted detonators into each glob, stringing a thin red electrical wire from patch to patch.

The detonating system was almost as simple as the plan. The heart of it was a small blue metal box with a red plastic button, much like a doorbell, only about three inches square. Andreason had wired both boxes—he had insisted on a back-up in case the first one malfunctioned—with two small flashlight batteries as the power source. A thick roll of electrical wire, long enough to stretch from the Monitoring Room out to the south fire exit, was connected to the clip at the edge of the blue box. From the other end of the wire dangled a small circuit board with a ten-second delay switch. Once connected to the wires leading from detonator to detonator, the circuit board required only one light push on the red button. The delay switch would activate, and ten seconds later a fury of explosive power would be unleashed. The device was simple, the results spectacular.

Almost a full minute later Eric heard Nicole cry, her voice muffled by the noise of the big units in the room. "I can't get access to the Guardian code. Someone has changed it."

"Try again!" he called. "We've got to know where they are."

"I've tried everything. They've changed it all."

Rod Loopes looked up, sweat pouring down his broad nose. "That's the Major's doing. He's nobody's fool." Then he turned his head and shouted, "Nicole, try tracking Travis with the regular monitor. See where he is right now."

Nicole's fingers flew over the keys, typing in the familiar number. Almost instantly the flashing light appeared on the board, and below came the sentence: PRESENTLY TRACKING TRAVIS OAKES, #G14332.

For a moment Nicole stared, trying to orient herself to the grid symbols appearing on the screen. Then her eyes widened in shock.

"Eric!" she shouted, "Travis is right across the square from us, in the Shalev Library." And then suddenly the light, which had been stationary, began to move. "He's coming here. Running!"

Clayne Robertson blinked once, then peered more closely through the glass doors out across the quad. The only light inside the lobby came from outside, making it difficult to see. "Don," he hissed, as he moved closer to the entrance, "someone's coming."

Don Brownley and Chet Abernathy both jumped to his side and peered out across the quad, unable to believe what they saw. The quad was suddenly alive with dark shapes running across the grass toward them, and they could hear the shouts of men through the doorway.

"We're under attack!" Clayne shouted as he pushed the door open and blasted off a shot at the nearest figure. As though he had used a cannon with an incredibly wide span of shrapnel, every figure suddenly disappeared, diving for cover or sprawling on the grass. Then, almost instantly, they returned his fire, and the front of Central Control exploded in a shattering spray of plate glass.

"Take cover!" Clayne screamed, diving for the sofa to his left. "Pin them down!"

The Guardians' opening volley had cleared the front entrance of everything but the metal framework, studded now with jagged shards of glass, and Don and Chet opened fire, the blast of the rifles deafening in the confinement of the lobby.

Clayne swept up his walkie-talkie. "Eric, we're under fire. It's a trap. We've got Guardians all over the place coming at us." He instinctively ducked as a bullet slapped through the back of the sofa, leaving a four-inch gaping hole not more than a foot from his nose.

With a cry he scrambled around the corner, glancing quickly at his two companions. Chet was behind the desk, while Don was in the corner almost totally without shelter, levering shells into the chamber and blasting away with a vengeance. "Don, get down!" Clayne yelled.

"Clayne!" the radio blurted.

He jammed the radio to his ear to hear over the explosion of the rifles and the angry whine of ricochets. "What?"

"We need another two or three minutes," Eric said. "Can you hold them?"

"Not here. We'll fall back down the halls, delay them at every corner. But it won't be long. There must be several dozen of them, and most of them have rifles."

"Do your best. We'll hurry. Give us two minutes, and we'll go out the back all together."

Eric slapped his last wad of putty against the base of one of the metal cases and turned around. "Leave the rest. Dick, wire up whatever we've got, and let's get out of here."

"No," Rod cried. "I can be finished with them all in another thirty seconds."

"And I'm right behind him," Dick added.

"All right, but hurry!" Eric darted out the doorway into the Monitoring Room. Nicole was standing at the door, looking anxiously up the hallway, rifle at ready. Eric grabbed his rifle and ran to her. "You cover the side doorway that leads to the back exit just in case."

The muffled blasts of rifle fire grew louder. Then suddenly the clatter of footsteps echoed in the corridor, and the three men dashed around the corner about thirty feet away and came pounding toward Eric. Chet whirled and fired a shot back the way they had come. In the narrow confines of the hallway, the reverberating blast was a sharp stab of pain against the eardrums.

"Come on, Chet!" Eric shouted. "I'll cover you. Don, get inside!"

An orange-clad figure hurtled around the corner, took one startled look down the corridor at Eric, and tried to change direction in midflight. He bounced off the wall and dove back behind the corner as both Clayne and Eric fired together. They ducked instinctively as the black snout of a rifle was thrust around the corner and fired wildly back at them.

"Inside!" As they dove through the door, Eric shouted through the opening of the doorway into the room with the CPUs. "Rod! Dick! Let's get out of here before they cut off the side exit."

Rod Loopes came out of the computer room in three strides. "That's it. Dick's almost done."

Andreason was right behind him, carrying the blue box and unreeling the spool of wire as he came. "Okay," he called. "It's hooked up." He handed the box to Rod Loopes. "You take this and let me take the rifle. Just don't bump that button!"

"All right, let's go," Eric commanded. "Don, check the hallway—see if we're clear. Clayne, you and I'll cover the rear while Rod unrolls the wire."

Don Brownley opened the side door that led out of the Monitoring Center, peeked around the frame, then nodded. "It's clear, let's go!" But as he stepped out, turning back to see if the others were coming, he suddenly flew backward and upward, jerked completely off his feet. He slammed back hard against the door, staggered once, then pitched face down to the floor.

"Don!" Nicole screamed.

In one leap, Eric was to the door, now propped half open by Don's body. "Help me, Nicky. I'll cover the hall while you pull him in."

He stuck the muzzle of his rifle around the door, fired two quick shots, then leaped over Don's form into the hallway. His first shots had sent the two Guardians coming down the hall frantically back around the corner where they had been hiding. He pumped another shell after them, hoping the screaming ricochet would drive them even farther back, then whirled and helped Nicole drag Don back into the room.

"Stay clear of the doors," Eric commanded. "Cover them from the center of the room." Then he turned to where Chet was kneeling over Don Brownley. "Chet, how badly is he hurt?"

Chet Abernathy pressed his finger into Don's throat just below his jawline, then removed his hand slowly and rocked back on his feet. "Dead."

"No!" Nicole gasped, her face white.

"Yes. They're using maximum power on the stun guns. He died instantly."

"Shhh!" Clayne commanded, pointing at the main door of the Monitoring Room. The lock rattled almost imperceptibly as he raised the rifle. The blast was like the explosion of a stick of dynamite in the small room, and the heavy wood panel of the door shattered. There was a sharp, muffled cry and then a heavy thudding sound. The smell of gunpowder filled the room.

"That's one for one!" Clayne said savagely.

"At that rate," Eric snapped, "we don't stand a chance. We've got to get out of here."

Suddenly the overhead speaker blared. "Eric!"

The six of them jumped in surprise and then stared at the ceiling.

"Eric, this is Major Denison. You're cut off in both directions. I can hear every word you've been saying. If you'll flip the switch on the control panel, you can talk to us. Nicole knows where."

Nicole swung around and stared at the switch in front of her but didn't move.

"Eric, it's foolish to go on killing each other. Let's at least talk about it."

Eric finally nodded, and Nicole stepped to the board and flicked the switch. "All right, Major," he said wearily. "Talk."

The Major shot Travis a look of triumph and covered the microphone. "Can you cut off the monitoring consoles from here?" he asked. They were in the confinement-cells section, sitting at the control panel Nicole had once used to trigger Eric's wrist computer.

Travis shook his head. "No, this gives us access only to the public-address system. But we can cut off the power upstairs."

"Do it! They can set off your punishment mode if they think about it. Shut the whole system down." He turned back to the microphone. "I must give you credit, Eric. You've been very clever. You didn't even open the doors to the cafeteria or the conference room. If you had, you would have seen that we had three squads of men waiting for you in here. What did you use to knock out the whole building?"

"Major," came the sharp reply, "you're not here to discuss tactics. What do you want?"

"True," the Major responded, almost amiably. "Actually, I wish to negotiate your surrender."

"Sorry."

"Look, Eric, you're no fool, never have been. A wise man knows when he's defeated."

"True. And so far, we don't see it that way."

A look of exasperation briefly marred the smooth features, but the Major spoke with a tone of patient goodwill. "We can come in there, overwhelm you with sheer numbers. I have over fifty men out here. But I don't want either my men or yours to die needlessly. You cannot win."

"Major, that depends totally on what you mean by winning." Now Eric's voice was easy, almost conversational. "We have one hundred fifty pounds of plastic explosives wired up to your little machines in here. We hoped to get away clear, but our primary objective is to wipe out the heart of your little psychological dictatorship. So we haven't really failed, have we?"

"You're sitting right on top of those explosives. You won't annihilate yourselves."

"Eric!" Nicole's whisper was muffled but still clearly understandable through the speaker, and the Major cocked his head to listen. "We have the monitors in here. We can trigger the punishment mode in Travis's wrist computer."

There was a moment of silence; then Eric's voice responded in a whisper. "Get Travis on line."

At that moment, the door opened, and Travis came back into the observation room. The Major shot him a questioning glance, and he nodded. "The monitoring terminals are shut down completely."

The Major nodded, unable to repress a tiny smile of triumph. For several minutes things had looked bleak, but they had turned them around. "Eric, the time for bluffing is over. You have a problem and no way out of it."

"No, Major. *You* have a problem. We're not bluffing. I'd like the side hallway cleared immediately."

"Or?"

"Or we'll push the punishment mode on Travis's wrist computer. We can terminate him just as you tried to terminate Cliff Cameron."

The Major shook his head. "Nice try, Eric, but it won't carry."

"As soon as Travis dies, we'll send your next man down. And the next and the next. We regret, Major, that you have been wise enough not to link *yourself* up to—"

A sharp cry of dismay cut him off. "The terminals are off!" Nicole cried.

The Major sighed. "Now, Eric, are you ready to negotiate? There's no way you can win."

For a long moment there was no response. "Give it up, Eric," he said softly. "It's pointless to die for nothing."

"Major, we didn't come here as a suicide squad, but you may not leave us much of an option. Suppose we do surrender. Then what?"

"You'll be arrested, of course. But there'll be no need for punishment. You'll simply be implanted once more, and then you'll not be any threat to us."

"Come on, Major," Eric said in disgust. "You said I wasn't a fool. We both know you'd never dare let me go around with nothing more than just implantation."

The Major sighed. "True, except for the fact that in your case—and I'll be honest with you—in your case it would be a

Stage Three implantation. It would be sufficient. It's not very pleasant to contemplate, but certainly better than death."

"Only in your mind, Major. I think we prefer the swiftness of high-powered explosives to any tender mercies you can promise. And at least that way, we would know that you hadn't won either."

"You're bluffing again, Eric." The Major spoke with arrogant confidence, but for the first time Travis saw his eyes cloud with worry.

"Am I? Two hundred thousand people out there are anxious to get their hands on you, Major. If I free them, it won't matter whether we live or die. Your empire is finished."

Travis grabbed the microphone. "If you care so much for those two hundred thousand people, you'd better not blow the central computers. It will automatically trigger Maximum Punishment Modes for everyone. And then, so much for freedom."

"Sorry, Travis." It was Rod Loopes' voice. "You forget I'm here."

Travis was unperturbed. "We've reprogrammed since you left, Rod, just in case something like this happened."

For a long moment there was silence; then in a whisper they heard Eric's voice. "Rod? Could that be true?"

The Major gave Travis a quick look of triumph, but it was instantly erased.

"No way!" Loopes said. "They couldn't risk that. Suppose they had a power failure and the back-up generators didn't work."

"Nice try, Travis," Eric called. "Major, we'll blow the computers unless we get a better alternative than what you're offering us now."

The Major stared at the microphone. "All right, Eric, we seem to have a standoff. What do you want?"

"Freedom for all of us," Eric said without hesitation. "Let us go, and we'll not blow your little game here. We'll leave the Alliance, and you'll be free of us."

"Now who is shamming who? But I think there's one other thing for which we might bargain."

"What?"

311

Very quietly the Major said one word. "Nicole."

"What's that supposed to mean?" Eric demanded, as Nicole gripped his arm.

"Travis," the Major's voice said over the speaker, "why don't you explain our little plan?" The flush of victory was so clearly evident in his voice that Eric felt his stomach drop. This was not just another bluff—the Major was pulling out his trump card. "Did Nicole happen to mention her little accident in the Monitoring Room the other day?"

Nicole's fingernails dug into Eric's arm as she visibly jumped, her face drained of color.

"It wasn't an accident, Eric," the Major broke in. "We put a little device in her back, which, like your explosives, is electronically controlled. We regret that you doubt our word and force us to provide a demonstration." There was a pause, and then with sadness he added, "I'm truly sorry, Nicole."

Before Eric could react, Nicole gasped, then screamed in agony as her back arched violently. She staggered against him, clutching wildly for his arm. He grabbed for her and held her as her body jerked in violent spasms, each wrenching shudder driving screams of agony out of her throat.

As suddenly as it started it left her, and she collapsed, nearly dragging Eric down with her, gasping in huge, desperate, hungry gulps of air. His face a twisted mass of shock and horror, Eric laid her down gently on the carpet. Chet and Dick leaped to help him. As Chet reached for her wrist to check her pulse, her eyes fluttered open.

"It causes us great sorrow to resort to that," the Major said softly, "but you leave us no choice. We'd like to start some serious negotiations now."

Eric leaped to his feet, his eyes wild. "You animal! What kind of monster are you?"

"My little kingdom, as you so condescendingly call it, happens to be very important to me," the Major said triumphantly. "*I will save it.*"

"Though we could, we will not kill her," Travis broke in evenly. "But we can produce that kind of pain at will and prolong

312

it indefinitely." Eric stared up at the speaker, his eyes wild. "Give it up, Eric. You've got one minute to surrender, or we turn it on again."

"Eric." Nicole's voice was a hoarse whisper. He dropped to his knee and gently cradled her head against him. "You can't surrender."

"Shhhh," he soothed, pulling her close against him.

"You can't give up!" she cried, trying to raise up.

Eric looked up and stared into the faces of the men.

"There's no choice," Chet said, his voice barely above a whisper. Dick nodded in agreement. Eric turned to Clayne. He started to shake his head; then he looked at Nicole and turned away quickly.

"Thirty seconds," Travis called.

"I've got to have more time," Eric shouted, not looking up.

"Twenty-five seconds."

"No, Eric," Nicole whispered. "Don't do it. Please! Not for me."

"I can't speak for my men," he shouted, staring at her. "We need time to discuss it. Give us five minutes."

Then the triumphant voice of the Major boomed over the speaker. "Talk. But you have exactly one more minute. Then we want your decision."

"We need at least three minutes."

"One minute!" the Major thundered.

Eric stood up and walked over toward the speaker in the ceiling. When he spoke, his voice was soft and menacing. "Major, I said we need three minutes. If anyone so much as pokes his nose in here before three minutes are up, or if Nicole twitches with even a flicker of pain, we'll blow this whole place apart and us with it. You'll hear from us in three minutes."

CHAPTER

36

Eric jumped to one of the monitoring stations and grabbed a pad of paper and a pencil. The others gathered closer as he scribbled furiously. He turned and held it up. THEY CAN HEAR EVERYTHING WE SAY! ROD, MAKE NOISE. THE REST COME WITH ME. Then he spoke, "We can't take a chance that they will move in on us while we debate. Block the doors with the furniture—anything you can move over there." He picked up one of the vinyl chairs near the corner and hurled it toward the door.

As they stared at him for a moment, he turned to Rod and mouthed the words while he pointed, "Make noise! But don't block the side door."

Then he motioned to the others, and they went quickly into the room with the CPUs, leaving Nicole lying on the floor, watching them anxiously. As Eric shut the door, Loopes carefully set the blue box in a far corner, then grabbed a table and pushed it across the floor, banging it into the consoles along the wall.

"Is there a speaker in here?" Eric whispered.

Clayne peered up at the ceiling. "No."

"All right," Eric said grimly. "For now, let's reject surrender as an option. Any ideas?"

Andreason spoke up first. "Nicole is the problem. If she was free, we could try and fight our way clear. But—"

"I could remove the implantation," Chet said, "*if* I had something sharp and some time to work on her."

"What if it won't come out? What if you trigger it automatically or something?"

"I doubt it," Chet replied. "They're controlling it from out there, which means it must be an independent device. I'll have to check once I see it, but my guess is it's a simple receiving device with electrodes implanted into her spinal column."

"I've got a pocketknife in my tool kit," Andreason said. "It's probably not very sharp though."

"It'll do," Abernathy said.

"She'll have to be kept absolutely quiet." Clayne sounded dubious. "If the Major hears her cry out, that will be it."

"And I've got to have time," Chet said. "I can't just start hacking away like a wild man. Three minutes isn't enough." He shook his head. "Two now."

"I'll get you the time." Eric's voice was hopeful again. "How much do you need?"

"Four minutes minimum."

"You know what you're asking of Nicole?" Andreason asked.

Eric's eyes flashed. "Is the alternative any better?" He turned. "Clayne, can you keep her quiet?"

"Yes, but how are you going to get us more time? The Major and Travis are through with any stalling."

"I'm going out in the hallway to negotiate with them."

"They'll cut you down."

"Not if I have the detonator button in my hand."

Before Clayne could answer, Eric spun back around to Andreason. "Dick, can you fix that control box so that it'll detonate when you release the button rather than when you push it?"

Andreason looked puzzled for a moment. "Yes, I guess I could. It should be fairly simple."

"Good, do it! Get me the back-up box and the extra roll of wire. I'll take that out into the hallway. You can fix the main one while Chet operates on Nicole."

"What are you going to do?" Clayne demanded.

"I've got an idea, a way to get the time we need, and maybe a way to get us out too."

"What?"

Eric shook his head. "Don't push me for details. I'm still working it out. But remember, if we can get out of here, we'll have an army of people waiting to help us."

"Who won't be able to do a thing for us unless we blow these computers," Andreason interrupted.

"I'm working on that too. But time is critical. Let's get moving." He jerked the walkie-talkie off his belt. "Stan, can you hear me?"

The building was interfering with the reception, and the answer was faint and full of static. "I've got you, Eric. Can you speak up? What's going on in there? We saw Guardians going inside after you."

"They've got us trapped," Eric said, jamming the mouthpiece against his lips so he didn't have to speak too loudly. "But we're going to try to break free. Stay down, but the minute we come busting out of that door, open fire on any Guardian you see out there."

"Roger. We're ready and waiting for you."

He looked back to the others. "Let's go."

They reentered the Monitoring Room just as Rod Loopes crashed a secretarial chair solidly against the door. "All right," Eric said clearly, "that should do it. It's time to make a decision. Let's hear how you all vote." He motioned vigorously with his hands for them to start speaking, even as he pointed to Chet to get ready.

Clayne spoke first. "I say no. Let's see it through. The Major will kill us, or at least turn us into vegetables like Cliff Cameron."

Andreason chimed in even as he got the pocketknife out of his small tool box and handed it to Chet. Eric tuned out the conversation, grabbed a pad of paper and a pencil from one of the monitoring stations, and wrote for almost thirty seconds. He dropped to his knee beside Nicole and gently raised her head so she could read it.

WE ARE STALLING. CHET WILL TAKE OUT THE IMPLANT. CLAYNE WILL COVER YOUR MOUTH. YOU CAN'T MAKE ANY SOUND. DO YOU UNDERSTAND?

Her eyes widened as she read and then looked up at him, seeing the anguish in his eyes. Finally she nodded.

He wrote again, I WON'T GIVE YOU UP, held it for her to see, then kissed her quickly. "Turn over," he whispered into her ear.

With an effort Nicole rolled over onto her stomach. Chet knelt down and raised the back of her blouse, exposing the red scar just above the small of her back. Eric stood up and motioned to Clayne.

"Don't be stupid, Clayne," Chet said loudly, as he opened the blade of the pocketknife, wiped it on his pants, then ran the blade along his finger and shook his head. "We've lost. We have to face that."

"We've got to surrender," Rod Loopes was saying hotly, understanding what they were up to. "Otherwise what will they do to Nicole?"

"They'll do it anyway!" Clayne shouted as he knelt down next to Nicole. His fingers gently touched Nicole's cheek; then he clamped his hand over her mouth.

As Andreason finished connecting the roll of wire to the second control box and handed it to Eric, the loudspeaker over their heads blared.

"Eric, your three minutes are up. What's your decision?"

Eric looked around at the four men. "Do you trust me to make our decision for us?"

"Yes." It was spoken as one.

He pulled Andreason next to his mouth and whispered, "Dick, take the end of the wire into the computer room. Connect it to anything; then come out and shut the door. It's got to look authentic. Then get the real button switched over as soon as possible."

As Andreason jumped to obey, Eric looked up at the ceiling. "Major?"

"Yes, I'm still here, Eric. What is your decision?"

"The detonator button for the explosives goes off if it's released. I'm holding it down at the moment. I'm coming out into the hallway."

"No, Eric!" the Major said loudly. "Your time is up."

"If I let go of the button," Eric continued calmly, "it'll close the circuits, and the whole place will go. If any of your men get jumpy and shoot me, it's all over."

"What is your decision, Eric?" the Major snapped. "No more talk!"

"I'm ready to negotiate," Eric answered, turning his head away as he saw Nicole's arms and legs stiffen and then start to tremble violently. "But I'm coming out to do it. Tell your men to hold their fire. If my thumb is knocked off this button, all negotiations will be over. There's no way to reverse that then."

Almost instantly, loudspeakers all over the building screamed out, "Hold your fire! Hold your fire!"

"Rod, clear me a way through to the door," Eric called, concentrating on uncoiling the wire carefully so as not to look in Nicole's direction.

"There's nothing to talk about!" Travis screamed. "Surrender or we'll terminate Nicole. We're not playing anymore, Eric."

"You're a real sweetheart, Travis. Major, I'm coming out." He stepped out of the door and into the hallway, tensing for the unseen blow. But the hallway was empty, and then a moment later, Travis and the Major stepped into view about thirty feet away.

Eric held up the box and uncoiled another foot or two of wire. "It's rather a bitter irony, isn't it?"

"What's that?" the Major said, searching Eric's face for any sign of surrender.

"You have a destructive device planted at the spine of something I treasure very much—" he paused long enough to note Travis's look of fury—"and I have a destructive device planted at the heart of something you treasure very much."

The Major's nod was barely perceptible.

"I have a suggestion. Why don't we trade boxes?"

The Major gave a short, humorless laugh. "I must admit, Eric, you don't give up easily."

Travis held up a black panel with a dial on the face of it for

Eric to see. "Tell your men to throw down their weapons and come out now, Eric." His hand went up to the dial. "*Now*, or Nicole begins screaming again."

Eric's eyes remained riveted to the Major's face. "You see, Major, I *am* willing to trade victory for Nicole, but you haven't offered me that yet."

"That's exactly what I am offering you."

"No. If we surrender, she will either be executed or at least put through a repeat of Cliff Cameron's ordeal. I'd just as soon see her dead."

The Major's eyes narrowed, and Eric knew he believed him.

"Suppose I promise you I won't do either."

"Sorry, Major. Trust is not the going commodity today."

"Suppose I promise nothing more than implantation. You know I'm a man of my word, just as you are."

"*Death is preferable to implantation,*" Eric roared, suddenly angry.

"He's bluffing!" Travis's fingers flicked up and rested on the dial. "Tell them to come out, Eric. Now!"

Eric's own hand came up slowly so the box and his thumb on the button were clearly evident, but again he refused to even glance at Travis. "Major, if I hear so much as a whimper from Nicole, that is it. Do you understand?"

The Major's hand darted out and grabbed Travis's arm. "Give the controls to me, Travis."

Travis turned around in shock. "He won't do it! Not with Nicole in there!"

"*Give me the controls, Travis!*" The two men stared at each other, eyes locked in anger, and then Travis finally lifted his fingers. The Major took the transmitter and turned away. He relaxed visibly, then turned to face Eric. "What is your proposal?"

"It's simple. I have about two hundred to two hundred fifty feet of wire tied to this box."

"Yes, go on."

"Clear the side hallway of all your men. We'll leave the Monitoring Room, unreeling the wire as we go. You and Travis can come around the corner into that side hallway and watch as I do it. One wrong move, one trigger-happy Guardian, and I let go of the button. But once I can see that my people are clear, I'll walk back down the hall to you. I hand you my box, and you hand me the transmitting controls. You save your computers, I save Nicole."

Both Travis and the Major considered for a moment. Finally the Major nodded. "Travis and I will confer on this for a moment to see if it's acceptable."

Eric shrugged. "Take whatever time you need. I'll be inside." Without a second glance, he went back in the room.

The Major turned and looked at Travis. "What do you think?"

"I don't know. It sounds too pat." His mind raced over the possibilities. "On the other hand, we've got a couple of surprises for him."

"Exactly," the Major said. "We can send our men out the front and still catch them outside. And I have another set of controls for Nicole in my office. I'm sure they plan to get the implantation out as soon as possible, but our transmitter has a range of ten to fifteen miles. That should give us plenty of time."

"What if he's pulling a fast one on us? Is there anything he can be doing in there right now?"

The Major frowned, then strode down the hallway to the door and pounded on it, leaning down to peek through the bullet hole in the upper panel. But someone was standing close to the door, blocking the view. "Eric, I want the door opened so I can watch you, see that you're not up to something." Then he whispered to Travis, "Clear the way to the fire door and then send Lieutenant Lowry and the men out the front."

As he turned back to the door, he heard Eric's muffled cry. "Open the door for him."

The door swung open to reveal Rod Loopes with a rifle pointing directly at the Major's chest. Eric was standing next to Nicole, holding her by the arm. Her face was chalky white, and the Major could see that she was leaning on Eric for support. Clayne was next to him and Chet Abernathy behind them.

"You can watch from there, Major," Eric called, "but if you try to come in—" He left it unfinished. "What have you decided?"

As Travis moved up to stand next to him, the Major nodded. "All right, we agree."

"Good." Eric turned. "Chet, you and Nicole go first, Dick and Clayne next. Rod and I will bring up the rear so the Major can see me and the box clearly." He looked up. "Is the way to the exit cleared, Major?"

"Yes."

"Okay, let's move out," Eric said. "Keep together."

As they moved toward the door, he stopped next to the dark form on the floor. He dropped to one knee and turned the body halfway over. "Major, will you give this man a decent burial? We are obviously in no position to do it."

"Of course."

"Thank you. I'm going out now. You and Travis move around to the side hallway where we can watch each other."

As they backed out into the hallway, Eric moved out of the Monitoring Room through the side door, unreeling the wire. "I might suggest, Major, that even though I can't see into the room now, if someone slips in and cuts the wire, you'll have the automatic detonation."

"I won't run that risk," the Major said evenly. "We'll play it your way."

Eric backed up the hallway as swiftly as he could unreel the spool, following the others. When he ran out of wire, he was about five feet short of where the hallway turned the corner and went out the door. He stopped. "Clayne," he called, "are you at the door?"

"Roger. We're set to go out."

Eric returned slowly, coiling the wire in big loops, and approached the two men. Halfway down the hall, the Major stepped forward to meet him. Five feet away from each other they both stopped. The Major studied Eric for a moment.

"Well, it comes to this, I guess," he said.

Eric nodded. "Yes."

"I thought I had planned so carefully, considered every factor. I was so sure that I finally had a foolproof system for creating the ideal society."

Eric shook his head. "This time you captured the wrong fools." He held out his hand with the box and the wire.

"You know we can't let you get away," the Major said, extending his own hand with the transmitting controls.

"I know," Eric responded. "But once we're clear of this building, we've got a chance. Out in the open, so far we've held our own pretty well."

Travis, still standing at the end of the hall, laughed derisively. "We'll see."

"Keep your thumb firmly on the button," Eric said as he transferred the box to the Major's hand. He held onto the wire until the Major handed him the control panel with the small dial. Both he and the Major backed away from each other slowly. Suddenly a fury gripped Eric, and he whirled, hurling the transmitting control against the wall with all his strength. It hit and shattered, spraying pieces across the hallway. Then he turned and darted down the corridor and around the corner.

"We have another one, you fool!" Travis screamed after him. "We'll still get your precious Nicole."

"Travis," the Major commanded, "get inside. Make sure no one bumps this wire until we can defuse it."

Moving quickly but carefully, the Major stepped inside the Monitoring Room, holding the red button firmly. As Travis moved over to join him, the sound of rifle fire came faintly down the hallway.

"We saved it, Major," Travis said, his eyes following the Major's as he looked round. "And we'll get them too."

"Let Lowry handle it for now," the Major said. "You stay right here until we get this thing unhooked."

He turned and surveyed the room with its scattered furniture, letting his free hand run lightly over the keys of one of the computer consoles. "We came so close, Travis," he murmured. "So close to losing it all."

"I know." As Travis turned, his eyes fell on the body near the side door, and he moved over to it. "Which one of them did we get?"

He dropped to one knee, grabbed the dead man's shoulder,

and turned him over as the Major came in closer to look.

"No!" The Major's cry and Travis's stunned gasp of surprise echoed in the Monitoring Room simultaneously, but it was not the face of Donald Brownley they stared at. A blue box was lying on the floor beneath the body—a blue box identical to the one held in the Major's hand, except that when they turned Donald Brownley over, the red button on that box popped up into its full position.

For several moments they both stood rooted to the spot, frozen with shock. Then Travis leaped to his feet. "Run!" he screamed, shoving the Major. He had barely cleared the doorway when the ten-second delay switch closed a fraction of an inch, sending the voltage from two small flashlight batteries racing down the wires to the detonators. With a stupefying roar of yellow and orange fire, the computer banks and monitoring consoles, the tracking screens, and most of the lower level of Central Control disappeared in a shattering blast of flying glass, broken bricks, shards of red-hot metal, and shredded silicon boards speckled with circuitry.

And in a time span so small as to be almost incomprehensible to the mind of man, two hundred fifty thousand silicon chips in the necks of the residents of the Alliance of Four Cities became nothing more than harmless disks.

CHAPTER

37

Lieutenant Fred Lowry was still fifty yards from the south exit and running hard, his men fanning out behind him, when the trees above them erupted with a withering fire. A bullet slapped past his ear so close that he felt the air smack against his cheek.

With a startled cry, he veered sharply to the left and dove for cover behind a thick clump of bush. "Get down! Get down!" he screamed. But the man behind him didn't have a chance to heed the warning. He was hit full in the chest, and his body jerked violently, the bullet hurling him back two or three feet before he tumbled to the ground. Another man screamed as a shot took him high in the shoulder, slamming him back against a tree.

"Take cover!" Lowry screamed again.

Had it been daylight, it would have been a massacre, but as it was, the Guardians still had the lights of the city behind them, silhouetting them faintly. Pinpoints of light flashed from several points above them as the rebels poured in the fire.

"Fan out! Circle around them!" Lowry's commands were nearly lost as the Guardian line erupted with return fire, shooting blindly at their unseen attackers. Lowry raised up on one knee and peered over the bush. Suddenly the south door flew open.

"They're coming out!" he cried, snapping off a quick shot in the direction of the exit. A hand with a rifle appeared from out of the doorway, stabbing upward at the overhead light. The bulb shattered, and the south side of Central Control was plunged into darkness. Taking aim this time, Lowry blasted off another round and heard a sharp cry of pain.

The rebels saw the flashes from Lowry's muzzle, and suddenly his position was under heavy fire. He jumped instinctively, rolling once, then came up in a darting, crouching run across a small open place and dove behind a tree where two other Guardians were firing up the hill.

For several seconds the fire fight raged unabated; then the ground beneath Lowry heaved upward, bouncing him hard against it. Looking up, he saw the building bulge outward, then explode, spraying bricks like straw in a hurricane. Both Guardian and rebel were momentarily stunned into immobility, and every person on the hill stared at the gaping hole in what had once been Central Control. Even as they stared, the flames cast an eerie light across the hillside and through the trees.

"Lieutenant Lowry!"

The booming voice rolled down to him over the crackling noise of the fire.

"Fred, this is Clayne Robertson! Can you hear me?"

He hesitated for a moment, then stood up, staying behind the tree. "I can hear you," he shouted.

"You know what that explosion means, don't you?"

Turning, Lowry stared at the inferno raging inside the smashed hulk of the building.

"The Major's gone," Clayne called. "So is Travis. It's over, Fred."

"We're still here!" he shouted back, but there was little conviction in his voice.

"The computers are gone, Fred. Central Control is gone. Think about that. Your families are free now. The people are free."

"Look behind you, Lowry." It was Eric Lloyd. "Here come the people of Shalev."

The flatness of Alliance Square gave way to the ridge behind Central Control. The point where Lowry stood was probably fifty or so feet higher than the quad. As he turned and looked down, he could see dark shapes pouring into the quad, outlined in the dim lights of the square and its buildings. There were hundreds of them, and swelling even as he watched, pouring toward them like an angry torrent.

"It's the people, Fred," Clayne shouted. "They're free now, and they're not coming to help the Guardians. Give it up, before you cause a bloodbath."

The two men who were crouched down next to Lowry stood up, transfixed at the sight below them. "Look at them!" one of them breathed in a mixture of awe and terror.

"Lieutenant Lowry!" It was one of his own men, somewhere behind him. "What about the squads of men unconscious inside the building? They'll be killed."

Clayne heard and replied, "We'll help you get them out, Fred."

Lowry hesitated, torn with indecision.

"Come on, man!" Clayne screamed. "It's over. Let's not make it any worse than it already is."

Lieutenant Fred Lowry looked at the two men next to him, who nodded quickly. He turned to stare at the shattered wall and the fire, which was swelling in size even as he looked. Suddenly he threw his rifle down and stepped out into view. "Guardians! This is Lieutenant Lowry! Throw down your weapons. Let's get those men out of that building."

Nicole stopped in front of the Fountain of Peace and watched the dancing waters, now edged with pink from the fiery sunrise that filled the sky. Eric stopped too, and she slipped her arm through his. Chet had stitched up the incision in her back and given her a pain pill, but her face was still pale and drawn. "The Fountain of Peace," she murmured, her voice barely audible over the sounds of the splashing water. "Maybe now it really can become one."

"I think—" Eric started to speak, but a shout cut him off.

"Eric!"

They both turned. Chet Abernathy had come out of the library and was running across the grass toward them. "Clayne's found them," he called.

Eric's shoulders sagged in relief. "Are they all right?"

Chet smiled broadly. "Yes, everyone's fine. They're bringing them down now. Your family will come first."

"Thank heavens," Nicole breathed. "Where were they?"

"Well, Clayne found Shirley Ferguson at the first campsite. Needless to say, she was quite surprised to see him. She had radioed Travis, and Stephanie caught her. So she ran, and the camp moved to the fall-back site. Clayne found them there."

"What a relief that is," Nicole said, squeezing Eric's hand.

"Do you want the other good news?" Chet said, barely able to hide his excitement.

"What?"

"President Dobson just finished talking with Mount Pleasant on the radio. The Guardian Forces have laid down their arms and agreed to submit to whatever government comes out of all this."

"So that's all of them!"

"Yes, every unit of Guardians has now surrendered. It's over, Eric." He clapped Eric on the shoulder. "Well, I've got to get back to the wounded. I just wanted you to know about your family."

Surprisingly, as Chet left them, the elation left Eric as abruptly as it had come, and he felt only a deep weariness settling in upon him. It was over. Don Brownley was dead. Cliff was bedridden and paralyzed. Richard Dawson had a bullet in his left leg, and Dick Andreason had been blasted into unconsciousness by a stun gun. The rest were exhausted but safe. On the other side, in addition to Travis and the Major, four Guardians were dead, several more badly hurt. But Central Control, with all that it implied, was a burned-out shell.

Eric pulled his thoughts away from all that and turned toward Nicole. "Hello," she said softly.

He reached out and touched her cheek. "We did it."

"Not we did it," she said. "You did it. You and Cliff."

He shook his head slowly.

"And now what do you do with Joe and Shirley?" she asked.

"Dr. Gould and any others who planned this must be dealt with, but as for Shirley and Joe, I'd say get them to a preacher as soon as possible, marry them off, and start them raising a family."

"Nothing else?"

"How can you punish people for being loyal? We don't need any more revenge at this point."

She smiled and leaned her head against his shoulder. "That's good. It's over now."

"Is it?"

Her eyebrows lifted. "Of course."

His eyes were dark and brooding. "You say we did it. What have we done?"

"What's that supposed to mean? You freed the people." Her voice suddenly dropped to a whisper. "You freed me."

He shook his head, half smiling. "You freed yourself. I only came along to watch." Then he was sober again. "Yes, we freed the people."

"Eric," she cried, "what's the matter with you?"

"Up in the mountains I told you that the Major had taken away the most sacred of all stewardships, the right to guard the gate of the mind."

"Yes."

"Well, we've just thrown open that gate and put man back in charge of his own destiny. Don't you find that just a little bit frightening?"

"I find you a little bit frightening," she said. "But that doesn't mean I want to go back to the way it was before."

He nodded. "You're right. Whatever we face in the years ahead, it won't ever be what it was before. And that has got to be worth it all."

"And what about the years ahead?" Nicole murmured.

"What?"

"Where will Eric Lloyd be in those years? Back in the valley?"

His eyes widened for several moments, and then he put his arm around her and pulled her close. "Is that what you think?"

"I don't know what to think. I have no right to ask that, but I want to know."

"Nicole, going back to the valley hasn't been part of my plans since you and I tangled with that old she-bear in the mountains."

"Really?"

"Really. I wouldn't miss the challenges and the excitement of what lies ahead now for all the valleys in the world."

"Oh." Her chin dropped, and she looked away.

He reached out and lifted her head, his eyes twinkling. "And I also promised one young lady I was going to start calling on her in a proper and acceptable fashion."

She looked up again, her eyes suddenly shining. "No more hiding behind the couch?"

"I promise."

"No more shattered doorways?"

"My solemn word."

"It sounds dull."

He laughed. "I know."

"But I'll cope with it somehow."

About the Author

Gerald N. Lund received his B.A. and M.S. degrees in sociology from Brigham Young University, and has done post-graduate work in the New Testament and Hebrew at Pepperdine University and the University of Judaism in Los Angeles, California.

Retired from employment by the Church Educational System, Brother Lund has been a seminary teacher, an institute teacher and director, and a curriculum writer. His Church callings have included bishop, stake missionary, counselor in a bishopric, and teacher development director.

Brother Lund has authored many books in addition to *The Alliance,* including *Jesus Christ, Key to the Plan of Salvation; One in Thine Hand; Leverage Point, The Freedom Factor;* and the best-selling *The Work and the Glory* series.